Tommie
+
Teddy

A
Marvelous
Hundred
Square
Miles

A Marvelous Hundred Square Miles

Black Hills Tourism,

1880-1941

SUZANNE BARTA JULIN

South Dakota State Historical Society Press

Pierre

Portions of chapter 2 and 4 appeared in different form in "'A Feeling Almost Beyond Description': Scenic Roads in South Dakota's Custer State Park, 1919–1932," in the *World Beyond the Windshield: Roads and Landscapes in the United States and Europe*, ed. Christopf Mauch and Thomas Zeller (Athens: Ohio University Press, 2008), and in "Art Meets Politics: Peter Norbeck, Frank Lloyd Wright, and the Sylvan Lake Hotel Commission," *South Dakota History* 32 (Summer 2002): 117–48. A portion of chapter 5 appeared in different form in "Building a Vacationland: Tourism Development in the Black Hills during the Great depression," *South Dakota History* 35 (Winter 2005): 291–314.

This publication is funded, in part, by the Deadwood Publications Fund provided by the City of Deadwood and the Deadwood Historic Preservation Commission.

Library of Congress Cataloging-in-Publication data

Julin, Suzanne.

A marvelous hundred square miles : Black Hills tourism, 1880–1941 / by Suzanne Barta Julin.

 p. cm.

Includes bibliographical references and index.

ISBN 978-0-9798940-6-0

1. Black Hills (S.D. and Wyo.)—Description and travel. 2. Tourism—Black Hills (S.D. and Wyo.)—History. 3. South Dakota—Description and travel. 4. Tourism—South Dakota—History. I. Title.

F657.B6J85 2009

917.83'9043—dc22   2009025881

Text and cover design by Rich Hendel

Please visit our website at http://www.sdshspress.com

13 12 11 10 09   1 2 3 4 5

To Joseph Harper Cash

Contents

Acknowledgments

I owe many thanks to professional colleagues whom I am also pleased to consider good friends. Nancy Tystad Koupal encouraged me to pursue this topic and discussed particular elements at length with me on several occasions. Richmond Clow shared with me his knowledge of South Dakota history, politics, and society. Bill Weikel helped me sort out the intricacies of early land titles and mineral claims and called in "markers" to help me meet deadlines. Diane Krahe offered insightful comments about several presentations based on this research—some of them offered in hotel hallways as I was about to approach a podium. Brenda Jackson-Abernathy listened to me think out loud over numerous late night burgers at Rico's, helping me to sharpen my focus and to sleep easier. Orlan Svingen, Leroy Ashby, John Kicza, and Janice Rutherford read the work, provided helpful suggestions, and shared their enthusiasm for the project.

I was fortunate to work with a number of people in archives and collections whose assistance was invaluable: Leonard Bruguier, Margaret Quintal, and Rebecca Anderson of the American Indian Research Project/ South Dakota Oral History Project, University of South Dakota; Amy Cooper and Anne Hinseth of University of South Dakota Archives and Special Collections, I. D. Weeks Library; Mark Henderson of the J. Paul Getty Research Institute for the History of Art and Humanities in Los Angeles; Bill Honerkamp at the Black Hills, Badlands, and Lakes Association in Rapid City; Randy Meeks, City of Deadwood Archives; Dave McKee at the Black Hills National Forest Supervisor's Office; Timothy Rives of the National Archives, Kansas City branch; Craig Pugsley, Sue Haas, Vicki Palmer, and Millie Wiley at Custer State Park; Stephen Rogers and Michelle Saxman-Rogers, formerly of the South Dakota State Historic Preservation Office in Pierre; Marvene Riis and staff at the State Archives, a program of the South Dakota State Historical Society in Pierre; Karen Rogsa at Jewel Cave National Monument; Ron Terry of Wind Cave National Park; Margo Stipe of the Frank Lloyd Wright Foundation in Scottsdale, Arizona; Jim Wilson, former Deadwood City Historic Preservation Officer; the staffs of the Rapid City Public Library and the Deadwood Public Library; and Judge Marshall Young who shared private papers pertaining to his grandfather,

Paul Bellamy, and the Black Hills Transportation Company. I also thank Patti Edman, Martyn Beeny, and Rodger Hartley at the South Dakota State Historical Society Press for their diligence, patience, and hard work.

My career as a public historian has afforded me the opportunity to conduct a number of research projects in Deadwood, allowing me to understand more fully the history of tourism there and in the Black Hills as a whole. I thank Deborah Gangloff, the Days of '76 Museum board of directors, Deadwood City Archivist Michael Runge, Deadwood City Historic Preservation Officer Kevin Kuchenbecher, the Deadwood City Commission, and the Deadwood Historic Preservation Commission for giving me the opportunity to explore Deadwood's past.

I also appreciate dear friends who have learned more about Black Hills tourism than they ever expected to know, but who still appear happy to see me coming. Their encouragement and enthusiasm for my work has been a source of real support. My heartfelt thanks to Christine Coffin and Rick Fuhrman, Frances Devore, Judy Dundas, Cindy Schultz, Dottie and Tom Hoshaw, and Roxane and Bill Weikel.

My sister and brother-in-law, Denise and Rick Askvig, graciously shared their Rapid City home with me for an entire summer while I conducted the initial research for this study, and they continue to provide me with a guest suite whenever I am working in the Black Hills. I pressed Denise into service as my research assistant several times; I believe she plans on keeping her day job. My sister Sandi Gallacher is my daily e-mail companion, and her words of wisdom helped keep me on an even keel while I wrote and then revised this work. She and her husband, Steve, have been my refuge from the storm on many occasions, and I am grateful to them for their love and care. My brother Jeff and his wife Kathy are another source of family support, and we have shared memorable times in the Black Hills. My daughter Holly has listened to or read many parts of this work and has given me frank and useful reactions. One of the nicest things she did for me during the years this work has been in progress was to marry Joel Rudnick, whose blunt faith in my abilities bumped me out of more than one period of self-doubt. Holly and Joel have given me two of the world's most beautiful grandchildren, Lucille and Henry, and I look forward to introducing them to the Black Hills.

I owe my greatest debt to my mentor, the late Joseph Harper Cash, former Director of the American Indian Research Project and South Dakota

Oral History Project, Doris Duke Professor of History, and Dean of Arts and Sciences at the University of South Dakota. When I was a new mother desperately in need of a job, he hired me—out of pity for a skinny young woman with a skinny baby, he later insisted—and within a few months set me off on a new course in life by transmitting his passion for the study of history to me. Throughout the years I worked and pursued my bachelors and masters degrees at the University of South Dakota, he helped me in innumerable ways without conferring any sense of obligation. Of all the lessons I learned from him, the most important may have been the value of aiding others while allowing them to maintain their dignity and indepen-dence. Without his assistance, my life would have taken another turn. This book is for him.

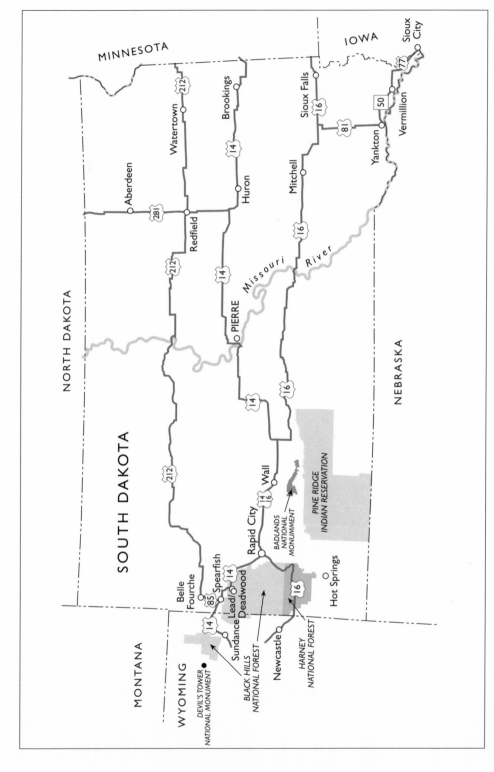

SOUTH DAKOTA, APPROXIMATELY 1940

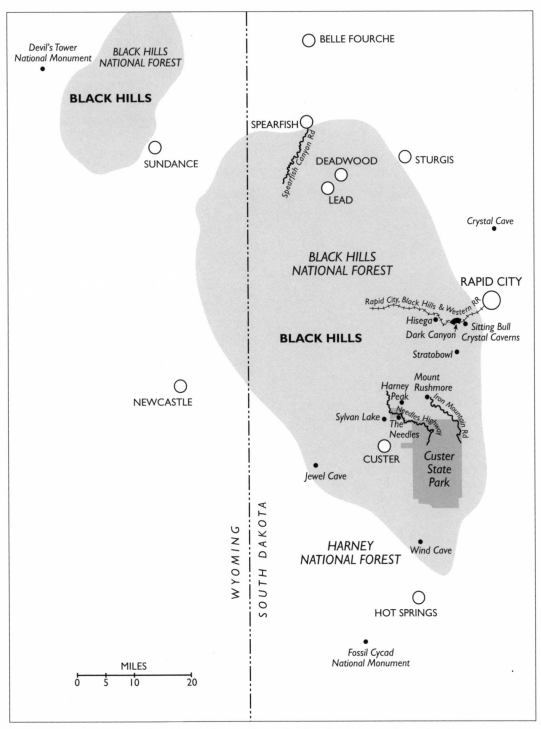

BLACK HILLS AREA, *showing parks, roads, and other features as they existed around 1940*

A
Marvelous
Hundred
Square
Miles

Introduction

Early one Sunday morning in the summer of 1959, my parents, my sister Sandra, and I loaded our '58 Chevy and left our southeastern South Dakota hometown of Dante for our first family vacation. My sister and I had each been allowed to pack a cardboard box of activities to keep us occupied during the drive across the state. The boxes also served as a barrier between us in the back seat, an attempt, I am sure, to limit squabbling and swatting. In the front seat, my parents installed a cooler with cold drinks, the fried chicken my mother had cooked late the night before, hard-boiled eggs, and celery sticks. We stopped to attend church services in the little town of Pukwana and stopped again to eat our midday meal at a picnic area in Badlands National Park. After we left the Badlands, we could see the silhouette of our destination—a dark and uneven smudge against the western sky that became more defined as we grew closer. Late that afternoon, we arrived in the Black Hills. We pulled in at the first tourist attraction we saw—Thunderhead Falls, a waterfall in a cave. We paid our money, donned waterproof ponchos, and listened raptly to our young guide's explanation of the geological and man-made forces that had created such a marvel.

I was eleven years old. I had never been more than ninety miles from home, and I had never seen a waterfall, a mountain, a fast-flowing stream, an evergreen tree that someone had not intentionally planted, or a log building. I was enraptured by the natural beauty of the Black Hills and captivated by its seemingly endless offerings for tourists. During that week, my family viewed Mount Rushmore, swam in the warm waters of Evans Plunge, fished at Trout Haven, posed for pictures at Dinosaur Park, and drove the Iron Mountain Road and the Needles Highway. One night we arrived in the northern Black Hills town of Deadwood after dark and took a room at the Terrace Motel. I awoke early in the morning and pushed aside the curtains to see the steep inclines of the historic gulch and to breathe in the intoxicating pine-scented air. Had my family announced at that moment that they were leaving me behind in Deadwood to fend for myself, I would not have been disappointed.

As that week went on, I became increasingly intrigued by the numbers of visitors drawn to the Black Hills. In fact, our favorite evening activity involved cruising a tourist attraction's parking lot to count the number of out-of-state license plates. Typically modest South Dakotans, we were not accustomed to much attention, and the fact that people from as far away as New York or California would travel to our state thrilled us. I loved my hometown, but no one vacationed in Dante unless they were coming to see relatives. The wide appeal of the Black Hills astounded me.

I was an eleven-year-old bookworm and questions began forming in my mind. How could a region in such a little-known and sparsely populated state attract so many people? Why were they here? When did they begin to come? And how did all these tourist attractions develop? At some point during that vacation, I decided that someday I would write about tourism in the Black Hills. Forty years later, I began to do just that, within the larger context of the history of tourism in the United States.

Tourism is one of the world's major industries, employing people, generating products and services, and offering new opportunities to undeveloped areas or areas in which traditional economic bases have eroded. Yet, many scholars consider tourism a less serious topic for study than, for example, banking, mining, logging, or agriculture. Some historians see tourism studies as a component of environmental history, concentrating on changes in the landscape and in land-use patterns. Others emphasize tourists' perceptions of landscape, places, and people and analyze how those views color the ways they—and we—see the world. There are additional reasons for examining tourism, however: this industry has profoundly influenced the growth and development of a multitude of cities, localities, and regions in the United States as well as throughout the world.

Critics blame tourism for despoiling local environments, creating low-paying regional service economies, encouraging outside investment at the expense of local control, driving community property values beyond the reach of long-time citizens, and increasing the use of fossil fuels. According to many of these judges, history is ill served in the process when purveyors of tourism create new myths and artificial ambiance to attract paying visitors, changing forever the landscapes and the identities of places from Africa to Alaska.

These criticisms are valid up to a point. All industries that dominate their locales, however, make particular alterations to the societies and the cultures in their areas. Therefore, it is instructive to examine tourism's impacts and how they have occurred in particular places. How do public and private decisions about this industry guide and mold the way a community or a region develops? How does existing public policy help form this development and how does the political process affect change and growth? What are the effects of social trends, economic cycles, and innovations in transportation? The Black Hills of South Dakota, which offers a well-defined example of the development of a specific tourism region, provides an opportunity to address these questions. By examining closely the political foundations of tourism in the Black Hills, this work illustrates how politics, policy, and national and local issues affected the growth of this industry in this place during the years before World War II.

I believe this study of Black Hills tourism identifies forces that forged the culture of tourism I experienced as a child in 1959, a culture that continues to define tourism in the Black Hills to the present day. The Black Hills tourism industry began in the 1880s with risk-taking entrepreneurs who founded a health resort, but its real foundation is the area's public lands and the political and policy decisions and actions that created a vacation mecca for motoring Americans of modest means. By the 1920s, the Black Hills included two national forests, a national park, two national monuments, and one of the largest state parks in the country, prompting the Standard Oil Company to promote it as "the most marvelous hundred square miles on earth." The leadership of Senator Peter Norbeck in developing Custer State Park set the stage for concentrated efforts to draw motoring tourists. His actions and those of other officials responsible for public lands encouraged private development that joined with public development in the Black Hills to result in one of the most defined tourism areas in the United States.

During the 1920s and the 1930s, tourism transformed this small mountain range, affecting its natural landscape, its built environment, its culture, and its society. The decisions made during these years defined tourism in the Black Hills and defined the Black Hills as a tourist region with a particular audience. This postwar transformation did not occur in a vacuum. Progressive politics and reforms at the national and state level, trends in art, architecture, and landscape architecture, the new availability of the automobile, and the ravages of the Great Depression influenced tourism development in the Black Hills and affected the ways in which the industry shaped the region. The growth of Black Hills tourism illustrates the interweaving of political, social, and cultural threads inherent in the ways industries and regions develop. In that sense, this study is not only an exploration of tourism development; it is an examination of the formation of a regional identity, an identity dependent to a large degree on the political foundations of regional tourism.

Thus, the examination of this small region's transformation to a tourists' locale sheds light on tourism and regional development in the twentieth-century United States as well as explores elements of the formation of regional identity. In many ways, the Black Hills is typical of other tourist areas, such as the Ozarks, the Florida coast, and the Minnesota lake country that achieved wide popularity during the period under consideration, particularly in its dependence on automobile traffic. The region's isolation, its preponderance of public lands, and the tourism industry's dependence on public policy and public funding, however, make the Black Hills a unique subject.

Birth of a Regional Industry
Tourism in the Black Hills through World War I

1

IN 1941, as the Great Depression came to a close, the South Dakota State Highway Commission issued an advertisement that invoked the names of Wild Bill Hickok and Calamity Jane and promised visitors petrified forests, gold mines, caves, and wild animals. "Cool Nights, No Mosquitos," the ad declared, touting the climate and the ambiance of the Black Hills. For hundreds of thousands of tourists during the period between the World Wars, this region was the place where the West began.[1] Its tourism industry was born decades earlier, however, as entrepreneurial visionaries in the Black Hills began to work to attract travelers. In the years before the end of World War I, tourism in the Black Hills was unorganized, largely unadvertised, and dependent on natural resources and nearby populations for its clientele. By the time the war ended, tourism in the Black Hills would be on the cusp of dramatic changes.

The Black Hills constitute a range of mountains in western South Dakota and eastern Wyoming, covering an area about fifty miles wide and a little over one hundred miles long. The ponderosa pines common on the slopes make the hills look black from a distance, and the Lakotas gave them the name Paha Sapa, "Hills that are Black." These are the highest mountains east of the Rockies. Harney Peak, the tallest summit, reaches an elevation of 7,242 feet. Perhaps the most unusual feature of the area's geography is its setting: surrounded by sparsely populated grasslands of the northern Great Plains, the Black Hills looks and feels like a forested oasis in an enormous, empty land.[2] Indeed, it seems a rare and "marvelous hundred square miles" to the weary traveler.[3]

The history of tourism development in the Black Hills through the end of World War I mirrors the growth of that industry in the United States. Early pleasure travel in the British colonies in America and in the new United States consisted mainly of health-related trips and included visits to natural hot-water spas at places like Saratoga Springs, New York, and White Sulphur Springs, West Virginia. As roads improved and greater numbers of people could reach the sites, many of these locations began to provide accommodations that attracted affluent citizens who could imitate the social life in the great spas of Europe. In the 1820s, the rise of the market economy and industrial technology led to increased wealth and better transportation systems, and more people could travel to more places. Railroad expansion after the Civil War made economical travel even more widely available, and the completion of the transcontinental railroad in 1869 opened up pleasure trips to the West—at least for those who could afford them.[4] This trajectory of tourism development, with some variations, was repeated in the Black Hills of South Dakota between 1879 and 1918.

Black Hills tourism began soon after the 1875–1876 gold rush brought permanent white settlement to the area. In 1879, several people claimed land near a group of warm-water springs in a scenic canyon at the southern end of the Hills. After one local man, Joe Larive, found relief from his rheumatism by bathing in the warm water, he and two other settlers began offering baths to the public. In 1881, five residents of Deadwood, in the northern Black Hills, formed a company to take advantage of this natural resource. Rudolphus D. Jennings, Alexander S. Stewart, Erving G. Dudley, L. R. Graves, and Fred T. Evans formed the Hot Springs Town-Site Company, dedicated to the goal of developing a health resort in the warm-water area of the southern Hills. Members of the new enterprise purchased one of the original claims and filed others, and Jennings and Stewart moved to the site.[5]

Jennings and his wife Mattie established a crude resort facility in a four-room log cabin next to one of the springs. They boarded customers, mostly

(opposite) Health-seekers enjoyed the scenery at Maiden's Leap, a rock formation in Hot Springs. The Gillespie Hotel can be seen in the background.

Frederick Taft Evans's name became closely connected with the growing town of Hot Springs.

local people who traveled there by stage or on horseback. Another settler, John Kohler, built a small hotel and provided services in competition with the Jennings. In 1883, the community of Hot Springs became the county seat of the newly created Fall River County, and two years later the Fremont, Elkhorn & Missouri Valley Railroad reached Buffalo Gap, thirteen miles to the east. The county-seat designation gave the settlement an air of permanence, and the proximity of the train terminus enabled travelers to reach Hot Springs with greater ease. This stability and accessibility initiated a burst of development of resort-related amenities.[6]

Fred Evans of the Hot Springs Town-Site Company led much of that development. An Ohio native who had worked in railroads and banking, Evans came to the Black Hills during the gold rush and established a successful freighting company. In 1886, Evans sold his business and shifted his attention to the new health resort. The original town-site company reorganized into the Dakota Hot Springs Company, with Evans as president, and built a two-story frame hotel, the largest in Hot Springs at the time. The following year, Iowa investors purchased the controlling interest in the enterprise.[7]

By 1887, bathhouses and three hotels provided services to guests, most of whom were Black Hills residents. The community also attracted a dentist, a general store, a drugstore, and a barbershop, among other businesses. The development of the health resort with its springs, hotels, and bathhouses overshadowed the business section of the town, located to the south of the resort area on a low flat and separated from it by a narrow canyon. The two sections of Hot Springs became known as "upper town" and "lower town," and the split became social, economic, and political, as well as geographical.[8]

Between 1889 and 1893, both sections grew rapidly. Upper town catered to health-seekers; lower town provided goods to the resort industry as well as to city residents and area ranchers and farmers. In 1890, the Fremont, Elkhorn & Missouri Valley Railroad extended its line to Hot Springs, and more than one hundred new businesses were established in the community during that year. The Burlington Railroad built a branch line into the city in 1891, and by the mid-1890s, Hot Springs had fifteen hotels and boarding

Opening in 1892, the palatial Evans Hotel raised the standard for accommodations in the Black Hills.

houses. A number of the new structures were built of red and pink-hued Lakota sandstone, quarried near town. The ornately carved, colored stone blended with the canyon cliffs to give the city a distinctive, sophisticated appearance. The Evans Hotel, which opened in 1892, was the most imposing of the new buildings. The five-story structure, built in an H-shape, boasted castellated trim and a wide verandah. With elevators, electric lights, and expensive interior decorations, Evans raised the quality of accommodations offered in the town to a new level.[9]

The baths were as important as the hotels. Facilities included the four-story Stewart Bathhouse with a central atrium and plunge bath and the Catholican Springs Bathhouse with "vapor baths." A three-story bathhouse addition to the Evans Hotel offered various treatments, including "electric baths," in which the bather held one electrode and placed another in the water, thus receiving an invigorating charge. In 1891, Fred Evans built his most enduring contribution to the bathing facilities, Evans Plunge. The wood, glass, and iron building covered a warm-water pool about one hundred fifty feet long and contained slides, rafts, and other paraphernalia for guests to enjoy. Unlike the traditional bathhouses that concentrated on well-being and sybaritic pleasures, Evans Plunge was designed as much for recreation as for healthful soaking.[10]

Bathers took the waters at the cavernous Evans Plunge in this early postcard scene.

As in other health-resort communities in the United States, the emphasis in Hot Springs soon shifted from the therapeutic warm waters to the social life offered by the local attractions. Hotels gave dinners and parties for guests and local residents. A curio-shop proprietor took visitors to the White River Badlands, southeast of Hot Springs, to search for specimens. The local opera house offered traveling productions. Tourists enjoyed day trips to nearby Cascade Springs, another warm-water area, and to Wind Cave, a large cavern north of town. The entertaining of travelers led to controversy in Hot Springs as saloons, gambling, and prostitution developed. While some citizens protested the illegal activities, others reluctantly acknowledged that they were probably necessary components of a pleasure resort. Attempts to eliminate these activities were intermittent and unsuccessful during Hot Springs's heyday. However, formal and informal means of control, including fines for saloons and brothels and an unspoken agreement that gambling should take place out of the public view, helped to temper the effects of the vices.[11]

Along with businesses that supported the tourist industry and the general population, Hot Springs attracted public institutions based on its reputation as a health resort. The Grand Army of the Republic selected Hot

Springs as the site of a territorial soldiers' home, and in 1889, over Governor Louis Church's veto, the legislature passed a measure establishing the institution in Hot Springs; it opened in November 1890. In 1902, President Theodore Roosevelt also signed a bill locating a national veterans' hospital in Hot Springs. The hospital, named Battle Mountain Sanitarium, was completed in 1907. It crowned the resort area with a complex of buildings in Mission-inspired architecture, set in a circular configuration on a plateau above upper town.[12] Hot Springs soon became a center for health and medical services as well as a warm-water resort.

Despite that reputation, the twentieth century brought changes that dashed Hot Springs promoters' hopes of continuing as a permanent health-resort town. As the public began to comprehend the bacteriological causes of contagious diseases like tuberculosis, they were less inclined to seek warm-water treatments in the company of strangers. Located in a sparsely populated region, the resort could not draw upon a large elite class to support it solely as a social center. A series of destructive fires and floods and divisiveness between the two areas of town threatened the community's growth. The agent most responsible for the decline of the health-resort concept, however, was the automobile. For large numbers of wealthy travelers, a lengthy automobile trip replaced an extended stay in the pink-walled canyon as a status symbol and as an ideal vacation. Personal automobiles also allowed people of more modest means to enjoy the area's features without spending significant amounts of time or money in hotels and spas. Residents began to tout good roads, rather than luxurious hotels or sophisticated entertainments, as attractions. By 1917, most of the tourists visiting Hot Springs were motorists, and most of them camped.[13]

The effect of automobile traffic on the resort industry of Hot Springs illustrated a permanent change in tourism in the United States. At the turn of the century, Americans owned approximately eight thousand automobiles. By the end of 1930, nearly twenty-six million cars were registered, one for every 4.63 people in the country.[14] This rapid expansion of auto transportation exerted a profound impact on American society. In 1932, the President's Research Committee on Social Trends said that the influence of the automobile "has . . . cut down railroad traffic, especially on short hauls, lessened the isolation of the farmer, aided the consolidation of small schools and churches, has helped, along with electricity, to disperse factories, and has developed a new kind of vacation."[15] Trains set fares, but with cars, motorists could manage their own travel expenses. Trains demanded adherence to schedules and routes; motorists could depart, pause, and stop for the day where and when they pleased.[16] Tourists who traveled by car could create and control their own experiences, schedules, and budgets. In an era of industrialization, the car provided an exhilarating freedom.

The automobile also offered a physical challenge, one that many Americans were seeking. In 1899, Theodore Roosevelt used the words "the strenuous life" in calling for American men to be strong and vigorous. Roosevelt's phrase created an antidote for what many people saw as the draining tensions of modern life.[17] In motoring, the quest for a strenuous life and the need to escape from structured society combined with the fascination for new technology and the burgeoning consumer culture to establish a satisfying and popular mode of travel.

Initially, car travel was restricted to the well-to-do, but by 1920, economical cars and improved roads opened motoring to greater numbers of people. Although their trips might remain shorter, more modest, and in areas closer to home than those of the first wealthy motorists, they shared the pleasures of car ownership and travel. The restrictions on their time compelled many of these tourists to reach well-known sights as quickly as possible during their vacation and to see as many of them as they could. The nature of car travel created a new kind of tourist as well as a new kind of vacation. Motoring travelers were restless and anxious to move down the road.[18] Traditional resort sojourns in places like Hot Springs did not appeal to them; new services and amenities soon developed to serve their interests.

In the early twentieth century, the national park system became a major attraction for automobile tourists, providing exciting destinations, wide-open spaces, and opportunities for adventurous motoring. The development of these parks stimulated automobile tourism in the American West and encouraged some of those travelers to come through the Black Hills. Until 1916, national parks were administered as separate units under a variety of agencies. In that year, the National Parks Act created the National Park Service, providing for the regulation and management of national parks and most national monuments and reservations under one entity. The National Park Service was charged with protecting the scenic, natural, and historic features of these areas while at the same time providing "for the enjoyment of the same" by the public.[19] A manifestation of the Progressive trend toward centralized management and planning, this administrative umbrella over the national parks and monuments was created at the same time that economical autos, a higher standard of living, increased free time, and growing road systems encouraged Americans to see their country. The National Park Act directly influenced the growth of modern tourism in the United States. From 1917 until 1928, the policies of Steven Mather, director of the National Park Service, established the parks as tourist destinations for the growing number of American travelers. Mather built relationships with political leaders and with railroad officials, who helped to advertise the parks and to develop visitor accommodations within them.[20]

The development of Wind Cave in the southern Black Hills provides an illuminating and complex example of one of those parks. Although Hot Springs did not fulfill its promoters' hopes, its success as a nineteenth-century resort helped to promote Wind Cave. Located about thirteen miles north of Hot Springs, the cave became popularized after nearby settlers Tom and Jesse Bingham noticed wind coming from the ground while on a hunting trip in 1881 and spread word of the phenomenon. For the next several years, area residents casually explored the cave for recreation, and by 1886, Hot Springs businessmen were promoting Wind Cave to visitors as an interesting and exciting day trip. In 1890, the South Dakota Mining Company, owned by the R. B. Moss family, bought three mining claims at the cave site and installed Jesse D. McDonald as manager of the property.[21] Two of McDonald's sons, Elmer and Alvin, became avid explorers of Wind Cave and developed maps of many of its subterranean passages.

In about 1892, John Stabler of Hot Springs also became involved in the operations, and the Stabler and McDonald families institutionalized touring at Wind Cave. They opened three routes through the cave, using explosives to widen the passages in some places. Their improvements allowed tourists to tour portions of the site with relative ease, even enabling women to enter the cave without donning overalls. In 1893, John Stabler, Jesse McDonald, and three other men formed the Wonderful Wind Cave Improvement Company and built a hotel near the cavern. Stabler also advertised the cave tours at Hot Springs hotels, and a stage brought passengers to the site. The operators devised colorful promotions to attract visitors' attention. One of the most unusual occurred in 1893, when a "mind reader" named Paul Johnstone spent seventy hours searching for a pin that had been hidden in the cave. He fell into a coma after finding the pin but fortuitously recovered

This tour group sought adventure in Wind Cave in 1917.

the next day. Newspaper publicity about the event helped to promote Wind Cave, making it a popular attraction.[22]

The success of Wind Cave stimulated a contentious and bitter rivalry over its ownership. Jesse McDonald filed a homestead claim shortly after the vicinity was surveyed in 1892, apparently at the request of the members of the South Dakota Mining Company, who had purchased and filed mining claims in the area and were trying to strengthen their legal ownership. However, McDonald did not contract to convey the land to the company and appears to have believed his claim gave him full right to the property. After he sold part interest in the cave to John Stabler, the Stabler family filed additional homestead claims in the area.[23]

In 1893, R. B. Moss of the South Dakota Mining Company sued the Wonderful Wind Cave Improvement Company, asking the court to restore the property to his company and to compensate him for specimens taken from the cave. At about the same time, another party, Peter Folsom, filed liens against the Moss claims due to nonpayment for assay work he had performed. Eventually, Folsom bought the insolvent South Dakota Mining Company's property at auction. In the meantime, dissension arose between the McDonalds and the Stablers, and the latter family joined forces with Folsom. The next several years saw ongoing litigation punctuated by confrontations and threats of violence between the two factions. The suits were particularly complicated because no one had used the land for the primary purposes for which they had claimed it; Wind Cave had never been a mine, and it had never been a farm.[24] From the beginning, it was a tourist attraction.

The conflict over the ownership of Wind Cave may have given impetus to its becoming a national park. In 1896, the *Hot Springs Star* noted that as long as the McDonald family continued to operate the cave, it could not reach its potential of drawing tourists. S. E. Wilson, a Hot Springs attorney, and Eben W. Martin, a congressman from Deadwood who owned property in Hot Springs, exerted political pressure on the federal government to take the cave out of private hands. At one point, Martin suggested that the area be incorporated into the newly designated national forest.[25] Later, Martin supported the establishment of a national park and complimented the secretary of the interior's office for saving the property from the "individuals and companies" who were trying to gain title to it.[26]

In January 1900, the secretary of the interior authorized the temporary withdrawal of Wind Cave-area lands from settlement, pending a decision to make the site a national park. Additional withdrawals were made over the following two years. Early in 1902, Senator Robert Gamble of South Dakota and Representative John F. Lacey of Iowa introduced bills to establish Wind Cave National Park, making it one of the earliest national parks. Gamble's bill passed the Senate and the House with little discussion, and Theodore Roosevelt signed the law early in 1903. Perceived scientific values of the cave strengthened arguments for creating a national park, but its importance as a tourist attraction also played a role. The legislation authorized the secretary of the interior to lease the cave and surface areas of land for development of tourist amenities, with the funds from such leases supporting park maintenance and improvements.[27]

Those improvements were slow in coming to Wind Cave National Park. Congress, the Department of the Interior, and the National Park Service took few steps to further the development of the site during its first quarter century of existence. Congressional appropriations were small, although in 1912 that body provided funds for the establishment of a game reserve at Wind Cave, to be administered by the newly created United States Biological Survey. The park's first superintendent, William Rankin, reported that Wind Cave's facilities included a log house at the entrance to the cave, a ramshackle hotel, and a few outbuildings for livestock. Poor roads and four unsafe bridges completed the park's infrastructure. Perhaps to supplement his salary, Rankin gave his wife a permit to sell lunches to tourists, and she used the otherwise abandoned hotel as a dining room and shelter. Rankin directed some further exploration of the cave, erected fences, made minor repairs, and, in 1905, constructed a superintendent's residence.[28] The dearth of financial support precluded more than these minimal improvements, and local controversies about services and facilities at the cave continued to simmer.

In 1905, a visitor complained to the secretary of the interior that his party had arrived at Wind Cave in the morning, but Rankin would not allow them to enter the cave until afternoon. To delay entry, Rankin had cited regulations, but the tourist suspected he was trying to coerce them into buying his wife's lunches. Seth Bullock, chief forester of the Black Hills National Forest with jurisdiction over the park, told the secretary he believed the disagreement was instigated by a Hot Springs "hack driver" who was disgruntled by the disruption of his former monopoly.[29] In 1908, the Interior Department's acting secretary reassured Congressman Martin that the department intended "to improve this reservation so as to make it a pleasuring ground for the people and carry out the spirit of the act establishing it."[30] In 1914, however, Acting Superintendent Frederick M. Dille informed the secretary that despite the intention of the law, the park had not been operated in a manner that served the public well. He reported that unqualified guides were collecting exorbitant fees, that the numbers of visitors had been inflated, and that, despite the fact that most of the visitors were women, "the ladies room has been a joke."[31] The national park was not fulfilling its promise as a tourist attraction.

In addition to lack of money, inconsistent administration and staffing contributed to the problems. Between 1903 and 1919, Wind Cave National Park had seven superintendents. The men were area residents, and most of the appointments were politically motivated. As an example, Rufus Pilcher served as superintendent from March 1910 to May 1911. He succeeded his father, who died while holding the post. Rufus Pilcher later wrote that he resigned after one of the senators succeeded in taking the patronage for the superintendency away from Congressman Martin. The use of the position as a source of political patronage contributed to the rapid turnover and retarded long-term planning.[32] Politics and resulting policy governed the administration of Wind Cave National Park.

The establishment of the National Park Service in 1916 did not appreciably improve conditions at Wind Cave. By mid-1918, Superintendent Thomas Brazell was the only regular employee at the park. Two or three rangers were hired on a seasonal basis, mainly to guide tourists through the cave. The buildings consisted of the superintendent's residence, a small administration building, the structure over the cave entrance, a barn, auto shelter, camp pavilion, and blacksmith shop; all except the auto shelter needed repair. Most of those who came to the cave were from South Dakota or nearby states. Nine thousand people reportedly visited Wind Cave in 1916, but two years later the superintendent noted a decline in visitors, which he attributed to wet conditions, bad roads, and war activities.[33] At the end of World War I, the park remained ill-equipped and sparsely staffed.

Ownership issues that plagued the early development of Wind Cave and helped lead to its establishment as a national park also affected other areas destined to become tourist attractions. The presence of national forest lands and the administration of the United States Forest Service were crucially important to the development of the tourism industry in the Black Hills. President Grover Cleveland created the Black Hills Forest Reserve in 1897 by the authority of the Forest Reserve Act of 1891. This reserve was unusual because it was established in proximity to significant settlement, compared to most forest reserves that were located in remote, unpopulated areas. The designation effectively removed from public use all timber and land not legally claimed in the reserve's 967,680 acres, representing most of the timbered lands in the Black Hills region.[34]

Black Hills residents were not pleased. They expected that the forest reserve would block individual access to the region's resources and retard development. Shortly after the establishment of the reserve became public knowledge, thousands of local citizens gathered in Deadwood and protested. Such opposition in South Dakota and in other areas of the West led to modifications in the laws governing forest reserves. South Dakota Senator Richard F. Pettigrew, for instance, successfully sponsored legislation that placed restrictions on further forest reserve designations, allowed the filing of mining claims on forest lands, and permitted prospecting and cutting of timber for mining-related purposes. By requiring active management of forest reserves and opening them to managed use, including sale of timber, these laws revised the earlier policy of simply protecting the areas. Subsequent Interior Department administrative policies allowed grazing, farming, and road and irrigation development under controlled conditions. In 1905, jurisdiction over the forest reserves was transferred to the Forest Service. Subsequently, the term identifying all the reserves was changed to "national forest." In 1910, President William Taft divided the Black Hills National Forest into a northern section, carrying the original name, with headquarters in Deadwood, and a southern section, designated the Harney National Forest, with offices in Custer.[35]

The United States Forest Service, by the terms of its organic act of 1897, had the authority to manage the national forest lands for mixed uses, including recreation. Under Gifford Pinchot, who headed the agency until 1910, the Forest Service concentrated on the management and control of its resources, rather than making national forests accessible to the public or preserving scenic lands. Although Forest Service officials and foresters under Pinchot and his successor, Henry S. Graves, recognized the validity of the recreational use of the forests, they continued to see that use as a low priority. In 1915, Congress authorized leasing lands in the forests for summer homes and businesses to serve visitors, and in 1917, the Forest Service engaged Frank A. Waugh, a landscape architect, to investigate the recreational promise of the nation's forests. The public's utilization of the scenic and recreational resources of the national forests, however, remained relatively insignificant in terms of forest management until automobile travel brought more people to the areas.[36]

That increase created a demand for services and amenities. In 1916, the Forest Service estimated that three million people had come to the national forests during the year; in 1925, visitation reached fifteen million. By then, fifteen hundred designated public campgrounds existed in the forests, about one-third of them enhanced by sanitary facilities, water supplies, and fireplaces. Many of these improvements, however, had been made by private or civic organizations. Although the Forest Service recognized and acted upon the needs of the increasing numbers of visitors, expansion of resources to serve them remained less important than other priorities and even controversial within the agency. Partially as a reaction to the creation of the National Park Service and its programs, the Forest Service's attention to recreational use focused increasingly on wilderness management, including limited development in wilderness areas. Such policies served different purposes than the Park Service's programs and therefore did not compete directly with that agency's goals.[37]

The presence of the national forests in the Black Hills offered residents and tourists opportunities to enjoy the scenery and to camp, fish, and hunt. Some people built cabins under the leasing law of 1915, which allowed the public to lease lots for recreational structures as well as for hotels, stores, and other services that catered to tourists. The Forest Service made little effort to promote the establishment of such services, however, emphasizing timber and land management, not public access. The Antiquities Act of 1906 allowed the president to establish national monuments to protect natural and built features of historic, prehistoric, and scientific value located on public lands and gave various federal agencies, including the Forest Service, responsibility for monuments created on lands under their control. This charge did not necessarily extend to supervision or development, and often the only protection accorded monuments were signs posted at the sites to warn the public against collecting and vandalism. The presence of vast tracts of public lands meant most of the earliest designated monuments were in the West, and as automobile tourism increased, the existence of the monuments helped pull motorists in that direction.[38]

To the United States Forest Service, then, fell the supervision of Jewel Cave in the southern Black Hills. The development of this cave, located about twelve miles west of Custer, South Dakota, had repeated the Wind Cave pattern of conflicts between early developers and local citizens concerned with degradation of resources. At the turn of the century, Frank and Albert Michaud, two brothers who had recently settled in the Custer area, came upon a cave entrance so small that neither of them could enter it. They enlarged the opening, explored the cavern, and decided the crystals within had no value as minerals but could be a lure for tourists and a source of revenue as specimens. The Michauds took on a partner, Charles Bush, and filed a mining claim on the property, calling it Jewel Lode, in September 1900. The Michauds subsequently filed other mineral claims in the same area, and another partner, Bertha Cain, acquired an interest in these properties.[39]

Over the next several years, Bush and the Michauds explored the cave, established passages in it, built a wagon road to the site, and constructed a two-story log building there. The building, probably designed as a hotel and dining room for tourists, featured a rustic but imposing two-story front porch with round arches and decorative detail suggestive of the Stick-style architecture popular in the late 1800s. The men promoted the structure

*The turn-of-the-century hotel at Jewel Cave
blended into its surroundings.*

as the site of the "Jewel Cave Dancing Club" in 1902. Despite these efforts, as well as some local advertising, the cave failed to draw enough people to make the enterprise worthwhile. The site was difficult to reach, and Wind Cave was better known and more easily accessible. Subsequently, Bush sold his interest in the cave to Frank Michaud in 1905, and at some point, the brothers apparently devised a new scheme to increase the attractions of the site: the development of a game preserve.[40]

The Michaud brothers garnered some political support for the idea, proposing the withdrawal of an area of sixty square miles from the Black Hills National Forest, including over sixteen thousand acres of timber. Local residents, however, were not enthusiastic about such a withdrawal, suggesting that opportunities for general development in that area of the Black Hills were better served if timber sales and grazing continued. A report produced at the time of the proposal stated that the cave was not scientifically significant because the same variety of specimens were available in Yellowstone National Park. It further concluded that the proposed area was not large enough for a viable game refuge and recommended that the area be designated a national monument instead.[41] Unfortunately for the Michauds, the interest generated by the game-preserve proposal, which threatened the interests of other local residents, undermined their attempts to develop a profitable tourist attraction. As a national monument, the cave and its environs would remain under the jurisdiction of the Forest Service, and its grazing and timber resources would still be available to the larger public. President Theodore Roosevelt signed a proclamation citing Jewel Cave's "scientific interest" and designating it a national monument on 8 February 1908.[42]

Immediately, the Michaud brothers and their partner Bertha Cain began asking for compensation for the loss of their claims as well as for the improvements they had made to the property. The Forest Service questioned the legality of the claims, citing a decision in the Wind Cave litigation that held that land claimed because of the presence of a cave and which yielded minerals which could be sold only as "curiosities" did not meet the definition of mineral land in mining law. Although the Antiquities Act said monuments created under the law were subject to valid claims, the validity of the Michaud claims could be questioned because of the family's use of the property.[43]

Giving up hopes for a resolution, Albert Michaud assigned his interest in the claims to his brother Frank and moved to Canada about 1910. Frank Michaud and his family continued to ask for reimbursement from the government, and the Forest Service debated the matter internally. If Michaud's claims were valid, he could have obtained patent to the property and the government might have been obligated to purchase the land. On the other hand, if investigation showed that the Michauds had tried to acquire Jewel Cave for development as a tourist attraction through the use of a mineral entry, the claims would be fraudulent. In that case, Michaud would lose any rights to the property and the government would owe him nothing. Apparently, Frank Michaud never applied for a patent to the land, and as a result the Forest Service did not formally investigate the claims, leaving their status in question.[44]

The Forest Service did not consider mining activity under Michaud's mining claims to be in contradiction with the government's interests in the monument and continued to allow the family access to the cave so that they could perform annual assessment work necessary to maintain the claims. Thus, the agency avoided interference with legitimate mining activity that might have become a factor in the controversy. The Forest Service was unwilling to extend those rights, however. According to Frank Michaud's son, the agency refused to enter into a lease that would have allowed the family to operate the cave as an attraction. Although the cave was open to visitors for periods of time, the confusion over the claims, the proximity of Wind Cave as a similar attraction, and the agency's emphasis on timber and land management discouraged the Forest Service from further developing Jewel Cave or tourists' services there.[45]

Similar to the circumstances surrounding the establishment of Wind Cave National Park, part of the impetus for the creation of Jewel Cave National Monument was its potential attraction for tourists. The Michauds, trying to expand that potential, lost control of the cave. The Forest Service, frustrated by the legal issues and less interested in providing public access to the lands under its jurisdiction than in managing its resources, did little to promote the site. Under federal control, Jewel Cave received even less attention than Wind Cave. While Wind Cave superintendents struggled to maintain the national park and the United States Forest Service protected but did not promote the national monument, state lawmakers created a new game reserve in Custer County that would eventually become one of the country's largest state parks and would play a more significant role in

Peter Norbeck personified Progressive Republican politics in early twentieth-century South Dakota.

the development of Black Hills tourism than did any of the federally designated areas.

South Dakota's first state park was the outgrowth of a state game reserve created largely through the efforts of Peter Norbeck, one of South Dakota's best-known politicians. In 1905, Norbeck and two friends were the first people to drive an automobile across western South Dakota to the Black Hills. Norbeck's visit there inspired him to promote the creation of a game preserve in the southern Black Hills and, in larger terms, to open the beauties of the Hills to motorists. In the process of pursuing that goal, he acquired beliefs and attitudes about park design and services for tourists that had a strong impact on the growth of tourism in the region.[46]

Peter Norbeck was born in Clay County, Dakota Territory, in 1870 to Scandinavian immigrant parents. Although his father was a lay minister, the family's farm was the primary source of income, and the Norbecks depended on their oldest son to help with the work. Consequently, Peter

Norbeck received little formal education, attending rural school for a few months each year and then three terms at the new University of Dakota. He was intellectually curious, however, and always a voracious reader. In 1894, he and a cousin began an artesian well-drilling business that eventually made Norbeck a wealthy man and a well-known one in the new states of North and South Dakota.[47]

Norbeck entered state politics during the Progressive period, an era from about 1890 to the 1920s. Although he was a successful self-made businessman, both his personal background and business interests were bound to agriculture, and he supported Progressive laws that restrained the power of corporations and railroads and favored farmers. In 1908, he ran for the office of state senator from Spink County on the Republican ticket. The primary election was marked by a division between Progressives and Stalwarts that constituted a deep rift in the Republican party. Although he was unpolished and largely unschooled, Norbeck's energy, work ethic, and political instincts served him well. He won the election in 1908 and was reelected in 1910 and 1912. In 1914, he successfully ran for lieutenant governor, and in 1916, he was elected governor by a wide margin.[48]

In addition to agricultural issues, Norbeck was also vitally interested in conservation and wild-game protection. In 1910, the state took title to lands in the southern Black Hills in lieu of state school sections located within the national forest. This agreement between the state and federal governments gave South Dakota jurisdiction over a rugged, heavily timbered area in Custer County that the state legislature designated a state forest. In 1913, with Norbeck's prompting, John Parks, state senator from Custer County, introduced legislation creating a state game preserve on the land. The legislation passed the senate, but failed in the house until Norbeck suggested that some supporters of the preserve vote for a pending temperance law in exchange for votes in favor of the game-preserve measure.[49]

The new game preserve comprised an area eight miles by twelve miles just north of Wind Cave National Park. The legislation also provided an appropriation for fencing and acquiring game for the preserve, and the commissioner of school and public lands and the state game warden had the responsibility for stocking and administering the area. Norbeck took a deep interest in the development of the refuge and spent a great deal of time in the Black Hills supervising the fencing.[50] Although the primary purpose of the preserve was to raise and protect game birds, fish, and animals, George Roskie, the state forester, noted that it was also a potential attraction for the "hundreds" of midwestern tourists who visited the Hills each year.[51]

At this time, only small numbers of tourists visited the Black Hills, as George Roskie's remark reveals. Bypassed by the major transcontinental railroad lines, the Black Hills did not benefit from significant railroad tourist traffic, large-scale railroad tourism promotion, or the development of accommodations by rail companies that other regions enjoyed. The Fremont, Elkhorn & Missouri Valley Railroad, owned by the Chicago & North Western, was the first railroad to bring passengers into the Black Hills, reaching Buffalo Gap in 1885, Rapid City in 1886, and Deadwood in 1890. The Grand Island and Wyoming Central line of the Chicago, Burlington & Quincy also entered the Hills from the south and extended into the northern Hills. The Chicago & North Western reached Rapid City from Pierre in 1903.[52] These regional lines provided transportation to tourists and publicized the area in brochures, but their audience and their effectiveness were limited. Until an automobile transportation system developed, western South Dakota remained a difficult region for tourists to reach.

In 1913, fewer than fifteen thousand automobiles could be found in South Dakota; by 1919, more than a hundred thousand had been registered. The need for good automobile roads in a rural, sparsely populated state was recognized early, but issues of local control over roads impeded development of a cohesive system and contributed to ongoing controversies. Legislative attempts to establish some form of centralized authority over road systems failed during the century's first decade, and road-building remained largely a local function.[53]

In 1911, the state legislature passed what was referred to as a "Good Roads Law" that gave the responsibility for road construction costing up to five hundred dollars to township supervisors and for construction for roads over that amount to county commissioners. Under this law, county commissioners had the authority to designate routes and to levy taxes for county roads. The state engineer supervised road work on state lands. In the mountainous areas of western South Dakota, the county could hire an engineer to plan and superintend the work. The legislation reflected the ongoing concern over local power, as each county could vote to exempt itself from the measure. Twenty-five counties held elections on the issue, and all accepted the new law.[54] By giving counties increased control over roads and road systems, the state moved toward a more comprehensive means of road planning.

J. W. Parmley was one of the supporters of this broader system. A state senator from Edmunds County, Parmley was also a regional leader in the Good Roads movement, which promoted responsible and organized road development. One of the effects of the movement was a proliferation of highway routes carrying particular names, and Parmley was instrumental in establishing the Yellowstone Trail Association, an organization devoted to the marking and construction of a national east-to-west route. The Yellowstone Trail, so named because it passed near Yellowstone Park, became one of the most prominently named highways in the area. Parmley himself painted large rocks bright yellow along the way. He even carried appropriate stones with him in the trunk of his car, to be used in areas where no such natural markers were available.[55]

As automobile travel increased in popularity, efforts of organizations like the Yellowstone Trail Association to mark routes and the competition among them to win the support of localities became almost frenzied. The South Dakota Highway Commission, created by the 1913 legislature, addressed this situation in its initial report. It was "high time," the report said, to establish rules governing the signage employed by the various organizations so that travelers would be guided by some uniformity. They disapproved of wooden signs on posts or fences because vandals shot holes in such signs or pointed them in the wrong direction. The commission established "one rule": highway associations should paint their emblems on existing poles and posts rather than erecting signs or arrows.[56] The commission's concern with uniform guidance for travelers indicates that road planning had moved beyond the local farm-to-market emphasis and was now addressing the needs of the long-distance traveler.

The lack of any appropriation hampered the effectiveness of the state highway commission during the first years of its existence. The problem was rectified, however, when South Dakota passed legislation in accordance with the Federal Road Aid Law of 1916, requiring states to establish highway departments in order to receive federal matching funds. To comply with the law, South Dakota amended its constitution to enable the state to fund internal improvements. The 1917 legislature established the highway department and a new highway commission with appropriate funding. Governor Peter Norbeck served as its first chairman. Two years later, the

GRAND OPENING
Spearfish Canyon Road,
Aug 28. 1930.
© BLACK HILLS STUDIOS INC
63

Cars waited bumper to bumper for the grand opening of the completed Spearfish Canyon Road in 1930.

legislature charged the commission with the responsibility of establishing a trunk-road system that would relieve counties of some of the responsibilities of road building.[57] In the ensuing years, the increased state authority led to a more efficient and integrated road system, though it also continued to stimulate rivalries between localities and politicians interested in road issues.

The importance of recreational driving influenced these issues. In 1915, a Sioux Falls newspaper lamented that eastern South Dakota motorists were "fairly crying" for interesting destinations, but because of the absence of good roads, they found little interesting. "For the sheer joy of driving," the article noted, "they will follow the smoothest path southward a distance of 90 miles—and find at the end of the trip what? Sioux City!" The newspaper urged the development of a road that would give eastern South Dakotans access to "the state's magnificent scenic resort" in the Black Hills.[58]

The road situation in the Black Hills was even more complex than elsewhere in the state, due not only to the rugged terrain but also to the federal and state jurisdiction over the bulk of the area. The United States Forest Service played a crucial role in road development there, particularly in building "forest roads" that served settlers and towns beyond the reach of main highways. Because so much of the area was encompassed by the national forests, federal funds paid for a great deal of road building in the Black Hills. Local efforts also remained important. For example, Spearfish residents who recognized the scenic values of Spearfish Canyon unsuccessfully asked its county commissioners to build a highway through the canyon as early as the 1890s. In 1910, the Spearfish Commercial Club began to develop the Spearfish Canyon Road.[59]

That city's initiative was typical of the area's commitment to road-building. Lawrence County, located in the northern Black Hills and encompassing the cities of Deadwood, Lead, and Spearfish, acquired a reputation for developing good roads, beginning a comprehensive construction program in 1911 after the Good Roads Law was enacted. County commissioners designed a road system with Deadwood as the hub. Among other accomplishments, the program succeeded in reducing some Deadwood-to-Spearfish highway grades from eighteen or twenty percent to less than seven percent. By 1919, Lawrence County had spent more than six hundred thousand dollars on roads and bridges. Officials in Pennington County, located in the central Hills and home to Rapid City, also instituted a road-building program, recognizing that their roads could not only aid transportation for local residents but also open up access to previously unappreciated scenery.[60]

As the tourism industry developed, the road system in the region and the state became increasingly important to its success. County and state efforts in road building joined the federal park and monument system, the national forest, and the state forest and game preserve in forming a basis for a tourism infrastructure through public works and public policy. Railroads, although becoming less important, still played a role. By 1920, travelers could journey through the Black Hills by a combination of rail, automobile, and stage. A comprehensive trip included the South Dakota School of Mines Museum and the United States Indian School in Rapid City; the mining and government community of Deadwood; the Homestake Mine at Lead; Spearfish Canyon; Fort Meade at Sturgis; and Sylvan Lake, Harney Peak, and Wind Cave in the southern Black Hills. Residents and visitors alike enjoyed riding the Rapid City, Black Hills & Western Railroad, a local narrow-gauge railroad built in the 1880s that carried sightseers as well as freight. Popularly known as the Crouch Line, the train ran from Rapid City to Mystic, twenty-five miles to the west, and became an attraction in itself due to its winding and scenic route.[61]

The Rapid City, Black Hills & Western Railroad operated both steam- and gas-powered engines. This gas-powered locomotive stands on a trestle in front of the Pierre Lodge at Hisega.

The first hotel at Sylvan Lake charmed visitors until it burned down in 1935.

Although public entities became increasingly important, enterprising individuals continued to be responsible for the birth of the region's tourist industry. Tourism had begun in the early 1880s with the health resort at Hot Springs, where private enterprise had stimulated the development of Wind Cave. Tourism also inspired efforts to promote Jewel Cave as an attraction. The forty years preceding the end of World War I saw additional private growth in the tourism industry, although that development was sporadic and intended mainly for local, relatively affluent audiences. Among these developments were resort or vacation hotels that offered people who could afford the time and money a retreat for a weekend, a week, or a summer. Sylvan Lake and Hisega are examples of two such sites.

Destined to become one of the area's best-known vacation stops, Sylvan Lake, near Custer, was the first of the numerous reservoirs eventually created in the Black Hills. In 1891 and 1892, Theodore Reder, who had filed mineral claims in a granite-rimmed valley northeast of Custer, hauled in cement to fill a narrow opening in the formations there. After the concrete dam was completed, a lake formed in the circular canyon. Elizabeth Reder,

A group
from Pierre
enjoyed a day's
diversion by a
Black Hills
stream in 1908.
During their
stay, they
named their
campsite
"Hisega."

Theodore Reder's wife, designed a simple frame, three-and-one-half-story hotel building with a gingerbread-trimmed, two-story porch, and Reder and his brothers built the structure. In 1896, the Reders sold the hotel to Joseph Spencer III, who leased it to various operators for a quarter of a century. Despite the fact that the rugged road to the hotel required an arduous trip, the hotel's location on the shore of a mirror-like lake bordered by dramatic granite cliffs and timbered slopes made it a popular gathering spot for Black Hills residents and guests. Visitors fished, hiked, canoed, and enjoyed the tranquil spot.[62]

Hisega, established west of Rapid City, became a favorite destination for residents of central South Dakota. In August of 1908, sixteen people from Pierre, including State Historian Doane Robinson, traveled to Rapid City on the North Western railroad and then took the Rapid City, Black Hills & Western to the mouth of nearby Spring Creek, arriving in time to make camp for the night. The ten-day vacation cost a total of $13.75 for each of the sixteen campers. Refreshed and exhilarated by their mountain stay, the group used the first letter of the first name of each woman in the party to create an appellation for the site: Hisega. Robinson's enthusiasm about the spot convinced a group of Pierre residents to acquire land there and build a summer lodge. Subsequently, other visitors erected cabins and tent camps, and the railroad adopted the name and established the Hisega station.[63]

Summer visitors to Hisega fished, hiked, played tennis, and relaxed away from the heat and humidity of the South Dakota prairie. In July 1918, for example, a number of Pierre residents, other people from central and eastern South Dakota, one family from Wisconsin, and two families from Iowa spent time at the Pierre Lodge.[64] Doane Robinson wrote a poem about the spot, some lines of which reveal the elite positions of its habitués:

> Gathered about the chimney blaze,
> Seeking amuse in devious ways,
> The capital's contingent gay,
> Out for the summer's holiday.
> A governor, a congressman,
> A judge or two, a ready clan
> Of merchants, lawyers, doctors wise,
> A jolly priest—you'd least surmise
> His cloth this night. Young matrons fair
> With trooping youngsters too, were there;
> Pert college men and maids demure,
> Spouting of love and literature.[65]

Hisega offered a pleasant summer vacation in socially acceptable company for those who had sufficient time and money to travel.

Genteel visitors like those summering at Hisega found entertainment in specific attractions. Dark Canyon, outside Rapid City, became a popular spot for day trips, walks, and summer camping. Frank Lockhart, who owned property in the canyon, added to the natural beauty of the site by planting berry bushes, shrubs, and flowers; creating moss sculptures of animals and birds; and building a small artificial lake that contained floating emblems of the Masonic order.[66] He also constructed a path "to make it easy for the delicate and those not accustomed to climbing" to enjoy the canyon.[67] Dark Canyon provided a spot for quiet strolls and contemplation of the natural environment and Lockhart's embellishments.

(opposite)
The wild beauty of Dark Canyon, outside Rapid City, gained early popularity with tourists.

Dark Canyon

Crystal Cave, about twenty miles north of Rapid City, also drew visitors. Unlike Wind and Jewel caves, it remained in private hands. Two brothers located the cave entrance in 1885, settled nearby, and explored and developed it. Although legal issues reminiscent of the Wind Cave and Jewel Cave situations arose, the family's possession of the property was confirmed in 1913. By 1920, seven miles of passages had been mapped, and Crystal Cave proved to be more accessible than Jewel Cave, the national monument.[68] Altogether, attractions such as Crystal Cave, the Crouch Line, Dark Canyon, Hisega, and Sylvan Lake entertained residents and visitors to the Black Hills who appreciated the scenery and features and had the means to enjoy them.

Well aware of the natural beauty of the region, Black Hills residents took pride in the fact that it attracted visitors. Until after World War I, however, tourism in the Black Hills was localized and relatively undeveloped, catering predominantly to local and area travelers and elite tourists. Little effort went into expanding existing offerings. Local boosting of the area's scenic attributes was often intended to attract permanent settlers and investors; drawing transient visitors remained a secondary goal. The *Rapid City Daily Journal* repeatedly printed an article during the spring of 1918 that illustrated this outlook. Entitled "The Black Hills of South Dakota, Rapid City Especially, an Ideal Place," the feature described the natural resources of the Black Hills, government offices, businesses and industries in Rapid City, gold mines in the area, and rich agricultural lands in the surrounding countryside. Except for a brief mention of trout-fishing, the article made no reference to recreational opportunities or the scope of the local tourism industry.[69]

Public officials displayed similar attitudes. In 1905, Governor Samuel Elrod received an invitation from the Salt Lake City Commercial Club to attend a 1906 conference that would gather western officials and business interests in planning ways to attract visitors. Elrod sent a brief reply saying he could not attend. Thus, although 125 delegates from western states went to the conference, no one from South Dakota was among them. An informal report of the state's commissioner of immigration to Governor Norbeck on 1 Jan. 1919 described that office's efforts to publicize South Dakota's assets to potential settlers, but it made no mention of the state's attractions for tourists other than a brief reference to hunting and fishing.[70] Governor Elrod's dismissal of the 1906 Salt Lake City conference and the

Turn-of-the-century Black Hills tourists waited outside the rustic entrance to Crystal Cave.

lack of attention to tourism by the commissioner of immigration's office in 1919 accurately reflect attitudes in the state before the 1920s. The state's isolation and the region's small population discouraged the serious consideration of tourism as an important undertaking.

The interruption of European travel during World War I, however, and the development of the economical car began to change these attitudes about tourism, at least in the Black Hills. In 1915, a writer in the *Pahasapa Quarterly* pointed out that Americans were accustomed to taking trips to Europe to satisfy their "touring habit," but war mobilization abroad had made such travel unsafe. He noted that Americans might consider it their "duty and pleasure" to see the attractions in their own country before traveling overseas. Therefore, "this magazine would not be worthy of its name did it not urge that among the multitude of those wonders our own Black Hills are not the least worthy of attention."[71]

The area's commercial organizations began to encourage these vacation visits. Deadwood's business club, for example, promoted good roads and rail transportation, sponsored special events, and published and distributed publicity about the attractions of the city and its environs.[72] Late in 1915, secretaries of commercial clubs in the Black Hills met and formed an association "for the purpose of not only creating a better feeling among the different communities, but to formulate plans for the better advertising of the Black Hills in the various communities in Eastern South Dakota for the coming tourist season." The association planned an advertising campaign that included the distribution of printed folders and newspaper advertisements in the eastern half of the state.[73] In 1918, Judge W. W. Soule, president of the Rapid City Commercial Club, chastised Sioux Falls citizens for vacationing in the mountains of Colorado and Wyoming and for fishing and hunting at resorts in Wisconsin, Minnesota, and northern Iowa—all the while ignoring the beauties and recreational opportunities of the Black Hills.[74] The commercial clubs had opened their eyes to the potential importance of tourism, but they continued to view it as an activity restricted mainly to state citizens.

Residents of the Black Hills also assumed that their scenery, some promotion, and good roads were the keys to attracting travelers. In reality, successful tourism demanded a new way of thinking: tourists needed to be served and entertained. In the summer of 1919, after visiting the Black Hills, a man from Gettysburg, South Dakota, complained that the people there, particularly in the so-called gateway to the Hills, Rapid City, "live in a state of mental passivity and indifference to the advantages of the Hills as a tourist resort that is difficult to analyze." He went on to say, "Absolutely no effort is made to make a tourist glad he came, . . . for all the use it makes of its opportunity it might as well be the gateway to the town cow pasture."[75]

At the end of World War I, as these comments illustrate, the nature of tourism development in the Black Hills remained casual. After the boom period of the Hot Springs health resort had ended, area citizens by and large failed to regard the industry as a potentially important one on more than a local level. They depended upon the scenery to attract affluent tourists who could afford transportation, camping outfits, and extended stays in the few available summer-resort areas and gave little attention to developing the infrastructure or services that would support the industry on a wider scale. That attitude changed as increased car ownership, better roads, and the lure of the national parks put more motorists on the roads heading west. Peter Norbeck applied his prodigious energies, his Progressive beliefs, and his political ties and skills to attracting them to the state, marshaling public resources to do so. By 1920, the Black Hills was on the verge of a tourism boom. During the 1920s and the 1930s, the "hundreds" of midwestern tourists that State Forester George Roskie noted became thousands, and then tens of thousands.

Black Hills tourism from 1880 to 1918 formed a framework for what would become a vital regional industry in the following two decades. Although private initiative had started tourism in the area, public control and public policy were essential in the creation of Wind Cave National Park, Jewel Cave National Monument, and the Harney and Black Hills national forests. The public lands in the Black Hills, and the policies that dictated the use and management of those lands, would become increasingly important in the development of the area's tourism infrastructure. Additionally, an integrated road system, built principally with federal and state monies, would prove essential to the growth of tourism. Public policies and public actions would drive changes in Black Hills tourism during the immediate post-war years, just as the National Park Service and its programs would increase western tourism in the country. In the Black Hills, however, the greatest momentum came from state efforts, and the results of those efforts profoundly affected the region's culture and society.

Looking for Tourists

Public Tourism in the Black Hills, 1918-1925

THE IMMEDIATE post-World War I era saw a distinct change in the nature of tourism in the Black Hills. Two major factors influenced the change: nationwide growth in recreational automobile travel and involvement by state officials and agencies in the development of the tourism infrastructure. The combination of these elements furthered the growth of the regional tourism industry despite the reluctance of federal officials to expend resources on development of federal lands.

During the first half of the decade, the increasing accessibility of the economical car stimulated a dramatic expansion of automobile travel and introduced recreational motoring to a large new segment of the national population. In 1920, the *Rapid City Daily Journal* had noted that most tourists enjoying South Dakota's Black Hills drove expensive cars such as Chandlers, Jordans, and Hudsons.[1] In his report at the end of the 1925 travel season, National Park Director Stephen Mather observed that visitation to national parks and monuments that year had increased by twenty-six percent over 1924 and that the automobiles themselves indicated the make-up of the clientele: "Among the thousands of cars nightly parked in the larger parks, the cheaper makes by far predominate."[2] Widespread automobile ownership had opened tour-

EDLES PARK AT CREVACE TUNNEL - HIGHEST HIGHWAY EAST OF THE ROCKIES
BLACK HILLS, S. DAK.

By the 1920s, car travel to the Black Hills had increased dramatically, influencing the development of scenic roads such as the Needles Highway.

ism to people of moderate means and created a new class of travelers, a new kind of vacation, and a new impetus for tourism development.

In the Black Hills, however, public policy exerted a strong influence on tourism development, due in large part to the presence of great tracts of public lands. Political alliances and rivalries affected decisions directing the course of that development, and not all policy makers were committed to tourism growth. The National Park Service's lack of attention hindered development at Wind Cave National Park, and the United States Forest Service continued to ignore Jewel Cave National Monument in favor of more pressing priorities. The most significant event during the 1920s was the creation and development of Custer State Park. The lack of a coherent state or regional strategy toward tourism and the political prominence and leadership of Peter Norbeck allowed a handful of motivated public servants to play an essentially entrepreneurial role in furthering the growth of the industry by successfully building a state park designed to appeal to automobile tourists.

Attracting these travelers was the essential element in expanding the post-World War I tourism industry. Although the same factors that were stimulating travel all over the country contributed to Black Hills tourism, the area continued to suffer from conditions that discouraged touring. Distance from major urban areas, the dearth of good cross-state roads, and the shortage of services and of attractions other than scenery limited the appeal of the area to potential visitors. In order to lure travelers into South Dakota and the Black Hills, more incentives had to be created. Peter Norbeck saw both the opportunities and the problems, and he would grapple with political and developmental issues inherent in building a state-controlled tourism infrastructure into the mid-1930s.

Norbeck had been elected governor of South Dakota in 1916 and re-elected in 1918, serving in the post from 1917 until 1921. His two terms as a popular and politically powerful governor provided ample opportunities for him to put his Progressive ideals into action. He implemented a state rural credits program that sold bonds to raise capital, using it to provide low-interest loans to farmers. He promoted state ownership of a coal mine and a cement plant to provide those resources and commodities to consumers at reasonable prices, and he oversaw the development of compulsory state hail insurance to protect farmers against crop losses. During his tenure as governor, Norbeck particularly intended to alleviate the economic burdens of farmers, but he also undertook efforts, employing the same principles of public ownership and management, that would ultimately have a profound effect on the development of tourism.[3]

In an address to the state legislature in 1919, Norbeck broached the idea of transforming the state game preserve in the Black Hills into a state park. "Sometimes to states, as well as individuals," the governor asserted, "come peculiar opportunities which may be grasped to great and permanent advantage, or be allowed to slip away forever." In his opinion, the state had such an opportunity in the Black Hills, and he urged lawmakers to take advantage of it.[4] In March 1919, the state legislature passed the law creating the park and establishing the Custer State Park Board, made up of the governor and two of his appointees. The measure gave the board the power to acquire the lands held by the state as well as privately owned lands within the area of the park. This authority extended to the power of eminent domain, which allowed the park board to take property through condemnation. The law also granted the board the ability to manage and develop the park, continued the sale of timber on the lands with the proceeds going into the state's general fund, and appropriated two hundred thousand dollars for land acquisition and park improvements.[5]

From the beginning, administration of Custer State Park involved a complicated web of political relationships. The South Dakota Game and Fish Commission administered the original game preserve, with the School and Public Lands Department overseeing timber management and sales. With the creation of the park, the Game and Fish Commission retained authority over game management, and the School and Public Lands Department continued to manage timber and grazing lands. The Division of Forestry under School and Public Lands hired and supervised the park's forester, and the gamekeeper was an employee of the Game and Fish Commission.[6] As road construction in the park began, the South Dakota Highway Commission exercised their own control. The involvement of these agencies meant the park could be funded from the various budgets, but it also created bureaucratic and political problems and tensions. Norbeck chafed under this complicated network of control and finances, complaining later, "If I could have foreseen all these things while I was Governor, we could of course have been a little farther along with our plan," adding that he was "impatient for the day when the Park Board will have complete control of the Park."[7] In the meantime, he used his political influence and skills to direct the park's development.

As governor, Norbeck served as chairman of the Custer State Park Board and appointed the other two members. In forming the first board, he named one man from the Black Hills and one from the eastern side of the state, a nod to the sometimes bitter political and cultural division between the agricultural and commercial "East River" section east of the Missouri and the ranching, mining, and logging "West River" side. Concerned with enhancing as well as protecting the area's scenic features, he particularly wanted someone from the Black Hills who "knows the value of the timber and who would protect same, but a man who also has an eye for beauty, and who is a nature lover."[8] As the east-river man on the board, Norbeck appointed his brother, Enoch Norbeck, to a six-year term. After both Chambers Kellar, chief counsel for the Homestake Gold Mine, and a local judge declined to serve, John Stanley accepted Norbeck's offer of a four-year term. Stanley was a newspaperman from Lead, a northern Black Hills town and the location of the Homestake. The board initially designated a board secretary, but in 1921 Stanley assumed that role, as well. He became Norbeck's main contact and the direct overseer of much of the development in the park during its first eight years.[9]

One of Norbeck's immediate goals after the establishment of Custer State Park was an extension of its land area. The sixty thousand acres of the original game preserve did not include particularly scenic parts of the region adjacent to the new park: the Needles formations in the area's most rugged heights; Harney Peak, the highest elevation in the Hills; and Sylvan Lake.[10] For assistance in acquiring the area containing these dramatic sites, Norbeck turned to Harry Gandy, Democratic congressman from Rapid City. Although the ostensible purpose of the proposed extension was to establish a game refuge, Norbeck had more ambitious plans for the area. "If you can secure the desired lands from the Federal Government, the State will take it over and make an ideal summer resort out of it for the benefit of the entire traveling public," he told Gandy.[11]

Gandy succeeded in negotiating an agreement with the United States Forest Service and in shepherding legislation through Congress. His bill passed on 5 June 1920, allowing the president to declare thirty thousand acres of the Harney National Forest as the Custer State Park Game Sanctuary. President Woodrow Wilson signed the proclamation establishing the game sanctuary on 9 October. Although the Forest Service retained authority over the timber, received the proceeds from timber sales, and handled fire control, the Custer State Park Board otherwise managed the area, avoiding some of the complications of mixed jurisdiction that existed in the park proper.[12]

(opposite)
Harney Peak,
the highest
point in the
Black Hills,
quickly
established its
utility as a
Forest Service
lookout post.

The game sanctuary lands acquired under the 1920 presidential proclamation surrounded but did not include the privately owned Sylvan Lake and the hotel there. A long-standing attraction for visitors, the resort constituted a focal point in the rugged country. Obtaining the property was crucial to Norbeck's plan for park development, and passing legislation to secure the surrounding lands was the first step in this process.[13] Whether fearing opposition from the public or an inflated price from the owner, Norbeck and others involved moved cautiously in their attempts to acquire Sylvan Lake. While Gandy was preparing the game-sanctuary legislation,

SD 10

REFLECTION ON SYLVAN LAKE
RISE PHOTO RAPID CITY S.D.

Starting in 1920, the state of South Dakota sought to acquire Sylvan Lake as a crowning jewel for Custer State Park.

the Forest Service's acting forester suggested he change the description of the area to "adjoining or in the vicinity of the Custer State Park," instead of describing it as "in the vicinity of Sylvan Lake."[14] When Gandy's office issued a press release about the pending law, he assured Norbeck that "nothing is said with relation to the contemplated purchase of Sylvan Lake."[15]

The careful wording of public information further indicates the officials' goal to procure the private property with little fanfare. This caution extended to the 1920 special session of the South Dakota legislature, during which the lawmakers passed an emergency bill appropriating fifty thousand dollars to purchase the 330 acres comprising Sylvan Lake and its environs, along with existing improvements.[16] Norbeck later recalled that, although the special session had been called particularly to "secure the purchase" of Sylvan Lake, that purpose had been kept secret.[17] The acquisition gave the Custer State Park Board direct control over the Sylvan Lake state property.

The establishment and expansion of the park and the purchase of the school and the private lands within it absorbed a great deal of time and attention from Norbeck and the Custer State Park Board. Throughout this process, however, Norbeck kept his larger goal in mind. In 1921, he reminded John Stanley, "We are looking mainly for tourists now."[18] To achieve this goal, Norbeck deemed improvements to be crucial. "A wilderness may be a thing of beauty," he once wrote. "It must be preserved, but it must also be made accessible to the public."[19] A Progressive conservationist, Norbeck advocated that resources be used, not simply protected.

Given his actions and influence in developing Custer State Park, Norbeck also clearly understood that a wilderness must be attractive to the public. He was convinced the park had to appeal to the interests of the increasing number of automobile tourists in order to draw them away from routes through more populated areas. A firm adherent of good planning and efficient management, Norbeck was determined the park be improved systematically and in an aesthetically pleasing manner. In the decade and a half following its establishment, "the artistic development" of the park became one of his major interests.[20]

Much of Norbeck's involvement in Custer State Park happened long-distance. In November 1920, Norbeck was elected United States senator from South Dakota. He moved to Washington, D.C., the following March, feeling somewhat homesick and out of place at first, due in part to his lack of formal education. The new senator eventually settled into his responsibilities, however, appreciating in particular assignments to the Agriculture and Forestry and the Public Lands and Surveys committees, which offered him opportunities to engage in farm and conservation issues. He quickly found that his focused interests, his high energy level, and the slow pace of the Senate gave him time to attend to constituents personally, to enjoy the cultural attractions of the city, and to read prodigiously. He was also able to continue his close monitoring of the development of Custer State Park.[21]

As governor, Norbeck had planned and promoted legislation, appointed the other members of the Custer State Park Board, and decided how appropriations were to be spent. Once he was elected to the Senate and his successor as governor, Republican William McMaster, became head of the park board, Norbeck's official role ended. However, McMaster had no great interest in park matters, and Norbeck advised John Stanley to include him only in matters of major consequence.[22] He also advised Stanley not to confer with unenthusiastic board members unnecessarily because such consultation would only delay action. He suggested the board secretary ignore "the advice of cautious men, and scared politicians." Rather, he should follow Norbeck's policy: determine what needed to be done and accomplish it "in spite of incessant opposition." Norbeck told Stanley, "Those timid fellows that are holding on to a man's coat tail and saying 'don't' are the first fellows to approve it after they see that it works out."[23] In these statements, Norbeck summed up his guiding principles of leadership and management. The public would normally accept, even admire, a *fait accompli*, but asking for opinions or permission was likely to stall the process. Norbeck doubted that others shared the breadth of his Progressive visions, but he was confident they would approve of his actions once they saw the results.

In 1923, McMaster appointed Norbeck to the Custer State Park Board, changing his role from that of unofficial advisor to one of authority in park matters. Norbeck looked forward to having more direct control of park growth.[24] By the end of that year, however, the responsibilities of the position were beginning to wear on the senator. He wrote Stanley that once the board had succeeded in acquiring lands necessary for its full development and a "real hotel" had been constructed, he wanted to be "relieved from service on the Park Board, if, indeed I do not from some political accident become relieved in the meantime."[25] Norbeck knew that park board appointments had become political rewards, and given the sharp divisions in the Republican party, he had every reason to expect his removal with any change of administration. In fact, however, Norbeck would remain on the board until his death in 1936. His dedication to the park and to its success in drawing travelers overrode his occasional wish to unburden himself of the duties involved. In meeting his personal commitment to the park and to tourism development, he filled the vacuum that apathetic governors had created and immersed himself in building up the accommodations, attractions, and roads in Custer State Park.

Good internal roads were crucial to the park's success and an integral part of Norbeck's long-range plan for the area. Late in 1920, he suggested that the state's Highway Commission designate engineer Scovel Johnson as a "responsible representative of the Highway Department" and contract with him to build the park's highway system. Johnson, Norbeck said, had proved his engineering ability, his honesty, his knowledge of local conditions, and his understanding of the need to produce "maximum work for minimum cost."[26] Norbeck's faith in Johnson's abilities enabled him to put the development of the park's road systems in the hands of a like-minded engineer. For the next several years, Johnson assumed the responsibilities and the pressures of building park roads, essential elements of the tourism landscape.[27]

In road-building, Norbeck revealed his love of motoring, his determination to provide tourists access to the park's features, and his artistic sensibilities, unformed though they might be. In general, he had more confidence in his own judgment and that of people he trusted than he did in the opinions of professionals. He disdained a rigid adherence to rules in road construction in particular, and on at least one occasion, he contemplated rejecting federal funds if accepting them meant conforming to standard engineering practices.[28] He was particularly concerned with the aesthetic qualities of park roads and became frustrated with those who did not appreciate the need to build them different from ordinary thoroughfares. Norbeck once responded sarcastically to the complaints of an engineer who objected to trees left near a road and who insisted upon a safe, but view-blocking, guard-rail: "I do not think it is necessary to make the guard rail so high that people can't jump off the bridge if they really want to," the senator chided. "They might jump off the rim of the canyon, or they might climb up those tall trees (that we forgot to cut down), and commit suicide in that way."[29] Despite professional highway builders' disagreements with Norbeck's plans, he rarely failed to secure his objectives.

Norbeck achieved his first major accomplishment in scenic design with the completion of a fourteen-mile long road winding through the Needles formations, located in the northwestern part of the area acquired as the game sanctuary. The park board began contemplating a scenic road in this remote, rugged area in 1919. Norbeck, often in the company of Scovel Johnson and Cecil C. Gideon, the park gamekeeper and manager of the Game and Fish Commission's State Game Lodge, explored the area by foot and on horseback in order to determine a route. He procured surplus explosives from the War Department for use in blasting the roadbed through the almost entirely granite environment. Work began on the road in late summer or early fall of 1920. M. L. Shade, a state highway commissioner, had responsibility for general supervision of the project, and Gideon and Johnson managed design and construction on-site. Norbeck followed the process closely, offering detailed suggestions about the scenic elements of the road and the engineering process.[30]

The most difficult part of the project, and the most dramatic part of the finished road, occurred in a one-and-one-quarter-mile section in the midst of the formations. This section of the road cost almost five times as much per mile as the rest of the construction due to sharp turns, switchbacks, and several tunnels. Most of the boulders had to be dynamited out, and the roadbed was blasted through solid granite ledges in several places. As many as 165 men in eight separate camps worked on the road, including convicts, who were used as labor in park road projects for at least two years.[31]

A few adventurous motorists were able to drive the Needles Highway by early November 1921.[32] The road did not simply provide tourists with a view of the Needles; it took them *into* the Needles, wound around the formations, and passed through tunnels painstakingly blasted out and finished by Johnson and his crew. The proximity to the granite outcroppings contrasted dramatically with the distant vistas, and the blasters left selected rock formations beside the road in several places to add contrast and drama. In one section, the road narrowed and threaded through a group of tall pines, designed to maximize the impact of the nearness and height of the trees. The tunnels, the twisting road, the numerous switchbacks, and the steep grades provided drivers with an exhilarating experience. One auto tourist and writer said that for motorists, "the sense of conquering all these, affords a feeling almost beyond description to the soul of the driver."[33]

Norbeck's instincts about attracting motoring tourists were accurate. Tourists enjoyed not only the scenery but also the challenges the road presented. One motorist, describing part of his drive, said, "Gee, that climb was risky business. It takes a good car to take this last Hill on high but it also takes a good driver." The same driver noted that the road "cost $80,000 a mile; no wonder, think of the dynamite required to loosen these rocks in order that you and I might enjoy a Mountain highway unsurpassed anywhere."[34] Norbeck and the others involved in the road's design and construction had created a new and exciting landscape for automobile travelers, one in which the road itself quickly became a dominant feature. By mid-decade,

(opposite) This car demonstrated the forbidding scale of the terrain that stood in the path of the Needles Highway

other park roads, while not as dramatic as the Needles Highway, served the same purpose of giving tourists access to exciting driving as well as scenery, hiking, and fishing.[35]

Despite its status as a game preserve, visitors could fish in the park with a license and hunt in season under controlled circumstances. Enabling tourists to view wildlife, however, became a major goal. In order to increase travelers' chances of seeing game, the Game and Fish Commission staff fenced fields in areas accessible to view and kept small numbers of animals in them.[36] As a game refuge, the area had been stocked with fish, birds, and mammals, and this activity continued when it became a state park. Norbeck and Game and Fish officials were more concerned about developing an interesting assortment of animals in the park than they were in reestablishing native species. These efforts illustrated their goal of providing viewable wildlife to visitors and highlighted some of the problems inherent in multiple jurisdictions in park management.

In 1921, the Game and Fish Commission brought moose into the park, but the animals disappeared shortly after their arrival and were soon sighted west of the Black Hills, perhaps trying to return to their Wyoming range.[37] Norbeck was furious about their loss, exclaiming, "To say that this moose business makes me sick would be putting it mildly. I feel like doing violence to somebody." He blamed their disappearance on the state game warden, who, Norbeck said, placed the animals in an inadequate pen, and on the School and Public Lands Department employees who, he charged, failed to keep fences repaired or gates closed.[38] The park was more fortunate in its plans for a buffalo herd. Three dozen bison, descendants of the last large herd in the state, had been brought to the reserve in 1914 from the Scotty Philip ranch in central South Dakota. The park board built a fenced pasture along one of the main roads into the park to house the growing herd, ensuring their visibility. Norbeck also encouraged stocking mountain sheep in the park, and a shipment of them arrived in March 1923.[39]

One of Norbeck's more novel goals was the creation of a park zoo, which he initially proposed to Phelps Wyman, landscape architect who advised the Park Board on the development of Sylvan Lake. Wyman, dubious about Norbeck's plans, consulted the director of Milwaukee's zoo as well as scientists at the University of Minnesota about the advisability of the venture. None of them supported the idea, but Norbeck's enthusiasm for such a facility remained undaunted, particularly after he went to Washington.

HERD OF WILD BUFFALO
290 RISE STUDIO - RAPID CITY S.D.

Once nearly extinct, American bison found a refuge, and an appreciative audience, in Custer State Park.

While living there, he passed through the national capital's zoo almost every day on his way to the office and noticed its ability to draw tourists and local residents. Norbeck envisioned a zoo in Custer State Park that served the same purpose, with travelers coming to view corrals of large native animals, enclosures with smaller mammals such as woodchucks and prairie-dogs, and cages of foxes, coyotes, and wildcats. All these animals could be obtained within the state. He also dreamed of obtaining more exotic species, such as yaks, water-buffaloes, and llamas.[40]

Despite the negative opinions of Wyman and other professionals, Norbeck led the effort for the establishment of a zoo near park headquarters. In 1923, personnel blasted a bear's den out of rock near the headquarters and fenced in an area for a female bear that Norbeck had acquired; he subsequently brought in a mate for her. By the spring of 1924, cages had

been prepared for additional animals and eventually held coyotes, badger, wolves, bobcats, raccoons, deer, antelope, and various other specimens, including some birds.[41] The creation of the zoo illustrated Norbeck's ability to develop the area according to his tastes and his determination to provide attractions for park visitors.

From the beginning, Norbeck's interest in the park extended to the most detailed aspects of its development. He was particularly concerned with planning details of improvements and changes. For instance, he approved of the idea of leasing lots to people who wanted to build cabins within Custer State Park, but he recommended that they be located only in designated areas on main roads and clustered in groups rather than spread throughout the park.[42] He suggested placing the west entrance gate to the park in a location where it would be almost invisible, "which," he noted, "is something desired at a Park entrance."[43]

Although the Custer State Park Board entertained requests for permission to build summer cabins, its larger concern was with tourists who would visit the area for brief periods of time. The Custer State Game Lodge was the first facility to provide lodging for tourists in the park. In 1917, while the area was a game preserve, the Game and Fish Commission had hired

Phelps Wyman to plan a headquarters complex, including a lodge for visitors and tourists. Wyman, a native of Vermont and a graduate of Cornell University with a degree in agriculture, had studied architecture and landscape architecture in Boston and worked for Frederick Law Olmsted's firm before relocating to Minneapolis. A specialist in garden and park design and town planning, he became an important influence on the development of Custer State Park.[44]

The first lodge was built in 1921, but it burned down within three months of construction. The fire occurred under mysterious circumstances, fueling fears about opposition to the park that continued through its early years. The area of the game preserve and then the park encompassed several private ranches, and their owners disliked the notion of sharing their homes with game animals and enduring other park restrictions. In addition, many Custer County residents resented losing the potential tax revenues of private lands being acquired by the park board.[45] One local man wrote park board secretary John Stanley in 1922, asking for a job and recommending that the park should have an employee on hand during the summer because of "the fire danger which I feel is going to be greater this Summer than ever, on account of the hard feelings toward the Park Board."[46] The cause of the lodge fire remained a mystery but illustrated the tensions surrounding park development.

In 1922, A. R. Van Dyck, a colleague of Phelps Wyman, designed the new Custer State Park Game Lodge. Cecil C. Gideon, a long-time employee of Wyman's who had helped to build the first structure and occupied it until it burned, also built the replacement lodge, with M. E. ("Monty") Nystrom supervising the stone work. Both Gideon and Nystrom stayed in the area after the job was completed. Nystrom moved to Custer and became well known for his masonry work on buildings in the Black Hills. Gideon assumed the role of gamekeeper at the park. He and his wife, Elma, became strongly identified with the State Game Lodge, running the facility for many years under a management and then a lease agreement.[47]

Cecil Gideon was a man of many talents. Besides managing tourist accommodations and services, he also designed a number of structures in the park and helped lay out several of the main roads. Norbeck relied on his judgment, and both he and Lydia Norbeck were particularly close to Cecil and Elma Gideon. After the fire in the original lodge, in which the couple lost most of their belongings, Norbeck sent Gideon a check for two hun-

STATE GAME LODGE

Arson may have destroyed the first State Game Lodge. The second, pictured here, was designed in 1922 by A. R. Van Dyck. It still stands today.

dred dollars, telling him he could pay it back over three years without interest. Gideon expressed profound thanks for the loan but returned the check several weeks later, after determining that he could get by financially.[48] The relationship between the Gideons and Norbeck, and Norbeck's reliance on Gideon's managerial and creative abilities, influenced much of the park's development and helped to insure the Gideons' long tenure at the game lodge.

That lodge, in its size and Craftsman-inspired design, was more sophisticated than most of the subsequent, smaller park structures. Situated on a low hillside a few miles from the eastern border of the park, the lodge was built with a cyclopean stone foundation, terrace, fireplace, and chimneys. The front of the lodge included a full-length porch with a smaller sleeping porch above. The gabled ends of the building held cantilevered sleeping porches, and a long dormer between stone chimneys highlighted the third

Cecil G. and Mary Elma Gideon (hat in hand), top center, posed with staff members in front of one of the later structures built near the State Game Lodge.

floor. The interior featured a central hall and stairway with parlors on each side.[49] The lodge became one of the park's major landmarks and played a crucial role in its history.

Other buildings constructed in the park would be both more modest and more rustic. Late in 1923, for example, Norbeck and Stanley agreed that the cabin they were planning to build at a tourist camp should be of log, although Stanley had originally suggested that a double-boarded, tar-papered building would be faster to construct and perhaps more economical because lumber was available in the park. Gideon developed the general design for the building, which was finished early in 1925. Nine hundred square feet, constructed of local logs, and containing a fireplace, the cabin was designed to serve as a community building that provided tourists a place for entertainment during rainy periods or at night. The building offered facilities for relaxing, reading, and dancing.[50] The rustic log style was typical of many of the other structures erected in the park in the following years.

Sylvan Lake was among the most important of the sites developed in the park, and the Custer State Park Board began working to improve the facility as soon as the state completed its purchase.[51] Norbeck solicited Phelps Wyman's assistance in recommending long-term changes in the property but remained deeply involved in the planning process for the complex. Norbeck outlined his ideas for "improvements of a less expensive nature" to be implemented over about a ten-year period. These included a half dozen "cottages" to be placed back from the lake and the small zoo, to be located at the lake each summer and kept at headquarters during the rest of the year. He and the park board also considered an aquarium in a nearby gulch, a simple building that Norbeck envisioned as a natural history museum, a fishing pool, a greenhouse, a pasture, and sheds for about twenty burros. The board planned to build a new hotel at some point, probably at the east end of the lake. Norbeck pointed out to Wyman that the lake itself was small and could not be increased in size; therefore, any improvements needed to fit into and complement the setting and aesthetics of the lake.[52] His suggestions indicate a sensitivity to the scale and appropriateness of improvements as well as a desire to provide entertainment and attractions for visitors.

Although Wyman commended some of Norbeck's ideas, particularly the proposal for a museum, the landscape architect gently steered Norbeck away from features that would detract from the natural atmosphere of the site. He said that attractions like an aquarium, if they could not be built with a natural appearance, were better grouped with the buildings than placed in otherwise natural settings nearby. Wyman was not drawn to "the picturesqueness of fish ponds as parts of the Lake," and he believed any zoo should be kept at some distance from the Lake, "even quite a distance if necessary." A greenhouse was superfluous because Sylvan Lake did not need "an abundance of exotic flowers."[53] Norbeck continued to insist that wilderness could be improved upon, but as he worked with Wyman and others over the years, his aesthetic sense would become more finely honed.

In submitting his plan for Sylvan Lake, Wyman acknowledged the difficulty in "keeping [the lake's] beauty unspoiled and yet opening it freely to be enjoyed." He suggested that the board, by ordinance or by law, prohibit the building of cottages within sight of the lake, saying such construction would defeat the purpose of state control of the location. His recommendations included a permanent natural history museum to be located on a shelf above the lake and the erection of a new hotel of native materials at the east end of the lake. The new hotel would replace the original hotel at the west end, which Wyman considered poorly designed. The plan indicates that Wyman assumed the work on the resort, including plans for a new hotel, would proceed quickly.[54] In reality, financial considerations required the Custer State Park Board to restrain its ambitions for Sylvan Lake to a renovation of the old hotel and some peripheral development to accommodate tourists.

Despite Phelps Wyman's advice, the board failed to preserve the largely unspoiled character of Sylvan Lake. Late in 1924, Will Doolittle, the managing editor of the American Institute of Park Executives, wrote to Norbeck about a recent trip to the Custer State Park, his first since 1922. He praised the park and the board in general but admitted disappointment in seeing "the intensive use to which the shores of Sylvan Lake have been put as a camping ground." Doolittle added, "To me it seems that fires and camp equipment have no place on the shores of this lake, that they should be kept free for a considerable distance from the water's edge."[55] As this description indicated, the board continued to struggle with the basic contradiction between the preservation of natural features and the assurance of public access.

When it acquired Sylvan Lake, the Custer State Park Board had a more immediate problem than the planning of the area's development: it needed to make the old wood-frame hotel suitable and attractive for tourists. The board initiated a remodeling of the interior, including a newly extended lobby, improvements to the heating, water, and electrical systems, the addition of baths in several rooms, and new paint and wallpaper. Carpenters also built an icehouse, a laundry, and a number of cabins. An inventory of the hotel's contents conducted in the fall of 1922 indicated that the board had acquired a considerable collection of hotel furnishings, although some were in bad condition. The acquisition of the hotel also gave the Custer State Park Board the responsibility of running a resort business. Members decided to lease the property to Myra K. Peters, who had managed it during a previous summer. As the operator of the hotel, Peters became closely associated with Sylvan Lake. Along with her son, Laurel, she ran the resort until the late 1950s.[56]

In August 1920, Myra Peters was touring as social director with an opera company when the state acquired the hotel and leased it to her. She wrote Senator Norbeck saying that she was "terribly interested" in the development of the lake and offered to resign her post and return immediately if she could be of service. "I will come back gladly for after all the Lake is the most vital thing to us and we must make it a wonderful place next year."[57] Peters's enthusiastic and often emotional attitude toward the resort continued throughout her tenure as its manager, and her strong opinions about

Burros were known in the Black Hills even before Peter Norbeck's time; this quartet patiently bears visitors to Hygeia Springs, a Hot Springs attraction.

how it should be operated occasionally irritated Norbeck and, more particularly, Stanley. In the spring of 1921, as hotel renovation neared completion, Stanley wrote Norbeck that he had "persuaded Mrs. Peters to make considerable reduction from her own ideas—after she had traveled all over the U.S. for that opera company." The hotel rates she had seen in her travels, Stanley said, led Peters to have "a high notion of things."[58] Norbeck agreed with Stanley that the cost of rooms, meals, and cabins needed to be held to a reasonable level: "Our tourists do not, as a rule, belong to the wealthy class—not even the well-to-do class."[59] Norbeck and the board intended to attract and serve tourists of moderate means.

Norbeck spent a good deal of time and thought trying to improve conditions at Sylvan Lake, suggesting to Stanley, for instance, that they acquire more burros. While burros were not as comfortable as ponies for transportation about the hotel and lake, he noted, they were more appealing to the eye. "In these days of Kodaks," Norbeck told Stanley, "they have an attraction of their own."[60] He tried to solve laundry problems, examining the equipment and looking for reasonable replacements. He also served as an ear for Myra Peters, who frequently became dispirited.[61] In his attention to Sylvan Lake and its hotel, Norbeck again displayed his involvement in the details of Custer State Park development.

That attention reaped results. In 1921, Norbeck had noted that the park's only shortcoming was its location, which was "about three hundred miles" from the populated portion of the state. "This has made it harder to get the public interested in the Park."[62] At the end of the 1923 season, Norbeck commented, "The tourist season has been very successful and we may expect a greatly increased crowd next year in the State Park, as well as other parts of the Black Hills—it is on the map now."[63] Within a few short years, the Custer State Park Board had succeeded in building a publicly funded park that appealed to automobile tourists with its roads, accommodations, and attractions such as Sylvan Lake and visible wildlife.

During this period of growth and development at the state park, the National Park Service continued largely to ignore Wind Cave National Park, directly to the south. Although some minimal improvements occurred during 1918, including a widening of the park road and new stairs in the cave, facilities at the park remained limited. In October of that year, the state ordered the cave closed because of the threat of Spanish influenza. By the time it opened again in April 1919, Superintendent Thomas Brazell, on the job since 1914, had resigned, and his son, Roy W. Brazell, had replaced him.[64]

The father-son succession gave Roy Brazell a unique perspective on the park. He was particularly cognizant of trends and changes in visitation patterns, which he recorded in his reports to the National Park Service. In addition, as a long-time resident of the area, he was involved in community dynamics and aware of the success of Custer State Park. His frustrations in trying to develop services and facilities that would appeal to the increasing numbers of motoring tourists during the first half of the decade were apparent in his reports. While the nearby state park benefited from Norbeck's organization of a board and an adequate system of financing, Wind Cave National Park languished in comparison to both it and other better-funded and more-popular national parks. The state's road building and park development accomplishments stood in stark contrast to the federal government's lack of interest in Wind Cave.

Roy Brazell proved to be an ambitious and energetic superintendent who particularly embraced the challenge of attracting tourists. Shortly after assuming the role, he joined the Hot Springs Commercial Club and enthusiastically supported its attempts to draw tourist travel by touting good roads and more interesting scenery. When 2,457 people came to the Wind Cave during August 1919, breaking the monthly attendance record, Brazell credited the increase to the club's advertising campaign. He kept a log of visitors to the park and instituted a "tourist bureau" that provided information about the area, helped travelers plan their routes, and located lodging and other services.[65] Although Brazell did not elaborate on his methods of counting visitors, his reports provide a valuable picture of tourism in the Black Hills during the early 1920s, and because travelers tended to visit several sites in the Black Hills, his figures reflect regional tourism as well as Wind Cave National Park visitation.

In 1919, Brazell reported the "biggest run" of tourists ever to come to Wind Cave. According to his counts, nearly two-thirds of the visitors that year were from South Dakota or Nebraska. The adjacent state of Wyoming accounted for only a little more than three percent of the visitation, perhaps a reflection of its citizens' proximity to Yellowstone National Park. Other states represented were Iowa with nearly nine percent, and North Dakota, Illinois, Minnesota, and Montana, providing between one and three percent each. In 1920, Brazell reported a decrease in visitors all over the Black Hills because of bad road conditions. A larger percentage came by train than the previous year; many tourists reported that they had to abandon their automobiles as far away as one hundred fifty miles and travel the rest of the way by rail because of wet roads. Brazell noted a sharp increase in motorists in 1921 and an equally dramatic decrease in railroad passengers, a condition he attributed to the rise in railroad fares after the war's end. He estimated that motoring and camping were up thirty-four percent and train travel down forty-six percent. Tourists made extensive use of the park's campsites, and the superintendent remarked that communities lacking free campgrounds did not attract much tourist business. Brazell also noticed more people taking trips that encompassed multiple parks; many Wind Cave visitors were on their way to Yellowstone or Glacier.[66]

In 1922, Brazell reported being "swamped with campers." More than eighty percent of the tourists that summer came from South Dakota and Nebraska, continuing the pattern of localized tourism. In 1923, he began to notice more people from distant states among the "phenomenal increase" in visitors. He estimated that more than ninety percent came in private cars and considered the number of people camping to be at its highest. In 1924 and 1925, Brazell again reported substantial increases in tourists. The park superintendent's observations about tourism in Wind Cave National Park echoed trends the National Park Service saw on a national level. Tourism in all parks and monuments increased significantly in 1925.[67] In the first seven years of his tenure at Wind Cave, Superintendent Brazell had witnessed the burgeoning automobile tourism, the decline in railroad travel, the growing popularity of automobile camping, and the effect of the National Park Service's western parks on tourism.

Brazell's deep concerns about the poor conditions and lack of services at Wind Cave National Park, however, tempered his gratification at the increasing numbers. The national office acknowledged this situation in 1920.[68] Arno B. Cammerer, the assistant director of the National Park Service, visited Wind Cave that year and reported to Director Stephen Mather that, although the park was neatly arranged and well cared for, it was short of money, due to "the many circumstances entering into our handling of the park and the small funds available."[69] The park operated on its tiny congressional appropriation and benefited little from other revenues.[70]

As tourism increased, Brazell became alarmed to the point of panic about the deteriorating situation and often voiced his personal humiliation over conditions in the park. He sounded a recurring theme that the neglect of the park by its federal overseers compared poorly to state development in the area. Nowhere was this more apparent than the road conditions. In 1923, Brazell reported that the unpaved Wind Cave roads were deteriorating, and he was "humiliated" to have to apologize for their condition and justify "the apparent lack of that progressive spirit so much in evidence all around us." Someone had made the statement that a section of the Wind Cave road was "the worst six miles stretch of road between Denver and Deadwood," a judgment that Brazell considered accurate.[71]

Although road conditions constituted Brazell's biggest problem, other issues also plagued him. As numbers of tourists increased, the park's water system could not handle sanitation needs. Visitors disliked the primitive conditions in the cave. They had to carry lanterns and candles during the

82 Buildings at the Entrance to WindCave S.D.
© O'Neill Photo Co.
O'Neill Neb.

A mixture of old and new buildings accommodated visitors to early twentieth-century Wind Cave.

tours because there was no electricity. After people emerging from the two-to-four-hour cave tour complained about the lack of food and drink, Brazell instituted a refreshment concession, operating in a temporary frame structure with a canvas roof. During the summer of 1921, the permanent help and the seasonal rangers were forced to live together at the superintendent's residence because of lack of housing. In 1924, Brazell had to spend more than sixty percent of the annual ten thousand dollar appropriation on personnel rather than on improvements. Even so, the money was not sufficient to hire enough men with suitable qualifications to serve as rangers. In 1925, Brazell managed to make some minimal improvements to the park, including a new structure over the cave entrance and refinements to trails and stairways in the cave.[72] He continued to be frustrated, however.

The conditions at Wind Cave National Park and Custer State Park offer notable contrasts. The Custer State Park Board had both money and power at its disposal and thus could institute development and maintenance programs, including roads that not only provided a way for motoring tourists to get around the park but actually enticed them with adventurous, scenic driving experiences. Roy Brazell recognized the need to provide tourists with services and assistance if they were to be drawn to the national park, but he lacked the ability to develop attractions or conveniences. In addition, no matter how many tourists visited the cave, the park's revenues had little relationship to its consistently small appropriation from Congress. While the Custer State Park Board was developing a park zoo, building the Needles Highway, renovating the Sylvan Lake Hotel, and installing burros for "Kodak" opportunities, Brazell struggled to maintain roads and provide barely adequate services for tourists with little federal support. Brazell reflected a determination to keep up with Custer State Park, a concern for local opinion, and a desire to attract tourists that his federal superiors did not share.

Jewel Cave National Monument, west of Custer near the Wyoming border, was even more undeveloped than Wind Cave National Park. Until 1933, when Franklin D. Roosevelt transferred national monuments under the jurisdiction of the United States Forest Service to the National Park Service, Jewel Cave remained under the Forest Service's protection.[73] The monument presented particular challenges that reflected changing public expectations. As automobile tourism increased in the United States, the Forest Service rather reluctantly recognized the need to develop recreational services and resources for the benefit of the public but continued to take a more passive role than did the National Park Service. Rather than actively attempting to attract visitors, however, the Forest Service remained more concerned with protecting its resources and the public's safety in light of the millions of people who were flocking to the forests in search of scenery and outdoor recreation. Statements made in an official Black Hills National Forest plan for managing the Custer State Park Game Sanctuary reflect this attitude. The plan stated, "The primary purpose for which the Sanctuary was established is the protection and propagation of game animals; therefore protection of game shall have priority over human use."[74] As the human use of resources in national forests increased, however, so did the pressure to manage those resources differently.

Forester Henry Graves, the chief administrative officer of the United States Forest Service, acknowledged in 1919 that most national forest districts had some particular appeal for visitors: scenery, outdoor opportunities such as fishing or climbing, or "other kinds of attractions."[75] Jewel Cave was one of these other kinds of attractions. While scenic and recreational sites such as trails and streams could be managed and maintained relatively simply and without much interaction between Forest Service personnel and visitors, Jewel Cave required attentiveness. People had to be guided through the cave, requiring a higher level of service than the service's mission normally demanded. In addition, the situation at Jewel Cave was complicated by the continuing requests from the Michaud family, who had originally developed the cave, for some kind of compensation for their claims and improvements.[76]

In contrast to attitudes held by Forest Service personnel in the early 1920s, J. F. Conner, the Harney National Forest supervisor, took an interest in Jewel Cave and saw in it an opportunity to attract visitors. Like Roy Brazell, his enthusiasm for tourism exceeded that of his superiors. In 1923, with automobile tourism to the Black Hills increasing, Conner discussed the situation at Jewel Cave with Peter Norbeck, who suggested he seek a small appropriation to pay off the Michauds, install ladders in the cave, and provide for a superintendent so that the site would be available for tourists. Conner supported such a plan, saying, "I believe that opening up this cave will be an additional drawing card and I should like to see it opened up to the public."[77] O. J. Stahl, the assistant district forester, suggested that the Custer Commercial Club be encouraged to urge development of such legislation. The club did contact Norbeck, who in turn consulted Congressman William Williamson of South Dakota about the matter. Williamson, after talking to both the National Park Service and the Forest Service, told Norbeck that the chances of obtaining any appropriation for the cave were unlikely. Conner then asked Congressman Williamson to write to District Forester A. S. Peck about the situation. When Peck, in turn, contacted Conner to report Williamson's concerns, the forest supervisor admitted he had instigated Williamson's letter. Peck tried to assist, notifying the chief forester that the highway leading to Jewel Cave had been improved and would mean increased visitation. He recommended that some attention should be given to the cave.[78]

Despite all this political maneuvering on the local and regional level, little federal support for improving the cave was forthcoming. Leon F. Kneipp, assistant forester, made clear to Peck he was not interested in attracting tourists but only wanted the property safeguarded. In the fall of 1923, the Forest Service had padlocked the cave to prevent vandals from removing specimens, and Kneipp was satisfied with this level of protection. Local and regional Forest Service officials expressed concern that locking up the cave would keep the Michaud family from completing assessment work on their mineral claims, which might complicate the legal situation if the agency decided to challenge those claims. In response to this reasoning, Kneipp simply wrote to Frank Michaud, telling him that he could work in the cave as long as he did no damage and instructing him to make arrangements for entry with the forest supervisor.[79]

Jewel Cave continued to be a national monument inaccessible to the public. While local and district Forest Service officials had begun to support development of the cave for the benefit of tourists, they received no assistance at the federal level. Kneipp continued to embrace the policy of protecting the resource rather than opening it to the public, and Norbeck and Williamson failed to initiate legislation leading to an appropriation that might have encouraged development.

In 1922, another national monument, Fossil Cycad, was established at the southern tip of the Black Hills by proclamation of President Warren G. Harding. The monument was a pet project of George R. Wieland, a Yale professor who had uncovered rare cycads, fossilized fern-like plants dating from as early as the Mesozoic era, at the site.[80] The National Park Service did not promote Fossil Cycad National Monument to visitors, but its establishment meant that by 1922, the Black Hills contained two national forests, a national park, two national monuments, and the largest state park in the nation. The presence of so much public land in itself was an attraction to visitors, but only Custer State Park was actively developed during the early 1920s.

As Roy Brazell's comments about road conditions indicated, public roads continued to be a primary concern during this period. The South Dakota legislature replaced the state's original highway commission with a new one in 1917, in part to take advantage of the 1916 federal law providing financial aid to states' road-building efforts. Subsequent legislation provided for the construction of a trunk-road system in the state. In 1921, the legislature passed a gasoline tax with the proceeds designated for road maintenance and construction without legislative oversight. This method of financing highway construction removed the necessity to fund roads by

Signs like this one guided motorists on the Custer Battlefield Highway.

appropriation, thereby limiting the political influence of the legislators over road building and enhancing the power of the highway commission.[81]

The identification, construction, and promotion of roads led to intense competition among localities vying for public funds and among the highway associations seeking local support for their routes. By 1920, several named highways, including the Black and Yellow Trail, the Custer Battlefield Highway, and the Sioux Trail, led from the Midwest through South Dakota and the Black Hills.[82] These highways and others like them vied for travelers and for local sponsorship. The highway associations particularly depended upon local support because they were identifying routes and encouraging local construction or maintenance rather than building roads. Rivalry among them could become intense, often creating frustration for local and state officials. For example, the Custer Battlefield Highway Association ran afoul of Governor Peter Norbeck in 1919 when its organizer, W. D. Fisher, asked that the route the association had identified be marked "12" across the state. Norbeck informed Fisher and his supporters that the state could not give a single number to the road because it incorporated many long-established highways, some with their own sponsoring organizations.[83] He tersely reminded Fisher that the South Dakota Highway Commission was "building roads—not painting roads."[84] The increasing importance of roads across the state made policies governing their establishment and construction crucial to a well-ordered system that could continue to bring travelers to the Black Hills.

Public tourism development in the Black Hills during the period between the end of World War I and 1925 illustrated many of the trends taking place on a national level, particularly the growth of state parks, the construction of road systems, and, in general, the attention to expanding recreational travel by automobile. The growth of tourism in the area, however, also illustrated a number of unique factors, particularly the problems inherent in the area's isolated location. Because Peter Norbeck and his colleagues determined to develop a state park that would attract automobile tourists, dramatic transformations took place in the natural landscape through the building of scenic roads and in the park's built environment through the construction and modification of hotels and campgrounds. Finally, Peter Norbeck's ability to influence the design and development process profoundly shaped the nature of development in the park.

The presence of public lands under the administration of various state and federal agencies in the Black Hills led to an uneven development of the tourism infrastructure, an absence of coherent regional planning, and a marked degree of political maneuvering designed to affect public policy. While the Custer State Park Board utilized every means at its disposal to develop the park to appeal to tourists, the United States Forest Service kept Jewel Cave, a likely tourist attraction, locked up, and Congress and the National Park Service maintained a paltry appropriation for Wind Cave, restricting its potential for drawing travelers. As the number of tourists increased and tourism became a more important component of the regional society, officials responsible for these sites and local residents became increasingly concerned about the federal agencies' reluctance to upgrade facilities or increase efforts to attract travelers.

In the first half of the 1920s, tourism in the Black Hills grew significantly, although it remained focused on attracting visitors from South Dakota and the immediately adjacent states. During the last half of the decade, Black Hills tourism would expand to a national audience, due in large part to a small cadre of men who took the term "tourist attraction" to new heights.

3

President in a Park
Calvin Coolidge and
the Summer of 1927

THE SUMMER OF 1927 was a pivotal season in the development of the Black Hills tourist industry. In that year, South Dakota politicians succeeded in convincing President Calvin Coolidge to spend three months at the State Game Lodge in Custer State Park, resulting in almost incalculable benefits in publicity for the state, improvements in Custer State Park, and upgrades in South Dakota roads. The Coolidge visit dominated South Dakotan's attention during the summer of 1927 and captured the attention of the nation as a whole.

In 1926, officials had invited Calvin Coolidge to come to the Black Hills for the summer, but the chief executive declined, saying the area was too far from Washington. The next year, the state's political leaders mounted a more strenuous effort. In January 1927, the South Dakota legislature unanimously approved a concurrent resolution to invite the president to spend his summer vacation in the Black Hills. The newly elected governor, William J. Bulow, forwarded the resolution to Coolidge. Congressman William Williamson, who often conferred with Coolidge in his role as chair of the Committee of Expenditures in the Executive Department, discussed the matter with the president unofficially. Coolidge told the congressman he had been disappointed in a previous vacation site

The State Game Lodge was set among wild, forested hills. This attractive approach greeted President Coolidge when he stayed there in 1927.

that had been highly recommended but was infested with mosquitoes and flies and overrun with people watching his every move. Williamson assured him that the Black Hills had no such pests, winged or otherwise. Paul Bellamy, owner of the Black Hills Transportation Company, traveled to Washington, D.C., and called on the president to make a case for the Black Hills vacation, and Senator Peter Norbeck provided Coolidge with information about the facilities available to him at the State Game Lodge. In May, Colonel Edward Starling of Coolidge's secret service staff traveled to the Black Hills to examine the area and the accommodations.[1]

As the end of May approached, the prospects for a presidential vacation in the Black Hills appeared increasingly possible. John Stanley, secretary of the Custer State Park Board, Charles Robertson, newly designated park superintendent, Black Hills legislators, and officials from the South Dakota Agriculture Department and its Game and Fish Bureau met with the chairman of the South Dakota Joint Appropriations Committee to prepare the agenda for a special legislative session in June. They planned requests for appropriations to compensate Cecil and Elma Gideon, the Game Lodge lessees, in anticipation of their loss of income while the president and his family occupied the premises and to improve the facility and make preparations for additional tourists in the park. The group explained to the press that the state itself had to provide for public accommodations in order to prevent "private enterprise from exploiting the park and also avoidance of commercialization." They added that the improvements would eventually pay for themselves through tourism revenue.[2]

These preparations proved timely. On 31 May 1927, the White House announced that President and Mrs. Coolidge would arrive in the Black Hills in mid-June to spend the summer at the Game Lodge.[3] With only two weeks to make final arrangements, state officials and citizens hurried to prepare for the presidential party. In the process, permanent changes were made in Custer State Park. The newly appointed park superintendent, Charles Robertson, had responsibility for most of the work at the park. "Be assured that in my acceptance of the position . . . I had no conception that I would this summer be host of the President," Robertson wrote his brother.[4]

Indeed, the new superintendent faced an enormous challenge. On the day of the announcement, the *Rapid City Daily Journal* reported that "a year's development program for Custer State Park . . . was underway today

PRESIDENT COOLIDGE WEIGHING HIS FIRST CATCH.

RISE STUDIO.

Vacationing in the Black Hills, Grace and Calvin Coolidge would examine the fruits of the president's favorite hobby.

at a speed that promised completion within three weeks."[5] Workers cleaned the Game Lodge and refurbished its lobby with new furniture, repainted the exteriors of the compound's buildings, and moved a sawmill from the grounds to another location. Robertson and the park board rushed completion of a new road to the top of Sheep Mountain, also called Lookout Mountain. The peak, the Black Hills' second highest, was located near the Game Lodge. In addition, crews graveled the road to Hermosa, the town nearest to the park. Twenty-five men worked day and night to construct a dining hall one-half mile west of the Game Lodge in anticipation of increased visitation to the park. When it was completed, the two-story building could accommodate two hundred people.[6] Workers also began building several tourist cabins. Edward Starling, back in the Hills to make final security arrangements for the president's trip, declared himself "tickled to death" at the preparations underway.[7]

These preparations extended beyond the borders of Custer State Park. Coolidge particularly enjoyed fishing, and Norbeck had advised Robertson that "fishing is going to be the one important event of the summer."[8] Accordingly, twelve miles of trout streams were designated and reserved for the president's use during his visit. The waters included streams in Custer State

Governor Carl Gunderson led the Stalwart wing of the Republican party from 1925 to 1927.

Park and the Harney National Forest and on privately owned lands. Telephone crews strung twelve hundred miles of telephone wire, linking the Game Lodge with communities in the surrounding area and with the presidential offices established in Rapid City. J. B. Greene, secretary of Rapid City's commercial club, had made arrangements for accommodations for presidential staff and reporters there. In anticipation of increased travel, the South Dakota Highway Commission rushed plans to gravel United States Highway 16, which crossed the state, and to gravel and increase maintenance on United States Highway 14, which led through Pierre, the state capital, to Rapid City.[9]

The speed and ease with which preparations in Custer State Park were accomplished contrasted sharply with the disorder and disruption that had reigned there during the preceeding two years. Between 1925 and 1927, the park had been the subject of criticism by legislators and other politicians; attempts to modify the administrative structure had resulted in the park becoming, in Peter Norbeck's words, a "political football."[10] These problems stemmed in large part from a deep division in the state's Republican party, one that pitted Norbeck and his supporters against a newly elected, ambitious governor who threatened the senator's power and influence.

Republican Governor Carl Gunderson had entered office in 1925 with aspirations to reorganize state government, root out inefficiency, and concentrate responsibilities under particular offices. Gunderson's general consolidation goals conformed with Senator Peter Norbeck's desire to see authority centralized in Custer State Park, eliminating some of the vexations that resulted from mixed jurisdiction involving the park board, the School and Public Lands Department, the Fish and Game Bureau, and the Highway Department. Initially, Norbeck was pleased with the governor's plan to appoint a park superintendent with responsibility for the functions in the park, and he was satisfied with Gunderson's assurances that he and John Stanley would remain on the park's board.[11]

Norbeck soon became uneasy. The Republican party in South Dakota remained divided along a Progressive-Stalwart split. Gunderson did not consult Norbeck about appointments, and friends warned the senator of opposition from the new governor and his supporters, who blamed Norbeck for the defeat of incumbent senator Thomas Sterling in the 1924 primary. Norbeck had supported his former lieutenant governor, William McMaster, causing many moderate party members, including Gunderson, to swing to the Stalwart, anti-Norbeck wing of the party. The senator had written several letters to the new governor encouraging him to take actions beneficial to the park, but he worried that Gunderson would be unwilling to share Norbeck's vision and his practice of moving ahead without the prior approval of constituents and politicians.[12]

Custer State Park came under fire during the 1925 legislative session, and turmoil in the park continued throughout Gunderson's administration, slowing the park's development and frustrating Norbeck. During the session, park-board secretary John Stanley worked to gain a twenty-five thousand dollar maintenance appropriation for the park. Despite his efforts, the appropriations committee reduced the amount to fifteen thousand dollars.[13] Stanley, discouraged and "disgusted" by the legislators, wrote to Norbeck, "They simply shut their eyes and vote for economy and don't know what the word means."[14] Political rivalries aside, economy was a crucial concern among the legislators, whose state was facing a financial crisis. The post-World War I drop in farm prices and adverse weather conditions had combined to threaten South Dakota's predominately agricultural foundation. From 1921 to 1925, 175 state banks had closed.[15] Taxpayers were nervous and legislators, indeed, were likely to "shut their eyes and vote for economy" rather than appropriate funds to the park.

Beyond their reluctance to spend money, however, some legislators were particularly critical of the park. For example, lawmakers took the park board to task for failing to insure the architectural integrity of private cabins built on leased lands in the park. One group suggested legislation requiring cabins to be "of rustic appearance."[16] This argument puzzled Stanley; he noted that there had been only seven cabins built on leased land, and although the structures were not of the same materials or design, he considered them appropriate in quality and style.[17] Norbeck scoffed at the attention to the issue. "I can hardly believe anybody takes this stuff seriously," he wrote. "If so, our people are getting more aesthetic than I thought they were."[18] The support Norbeck had ensured for Custer State Park in its first years was in danger, a victim of difficult economic times and political divisions. The tensions over park affairs grew even more acrimonious after the session ended.

Although Gunderson's statutory reorganization of state government did not extend to the administration of the park, he attempted to accomplish consolidation through the Custer State Park Board and agreements with the various departments involved. With the governor's urging, the board appointed M. L. Shade as the park's first superintendent. To avoid legal challenges to gubernatorial creation of an important state position, Gunderson suggested the post be referred to as "maintenance superintendent." The Highway Department, the School and Public Lands Department, and the Department of Agriculture, which had incorporated the Game and Fish Commission, agreed to make Shade their emissary in the park. In addition, Game and Fish and the Highway Department earmarked a portion of their funds for park purposes. Cecil Gideon, who had served as park superintendent *de facto*, stayed on as manager of the Department of Agriculture's Game Lodge.[19]

Norbeck saw the appointment of Shade, a controversial highway commissioner, as a political move by Gunderson. Shade, he wrote, "is a load for the Governor to carry and I think the Governor wants to stick him out among the big trees where he will not be seen so much."[20] Despite this assessment of the situation, Norbeck admired Shade, who had supervised the construction of the Needles Highway in 1920 and 1921 and whose administrative style matched his own. He saw Shade as one of the few men in the state willing to move ahead with development in spite of criticism and opposition.[21] Norbeck hoped that a decisive man with an independent mind could further his goals for progress in the park.

Those very qualities in Shade, however, helped thwart Gunderson's intentions to streamline operations in Custer State Park and slowed the very progress Norbeck hoped to accomplish. Shade and other officials soon began disagreeing over park policy, and other departments eventually stopped cooperating with the new superintendent, bringing much of the park development to a halt. Norbeck was pleased with Shade's accomplishments in road work as superintendent but regretted the fact that Shade had contributed to the turmoil in the park. The larger part of the blame, however, he placed on Gunderson. The governor's failure to follow through on consolidation, his use of political patronage, which had replaced loyal employees in the park with political appointees, and what Norbeck saw as Gunderson's determination to ignore the park board and to manage the park from the state capitol annoyed and frustrated the senator.[22] He told Gideon, "I am so disgusted with the whole situation out there I hardly know what to write or say."[23]

Shade was forced to resign after a year and departed blaming the situation on the refusal of the state department heads to cooperate with him. "It will take years," he said, "to overcome the damage to the Park that has been done" by the failed attempt at consolidation.[24] Norbeck feared further harm to the park at the hands of the governor and Game and Fish officials, whom he accused of using the traditional political split between the eastern and western sections of South Dakota for political purposes. In his opinion, they were encouraging opposition to the park in the eastern part of the state by implying that the east-river population was being deprived of recreational development because their funds were supporting the western park's growth.[25] Norbeck acidly commented to a newspaper editor, "It is equally unfortunate that the Yellowstone Park is located in Western Wyoming and Idaho instead of in Illinois or Pennsylvania, but the Government has not abandoned it for that reason."[26]

Gunderson's opposition to Norbeck and his goals earned him the enmity of the senator and his supporters, and that enmity played a role in his 1926 defeat for reelection, when William J. Bulow became the state's first Democratic governor. Norbeck, in the meantime, successfully countered the challenges of his political rivals, won the Republican primary by a wide margin, and was reelected United States senator. Norbeck had met the threat to his political power. With the end of the Gunderson term and the advent of the friendly, although Democratic, Bulow administration, the senator reasserted his influence in Custer State Park.[27]

Bulow reappointed Norbeck, whose term on the Custer State Park Board had expired. The new governor replaced J. C. Denison, the park superintendent who had followed Shade, with Democrat Charles Robertson, the president of a lumber company in Midland, South Dakota. Norbeck knew and liked Robertson, but he initially disagreed with this decision, for he considered Denison an effective park administrator. Norbeck also opposed the use of political patronage in what he considered a professional position. However, Bulow instructed Robertson to maintain a good relation-

Paradoxically, in State Park affairs, Republican Peter Norbeck found Democratic governor William J. Bulow more cooperative than his Republican predecessor.

ship with the senator[28] and sweetened the transition by telling the new superintendent that he and Norbeck "would be given the reins" in the park.[29]

In short order, Norbeck accepted the change in superintendents, and he proceeded to give Robertson detailed information and instructions about park operations. Calling it "no ordinary Park," Norbeck cautioned Robertson that it was larger than other state parks and contained hotels, electric and water systems, fences, game animals, and private land owners. In addition, the mixed jurisdiction created special issues of management and finance. The senator gave Robertson advice on dealing with Sylvan Lake Lodge-lessee Myra Peters, told the new superintendent he did not want a dense network of roads in the park, and instructed him to purchase burro saddles with safe stirrups.[30] To handle the horses, Norbeck suggested that he hire a careful, polite man who had "business instinct . . . with an ability to 'sell' to the public."[31] Robertson did not object to these pointed instructions, and he and Norbeck formed a good working relationship. With the autonomy granted by Governor Bulow, Norbeck was able to continue guiding the park's development as a site attractive to tourists.

The pending Coolidge visit enabled Norbeck to further strengthen that power and finally consolidate administrative control in the park. In late May 1927, as the president's decision about a vacation site narrowed to the Black Hills or Colorado Springs, Norbeck informed Governor Bulow that officials making the arrangements for the trip "found out somehow" about the management of the park being divided among several agencies and said that it was "unthinkable" for them to deal with so many sources of authority. The senator recommended that one person, probably the park's superintendent, be given the power to speak for all the interests in the park.[32] Bulow responded almost immediately that other departments who had authority in the park stood ready to cooperate by placing its management in the hands of the superintendent during the presidential visit.[33]

Building on that success, Norbeck sought to institutionalize changes in the Custer State Park administration during the June 1927 special session of the South Dakota legislature, called to address funding of the presidential visit. The senator personally designed legislation that legally created and defined the post of park superintendent and gave the park board comprehensive management authority, including hiring the forester and game warden and making decisions about highway construction within the park. The measure provided for up to twenty-five thousand dollars to be set aside each year from Game and Fish license revenues for use by the Custer State Park Board and appropriated funds to purchase privately owned lands within the park.[34]

Despite the positive political climate surrounding the securing of the presidential visit, the bill had some opposition and failed on the first vote. Norbeck determined that several legislators had different objections to the bill—particularly the concentration of power in the board and the transfer of funds from license revenues—but that there was sufficient support for each section of the legislation to pass independently. The senator suggested that the measure be split into four separate bills. Each one passed. "Nothing left to do now but paste them together and it will look very much like the original bill introduced," he told Cecil Gideon.[35] As a masterful politician, Norbeck skillfully utilized the events surrounding Coolidge's vacation to concentrate power in the Custer State Park Board and obtain additional funding for the park.

South Dakotans, honored that the president had chosen their state for his summer White House, were well aware of the potential side effects of the vacation. The chief executive's visit promised unprecedented national publicity and economic benefits from the tourists it enticed to the Black Hills. Before Coolidge arrived, Governor Bulow urged citizens to "put themselves out" to look after the travelers. "This will prove to be the biggest advertising feature," the governor proclaimed. W. C. Lusk, president of the state chamber of commerce, asked residents across the state to prepare for the influx of motoring visitors by "cleaning up and beautifying with a thoroughness never before attempted." He encouraged people to cut weeds along main roads, keep dirt roads dragged, and complete graveling projects, thereby assuring their cities and towns presented "a trim appearance." Lusk said the presidential trip would be "the greatest opportunity South Dakotans ever have to sell their state to the rest of the country."[36] Early predictions

PRES. COOLIDGE AND GOV. BULOW, JUNE 15, 1927
PIERRE, SOUTH DAKOTA
PHOTO BY MILLER 167

President Coolidge and Governor Bulow walked alongside the train during Coolidge's stop in Pierre on his way to the Black Hills.

of large numbers of visitors quickly proved warranted. Almost immediately after the announcement of the Coolidge's visit, the *Rapid City Daily Journal* noted an increase in tourists, particularly from the East Coast and the South. The paper estimated that fifty percent more cars were traveling through the city than at the same time the previous year.[37]

Coolidge and his party arrived by train at Rapid City on 15 June 1927 to a colorful welcome featuring a twenty-one-gun salute, rough-riding cowboys, and formations of National Guardsmen in the area for their annual summer encampment. That night the Coolidges settled into the Game Lodge. Soldiers from Fort Meade in the northern Hills guarded the couple around the clock, redirecting sightseers who tried to approach the lodge from the road running directly in front of it. The president arose early on his first morning in Custer State Park. In the company of Cecil Gideon and Edward Starling, he went to a nearby stream and caught five rainbow trout.[38]

Thus began the president's summer vacation. Throughout the next three months, Coolidge combined business and pleasure, motoring to Rapid City most mornings to conduct the nation's business from a suite of offices established in the city's high school building, spending the afternoons and evenings enjoying the fishing and scenery of Custer State Park, and attending local events and celebrations on weekends. Two of the most notable of these weekend festivities were the Belle Fourche roundup and the Deadwood Days of '76. At the roundup, one of the area's oldest rodeo celebrations, Coolidge watched the activities in a tall gray beaver cowboy hat that the event's organizers had presented to him. At the Days of '76, a community celebration instituted in 1924, the president was adopted into the Oglala (Lakota) tribe and given the name *Wamble-To-Ka-Ha,* Leading Eagle.[39] Norbeck noted that the annual community events were "heavily attended" during the Coolidge visit, and he described Deadwood during the Days of '76 as resembling New York City: "Automobiles absolutely filled the gulch . . . and walking was faster than riding."[40]

The president's identification with the American Indians continued when Coolidge and his party traveled to the Pine Ridge Indian Reservation, just east of the Black Hills, on 17 August. The trip took place after consultations among Norbeck, Williamson, E. W. Jermark, the Pine Ridge superintendent, and Charles Burke, South Dakota native and United States commissioner of Indian affairs.[41] Burke, who joined Coolidge on the reservation, found the president's visit particularly gratifying because the choice of South Dakota as the president's destination had been discouraged, he had discovered, "based on the statement that it was in the Indian country and that the Indians would be constantly visiting the State Park and annoying the President." Burke predicted that the president would be much more annoyed "by white people who will wish to see him."[42]

Stories about the events of the summer and news photographs of the dignified, taciturn president wearing cowboy hats and feathered headdresses not only kept the nation apprised of Coolidge's summer experiences, but they also introduced the nation to this little-known, compact region on the eastern edge of the West. The impact of the publicity surrounding Coolidge's vacation added immeasurably to local promotional efforts. Advertising had become more sophisticated during the growth in tourist traffic in the early 1920s, largely due to the work of the area commercial clubs, the forerunners to modern chambers of commerce. In 1927, for example, even before

WAMBLE-TO-KA-HA
or
CHIEF LEADING EAGLE.

PHOTO BY
RISE
C-38.

Chief Wamble-To-Ka-Ha wore his new regalia after being adopted into the Sioux tribe. Also present were Lakota notables Rosebud Yellow Robe (standing next to the president) and Chauncey Yellow Robe (second from right).

Coolidge's visit was confirmed, the Associated Commercial Clubs of the Black Hills had planned a program of advertising for the region. Chauncey Yellow Robe of Rapid City and Mabel Rewman of Deadwood took a Black Hills booth to an outdoor and sportsman's show in Hastings, Nebraska, and the organization sent Myra K. Peters of Sylvan Lake Lodge to an outdoor-life exposition in Chicago. The clubs ordered 185,000 photograph sections to be placed in South Dakota newspapers as well as in the *Omaha Bee* and the *Cincinnati Tribune*. Radio broadcasts from Omaha and Chicago featuring South Dakota people talking about the Black Hills resulted in about sixteen hundred inquiries.[43] In the absence of organized state or regional organizations devoted solely to tourism promotion, these efforts filled an important need. Significant as it was, however, the work of the commercial clubs paled before the barrage of publicity surrounding the presidential vacation.

Between 1 April, when Coolidge's prospective trip to the Black Hills became serious news, and 1 October, after that vacation had ended, the president's summer in the Black Hills generated more than one hundred articles or photograph features—more than one each day—in the *New York Times* alone. Stories about the Black Hills appeared in popular periodicals, including the *Literary Digest, National Geographic,* and *Saturday Evening Post.*[44] One reporter noted, "It is a common saying that the State has received millions of dollars' worth of advertising thorough [Coolidge's] sojourn in the Black Hills. . . . The motor tourist trade of the State has increased by leaps and bounds this summer."[45] Roland M. Jones, an editorial correspondent for the *New York Times,* reported that the local newspapers were full of columns of "self-congratulation" about the free publicity and added, "This vacation is costing South Dakota what for a State of its population and taxable wealth is a fairly snug sum, but if there is a taxpayer who doesn't think it money well spent, he hasn't made himself vocal yet."[46] Nearly every newspaper story about the president and his decisions that summer originated from Rapid City; by the end of his stay, newspapers reporting about his activities had sent out over two million words, nearly twice the number generated during his vacation in the state of New York the previous summer.[47] As Jones indicated, South Dakota residents had every reason to feel well rewarded for their efforts in providing the president a vacation site.

Coolidge added to this outpouring of newsprint when, on 2 August, he called reporters to what was normally a French teacher's classroom in the Rapid City High School and handed them slips of carefully folded paper. Upon unfolding the notes, the reporters read a startling, twelve-word statement: "I do not choose to run for President in nineteen twenty-eight." The President did not elaborate on the reasons for his surprising decision, but one newsman speculated that Coolidge's vacation provided the impetus for the announcement: "The solitude of his mountain retreat, the change in environment and his communion with the mysteries of nature have given the President opportunity for introspection."[48] Whether or not this rather poetic interpretation of his motivations reflected reality, Coolidge had brought the presidency to the Black Hills and relinquished it there, and the region enjoyed the fruits of both actions. The Black Hills were on the map.

Those South Dakotans who arranged the president's vacation in the state knew that his visit would mean increased travel and traffic. The politicians

"CAL" TAKES RIDE IN LUMBER WAGON.

President Coolidge enjoyed a ride in a lumber wagon during his Black Hills trip.

also knew that their proximity to the president during the summer would help them familiarize him with particular issues, especially agricultural problems.[49] For Norbeck and a handful of others, however, one of the most important promises of Coolidge's trip was the impetus it could give to the Mount Rushmore project, the proposed carving of a massive monument to four presidents in the Harney Range of mountains, located in the Custer State Park Game Sanctuary. Doane Robinson, a prominent South Dakotan who had initially proposed the memorial, wrote Norbeck that Coolidge's visit would not only "sell the state park to the world, but it would insure the Borglum memorial."[50] Norbeck, convinced that private funding alone would not allow for completion of the project, told Gutzon Borglum, the sculptor, that a presidential trip to the site "will be a big advantage when it comes to getting any governmental assistance in financing the proposition."[51] Indeed, Coolidge's residence in the Black Hills provided the promoters of Mount Rushmore priceless publicity and a tangible link to the presidency and the national government.

The idea for a monumental public sculpture in Black Hills granite originated in 1924 with Robinson, the state's official historian and one of its most relentless boosters. Born in Sparta, Wisconsin, in 1856, Robinson came to

Dakota Territory in 1883. A lawyer by profession, Robinson became better known as a poet, orator, and amateur historian. In 1901 he was appointed the first secretary of the state's Department of History, a post he filled for twenty-five years, devoting himself to the promotion of his adopted state and to its development.[52]

Robinson introduced the idea of the giant carving at a meeting of the Black and Yellow Highway Association early in 1924. He suggested that the Needles, the granite spires in the Custer State Park Game Sanctuary through which the Needles Highway threaded, could be transformed into massive statuary figures representing heroes of regional history. He envisioned figures of Lewis and Clark, Jedediah Smith, Buffalo Bill Cody, and other notables silhouetted against the sky. Robinson believed the carvings

Gutzon Borglum signed this photograph at the foot of Mount Rushmore to Doane Robinson. The group included Robinson (middle left, black bow tie), Gutzon Borglum (center, with hat), and Congressman William Williamson (behind Borglum).

would enhance the area's natural beauty and create a legacy for future generations. Robinson was also convinced that the process of the work itself would pay for the project by attracting a significant element of the automobile tourists driving west.[53] He theorized that those travelers would respond to a certain stimulus. A region catering to tourists must have a number of "definite" attractions located in isolated areas, he said, because "Men are so constituted that they evaluate things by the effort involved in getting them."[54] He also believed that these attractions needed to add novelty to the natural environment. "Tourists soon get fed up on scenery," Robinson asserted. The proposed sculpture would add the "special interest necessary to keep their attention."[55]

Robinson enlisted Norbeck to support the cause. His suggestion intrigued the senator, who had strong interests in art and scenic development. Almost immediately, however, state residents began protesting the destruction of the natural features if the Needles were carved into figures. Both Robinson and Norbeck distanced themselves from that particular proposal, but they did not abandon the idea of creating a work of public art in the Black Hills. A few months after proposing the project, Robinson contacted sculptor Gutzon Borglum, at work carving a memorial to the Confederacy at Stone Mountain, Georgia, in an attempt to interest him in the concept.[56]

Borglum was born John Gutzon de la Mothe Borglum in Idaho in 1867. A restless and somewhat rebellious young man, he received a disjointed education before studying with artists in California and in Europe, including the sculptor Auguste Rodin. His years in Europe occurred during a period of influential international expositions that fostered interest in monumental art. Borglum's temperament and ego were well suited for such work. He returned to America in 1901 and eventually abandoned painting for sculpture. During the early decades of the twentieth century, he completed several significant pieces, including the marble head of Lincoln installed in the rotunda of the nation's Capitol and a bronze of Philip Sheridan, also located in Washington, D.C. His work, realistic and emotional, was more popular with the public than with art critics. Intensely patriotic, Borglum proclaimed the need for an American art based on American motifs. Restless, active, and a proponent of the "strenuous life" in the mold of Theodore Roosevelt, Borglum sought the challenge of a purely American art in a form that would stir the hearts of his countrymen.[57] "Volume, great mass, has a greater emotional effect upon the observer than quality of form," he once wrote. "Quality of form (when it is understood) affects the mind; volume shocks the nerve or soul-centers and is emotional in its effect."[58] Borglum wanted to touch the souls of his fellow citizens and saw "volume" as a means to this end.

In 1916, Borglum put these ideas into effect when he began carving a panorama honoring the Confederacy on Stone Mountain in Georgia. The project, first broached by a Georgia newspaperman and then supported by the United Daughters of the Confederacy, was unprecedented in modern art. Borglum's original design called for a bas-relief carving on the mountain that would stretch for fifteen hundred feet, representing the marching Confederate Army. The head of Robert E. Lee alone would extend twenty feet. World War I delayed the project, and serious work did not begin until 1922, after the original board overseeing the project was reconfigured. The Stone Mountain Monumental Association, made up of a group of Atlanta business leaders, formally contracted with Borglum to carve seven figures.[59]

Borglum was an artist rather than a businessman, and the difficulties of carving a mountain were less taxing to him than the difficulties of working with board members concerned with financial accountability and steady progress. Like Peter Norbeck, Borglum had great faith in his own ideas and proceeded according to his own decisions. Unlike Norbeck, however, he did not have the political or diplomatic skills to avoid almost constant conflict with the people overseeing the project. As his relationship with the Stone Mountain Association began to deteriorate, Borglum received the letter from Doane Robinson, suggesting a monumental work of art in the Black Hills.[60]

Borglum greeted the idea enthusiastically. In the fall of 1924, he visited the Harney Range in the Custer State Park Game Sanctuary. The artist agreed that the mountainous area presented the opportunity for a major work and proceeded to convince Robinson that the conception for the sculpture should change from a local to a national theme. Borglum, who had long hoped to create a national memorial, hinted that he could obtain financial support from wealthy patrons for such a project. As he departed the Harney Range, Borglum looked back and told Robinson that the features of Washington and Lincoln would someday be visible over the long distance. Won over by the sculptor's enthusiasm, Robinson embraced the notion of memorializing two of the country's most notable presidents.[61]

The Harney Range lay within both the Harney National Forest and the

Sculptor Gutzon Borglum paused on the platform after his arrival in Rapid City.

Custer State Park Game Sanctuary. Borglum, Robinson, and Norbeck all agreed that the location required federal legislation to authorize a public carving. In addition, Norbeck advocated that the state needed to provide a portion of the financial backing for a memorial located within its boundaries. Given the political and financial conditions in South Dakota, he anticipated some resistance. In order to make the proposition more palatable to state lawmakers, Norbeck, Robinson, and Congressman William Williamson of South Dakota carefully crafted federal legislation with a focus on state control of the project, rather than on its funding.[62]

In January 1925, Norbeck and Williamson introduced legislation in the United States Senate and House of Representatives that would authorize the South Dakota State Legislature to create the Mount Harney Memorial Association with the power to name, locate, design, and carve "a memorial in heroic figures commemorative of our national history and progress" in the Harney National Forest.[63] To avert political conflict, they intentionally avoided naming potential subjects of the proposed public memorial. On 16 February, H. R. 11726 came before the House. Thomas Blanton of Texas asked whether the events to be depicted would be controversial in any way. Williamson replied that he knew of nothing planned that would be objectionable. No other questions arose. The bill passed the House with an amendment ensuring that the location of the monument would not interfere with the administration of the Harney National Forest. Eleven days later, the Senate approved the bill, and President Calvin Coolidge signed the measure on 3 March 1925.[64]

The reasons for the relative ease with which this legislation succeeded are revealed in its language. The bill provided that the South Dakota legislature would create the committee to make the decisions about location and design, placing the responsibility for administering the project in state hands. More importantly, the law provided that "the United States shall be put to no expense in respect of such memorial."[65] Despite its national theme, the law clearly established the undertaking as a state project; the federal government would have no role in its design and no responsibility to finance the monument.

At the state level, however, the project faced serious obstacles. The 1925 South Dakota legislative session was a dramatic one due to the acrimonious split in the Republican party and the efforts of the new governor,

Carl Gunderson, to reorganize state government. Norbeck urged Gunderson to take a leadership position in the matter of the national memorial, telling him, "The possibilities of this matter are greater than anything else effecting [*sic*] South Dakota—except the price of farm products."[66] Whether from personal conviction or because of his political rivalry with Norbeck, Gunderson refused to support the project, although he told the senator he would not oppose favorable action on the part of the legislature.[67]

At the same time, South Dakota citizens who criticized the proposal because it would desecrate the natural landscape provided another obstacle. Cora B. Johnson, a Black Hills journalist, led the opposition in the western part of the state.[68] She resisted Doane Robinson's entreaties to consider the pending monument another Colossus of Rhodes, sarcastically stating that the project reminded her of college students trying to locate their class emblems in difficult places. "We look tolerantly on their scrambling," she observed dismissively, "knowing that they will learn in time to differentiate between physical altitude and real accomplishment. But we do not emulate them."[69] She also found unimpressive Robinson's promise that the people of her community, Hot Springs, would "reap a harvest of gold forever" from the proposal.[70] Johnson quickly became Robinson's nemesis. He complained of the "dribble of foolishness coming out of the Black Hills all of the time," for it engendered negative publicity and inspired others to voice their displeasure with the proposal.[71] For his part, Norbeck considered the opposition hypocritical, given the mining, logging, and general development that had taken place in the Black Hills after the beginning of white settlement in 1875. "It was the Indians," he said, "and they alone, who insisted that the Black Hills should be left as the Lord made them. A great deal of mutilation has been done the last forty years and the people out there seem perfectly willing some more shall be done, just so it is not called 'art.'"[72]

As Johnson's attack against public art in the Black Hills escalated, Norbeck, for several reasons, withdrew from open support for the state bill. In light of Gunderson's attitude toward him, Norbeck decided to distance himself from Custer State Park matters in order to avoid political reprisals that might harm the park. At the same time, the state legislature authorized an investigation of the Rural Credits Board, one of the Progressive programs implemented during Norbeck's gubernatorial term. After the board treasurer, a Norbeck appointee, was arrested and charged with violation of national banking statutes, the senator's political foes used the issue as ammunition against him. The upheaval weakened Norbeck's bargaining power during the legislative session, forcing him to keep a low profile while the controversy ran its course.[73]

As a result, the chief responsibility for the passage of the national memorial bill in the state legislature fell to Doane Robinson, an influential force in South Dakota politics. On 7 February 1925, he spoke before the joint appropriations committee, asking members to introduce the bill establishing the Mount Harney Memorial Association, designating Washington and Lincoln as subjects for the carving and appropriating ten thousand dollars for an initial survey. He wrote Norbeck that the men were "tremendously interested" in his remarks.[74] Robinson's report the next day, however, was not so encouraging. The committee refused to sponsor the legislation, although the members assured Robinson they would not block it. Robinson was convinced that without support from either the appropriations committee or the governor, the appropriations portion of the bill, at least, was doomed.[75]

A Rapid City legislator, J. L. Robbins, agreed to introduce the legislation in the South Dakota House on 9 February, but it was defeated. Upon Norbeck's advice, the appropriation request was reduced to five thousand dollars. C. D. Erskine introduced the modified version in the state senate; that measure was defeated on 24 February.[76] Robinson laid part of the blame on the traditional rivalry between the eastern and western sections of the state. He wrote Norbeck that other appropriations for public institutions in the Black Hills led east-river legislators to feel their area was being neglected, and he claimed that "they took it out on our little bill." Robinson declared to Norbeck, "I have had my share of legislative experience, but I have never gone up against a situation comparable to this."[77]

As Robinson struggled to save the legislation, Gutzon Borglum's work at Stone Mountain ended in a furious disagreement between the artist and the Stone Mountain Memorial Association. The artist's work habits, financial irresponsibility, and independent temperament continued to create friction between him and the association members, and on 25 February 1925, the group fired him. Borglum responded with a temper tantrum, smashing the head of his studio model of Robert E. Lee and throwing the body and his other models over a cliff. The association secured a warrant for his arrest and brought suit against him. Borglum hurriedly left Georgia. The resulting adverse publicity further soured South Dakota lawmakers and citizens on the proposal for a Borglum-carved monument.[78]

Despite these problems, a modified bill survived. Erskine reintroduced the legislation without the appropriation for the survey, and the legislature approved it. An unenthusiastic Gunderson signed the measure on 5 March 1925. The act created the Mount Harney Memorial Association and stipulated that the association would pose no cost or risk to South Dakota, even though title to the finished sculptures of Washington and Lincoln would be vested in the state.[79] South Dakota lawmakers thus established ownership of the proposed monumental sculpture without risking public funds on such an uncertain venture. The project became a state-owned national memorial with no funding whatsoever, forcing its supporters to seek financial backing privately. For the next two years, proponents struggled to keep the project viable.

After the federal legislation had authorized the carving and the state legislation had created the Harney Peak Memorial Association, Borglum visited South Dakota and selected a mountain suitable for a national public monument. Broad, relatively smooth, and high in the Harney Range, within the Custer State Park Game Sanctuary and the Harney National Forest, the peak carried the name of Charles E. Rushmore, a New York attorney specializing in mining law who had made professional trips to the Black Hills during the 1880s. On 1 October 1925, the sculptor and his supporters held a dedication at Mount Rushmore. Borglum and Doane Robinson hoped President Coolidge or some national figure representing him would attend. Only state officials participated, however. Eben W. Martin, former South Dakota congressman from nearby Hot Springs, served as Coolidge's representative at the ceremony, and despite constant references to a national memorial, the project remained a state and local proposition.[80]

The actual carving could not proceed without funding. Borglum had assured Robinson from the beginning that he had wealthy supporters who stood ready to finance the project, and Robinson had taken that position while discussing the matter with Black Hills residents. Both Robinson and the local people believed that if the Black Hills raised five thousand dollars, the sculptor's friends would donate the rest. Then one evening in early October, after Robinson had left a dinner of Black Hills residents interested in the project, Borglum revealed to the group that he expected no help from outside the area until some progress had been made on the work at the monument. He estimated the cost of that work at about fifty thousand dollars. The Black Hills men protested that they could not take this request back to their communities. When Robinson learned of the revelation, he was embarrassed and distraught. He continued to consider the project feasible, but he finally realized that Borglum could not produce the necessary financing. Robinson excused himself from active fundraising, saying he needed to concentrate on compiling the state census. For his part, Norbeck believed that the main problem was the Gunderson administration's continuing lack of support. Some state newspapers picked up the story, criticizing the concept of the project and its prospective costs to the state and its citizens.[81]

With the financial burden resting on local residents, much responsibility for the initial fundraising fell on Frank J. Hughes, a Rapid City businessman and a member of the Associated Commercial Clubs of the Black Hills. Hughes was initially optimistic about the prospects for raising money, but by the end of May 1926, eight months after the memorial's dedication, he had succeeded in gathering a paltry five thousand dollars, far short of the fifty thousand dollars Borglum said he needed. Hughes faced several problems. With South Dakota's agricultural depression and the problems in the Rural Credits system that had burdened the state government with foreclosed property, bad loans, and interest payments, residents were wary of further obligations. They feared that state taxpayers would ultimately have to pay for the public monument in the Black Hills. In addition, resistance to the memorial itself continued. In April 1925, shortly after the passage of the state legislation, the Black Hills chapter of the General Federation of Women's Clubs adopted an official position that opposed the carving because of its destruction of natural scenery, and the opposition in general became even more outspoken after the October 1925 dedication.[82]

Economic and aesthetic reasons aside, many Black Hills residents were simply disinterested in the proposal. As Frank Hughes drove from town to town trying to raise money, the communities in the southern Hills, closer to the site of the memorial, pledged only small amounts, and northern Black Hills people remained almost entirely uninterested. One of Rapid City's wealthiest citizens assured Hughes that the project had his moral support, but he declined to contribute financially until the project was well on its way. A prominent Black Hills businessman, Isaac Chase, remembered later that some people were afraid that too many tourists would ruin the hunting and fishing in the Hills, and they therefore hesitated to support an undertaking designed to attract more of them. Chase himself reluctantly contrib-

(opposite)
The sculpture
of Theodore
Roosevelt—a
hero to both
Norbeck and
Borglum—
took shape
behind a veil
of tackle and
scaffolding
late in the
carving
process.

uted one hundred dollars, but he thought at the time that he might just as well have thrown his money into the local creek.[83]

Political and administrative problems also plagued the effort. The South Dakota Highway Commission refused to consider building a road to the site until the fundraisers could show pledges of at least twenty-five thousand dollars.[84] Governor Gunderson also withheld his support from the road, prompting Peter Norbeck to declare that "we will either get the road or Gunderson will suffer much politically in the Black Hills."[85] Norbeck and his supporters turned their backs on Gunderson in the 1926 gubernatorial election, paving the way for Bulow, the state's first Democratic governor.

Other political complications arose concerning the Homestake Mining Company, which operated one of the world's largest gold mines in the northern Black Hills. Vitally important to the region's economy, it was a logical target for the fundraising effort. However, officials of the company were smarting from the state legislature's attempts to pass an ore tax as well as from local criticisms of their expenditures for a fifty-year anniversary celebration in 1926. They warned Hughes that they "would not try to do anything except just look after their own business."[86] The inability to raise funds delayed progress on the project and frustrated the memorial's promoters. Frank Hughes called it "heart-breaking work."[87] By 1926, the memorial existed as nothing more than a proposition—supported by a few fervent believers, largely ignored on the national level, and often derided as folly by local citizens.

While the need to raise money delayed work on the memorial, it also influenced its design. Norbeck supported the incorporation of additional figures into the carving, in part because the expansion allowed his personal hero, Theodore Roosevelt, to be enshrined, but also as a way to attract contributions. He anticipated that Roosevelt's image would generate interest from the Northwest and the East. In addition, he asserted that more figures would enable the fundraisers to "divide the work into several units and accept contributions for any one of these units."[88] The final conception featured George Washington, Abraham Lincoln, Thomas Jefferson, and Theodore Roosevelt.

Throughout the struggle to make the memorial a reality, the promoters viewed its value as a work of art, its significance as a patriotic symbol, and its potential as a tourist attraction as equal parts inseparable from each other. At one point, Borglum reminded Robinson that South Dakota sup-

porters were trying to do two things: "arouse the intellectual and cultural interest in the United States in South Dakota" and "sell South Dakota to the traveling world."[89] In August 1926, Borglum appealed to a group of potential supporters in Rapid City. Because of art, he claimed, Italy's "biggest crop" was the tourist, and South Dakota could have the same experience. "If you build the statues," Borglum explained, "you will have bequeathed a whole gold mine to your children for the wealth of dollars it will bring into your state."[90] Norbeck agreed. "I believe the undertaking . . . would become one of the great national attractions—so much so that the State Park would be just an incident: it would simply be the place where the monument is located," he wrote.[91] Herbert Myrick, owner and editor of the popular *Dakota Farmer* based in Aberdeen, South Dakota, summed up the attitude in a magazine article. "Aside from its value as a work of art, it is nothing against the continental memorial—that it shall also be an equally enduring advertisement which," Myrick opined, "will attract millions of people to the Dakota Farmer Empire in general and to the Black Hills country in particular."[92]

These predictions about the benefits of the memorial brought no great burst of financial assistance, although attitudes did begin to change. By 1927, Frank Hughes later wrote, "the Hills people began, so slowly, to thaw, but the warmth had not yet reached their pocketbooks."[93] Despite local residents' reluctance to donate money, sufficient contributions had accumulated to allow carving plans to proceed. Peter Norbeck, however, had concluded that only financial aid from the federal government would ensure the completion of the monument. Despite the terms of the original act, which precluded federal financial support, he began preparing bills to gain such funding. In February, Norbeck was hospitalized following a car accident, and Senator William McMaster and Congressman Williamson introduced the legislation, which called for an appropriation of two hundred fifty thousand dollars as matching funds to money raised from other sources. McMaster also introduced a bill providing for the issuance of memorial coins to be sold for more than their value as a funding mechanism. Norbeck knew the coin measure was doomed, but he designed it to publicize the project while drawing attention away from the request for a direct appropriation, thus increasing the latter measure's chances of success.[94] His ploy failed; neither bill passed.

At this dark hour, politics and providence smiled on the Mount Rushmore supporters. President Coolidge came to the Black Hills for his summer vacation, and the nation turned its attention to the region. On 10 August 1927, the monument and the federal government became linked when the president, in boots and cowboy hat, rode on horseback to a vantage point near the site and spoke at the ceremony marking the start of the carving.[95] Coolidge referred to Mount Rushmore as a national memorial and emphasized the site's geographic significance and central location. "We have come here to dedicate a cornerstone that was laid by the hand of the Almighty," the president intoned. "This memorial will crown the height of land between the Rocky Mountains and the Atlantic seaboard, where coming generations may view it for all time." Straining to make a historical connection between the location and the four figures that would grace it, Coolidge speculated that no white man had seen the area during Washington's day, that the site was located in territory Jefferson had acquired, that the area had "remained almost an unbroken wilderness" beyond Lincoln's time, and that it had been "especially beloved" by Roosevelt. Perhaps most importantly, Coolidge eased the minds of the memorial's promoters by making a case for federal financial support. He told the audience that South Dakotans, because of their strong "American spirit," were leading the establishment of the memorial despite their "meager resources." They deserved, he concluded, "the sympathy and support of private beneficence and the national government."[96]

Coolidge's appearance at Mount Rushmore was a crucial step in the transformation of the carving in the Black Hills from a local tourist attraction to a monument of national significance. In 1927 and again in 1928, South Dakota congressmen introduced legislation replacing the Mount Harney Commission with the Mount Rushmore National Memorial Commission, with members to be appointed by the president, and providing $250,000 in federal money to be matched by funds raised from other sources. Coolidge lent his assistance to the successful passage of the legislation, which became law in 1929.[97] He later wrote Norbeck, "I am glad they are making some progress on the Mountain. I was delighted that I could help you about it."[98]

With a national commission replacing the state version, and with federal financial sponsorship, the monument gained a wider potential base of

*Members of the first Mount Rushmore Commission
and other supporters posed outside the State Game
Lodge. They included Peter Norbeck (third from left),
William Williamson (ninth), and Doane Robinson
(eleventh).*

support. Despite the federal backing, private and state funding remained inadequate, however, and in 1934, an amendment to the 1929 legislation provided for $250,000 in federal funds with no matching requirement. In 1935, Congress appropriated another $200,000, and in 1938, it gave a final $300,000 and turned the administration of the project over to the National Park Service. By the time Gutzon Borglum died in 1941, $836,000 of the nearly one million dollars expended on the project had come from the federal government.[99] Coolidge's presidential patronship, initiated during his 1927 Black Hills vacation, had opened the door for this funding and made the Mount Rushmore National Memorial a reality.

The summer of 1927 was thus a pinnacle of success for Norbeck, for Custer State Park, and for the Black Hills as a tourist destination. The park's infrastructure was enhanced with a new dining hall, several new cabins, new or improved roads, and a refurbished State Game Lodge. Norbeck consolidated the park's administrative structure and secured important state appropriations. The Coolidge visit also brought inestimable free publicity for the region, presidential support for the Mount Rushmore Memorial project, and an increase in visitors to the area. While tourism had been on a steady rise, with Black Hills Commercial Club members estimating a three hundred percent increase in the number of tourists from 1922 to 1926, the 1927 season brought an unprecedented surge in travel to the area. The *Rapid City Journal* at summer's end estimated that even with a decline in August blamed on heavy rains, four hundred thousand tourists had passed through the city. The reporter based his statistics on records of local tourist parks and the fact that local hotels remained full throughout the season.[100] The *Saturday Evening Post* compared the effects of the Black Hills gold rush of 1876 with the Coolidge-inspired tourist rush of 1927. "The latter may be more lucrative," the author said, pointing out that the establishment of services and businesses aimed at tourists would also provide better "marketing facilities" for the local population on an ongoing basis.[101]

The president's summer in the Black Hills further enhanced Peter Norbeck's reputation as a park developer and promoter of tourism. When he departed Rapid City for Washington, D.C., at the end of the vacation, Coolidge acknowledged Norbeck's role in the creation of Custer State Park. "It is a fine thing to have a park of that kind," the president told his South Dakota listeners. "You will appreciate it more perhaps in the future than you do now." Coolidge added, "I am especially grateful to Senator Norbeck.

I regard him as one of the great men of the nation that your State may well honor him in any way that you can."[102] Coolidge's endorsement of Norbeck's accomplishments afforded the senator much of the credit for the successful Black Hills summer. Any lingering doubts South Dakotans might have harbored about the cost to them of the presidential visit evaporated a few weeks after his departure when Coolidge unexpectedly reimbursed the state ten thousand dollars for the expense of his vacation.[103]

The president had summered in an area where the federal government controlled most of the land, but he had spent his vacation in a state park, not a national park or national forest. Federal policies had precluded the development of facilities that he might have used in those areas, but Peter Norbeck and a handful of others had used political avenues to create in Custer State Park a pleasant, comfortable, scenic site attractive to a president. Coolidge's support of Mount Rushmore, his accolades for Norbeck, and his obvious satisfaction with his South Dakota summer reinforced Norbeck's vision for the Black Hills and the tourist industry. The effects of that visit reverberated long after Coolidge's train disappeared to the east.

(opposite) Suspended from the top of Mount Rushmore, a worker applied a drill to the emerging monument. The project was remarkable for its safety record: there were no fatalities.

4

Federal Funds, Federal Control
Politics, Policy, and Art Collide during the New Deal

ORD IN THE BLACK HI

PUBLIC DEVELOPMENT of tourism in the Black Hills changed dramatically during the 1930s. The Great Depression of that decade, particularly severe in South Dakota, toppled the state and federal Republican power structures and introduced congressional New Deal programs that employed professionals who assumed decision-making roles in local tourism development. The Franklin Delano Roosevelt Administration instituted a new emphasis on planning and recreation, and the National Park Service implemented master plans in the parks and assumed responsibility for recreational development on public lands. In the Black Hills, these principals superseded Peter Norbeck's philosophies about scenic design and art as important components of tourism. The era brought profound changes to Custer State Park, Wind Cave National Park, and Jewel Cave National Monument.

President Calvin Coolidge's 1927 summer stay in Custer State Park fixed the Black Hills as a vacation destination in the minds of Americans. However, the benefits of the presidential visit initially bypassed Wind Cave National Park. During 1927, the number of tourists in the national park decreased for the first time since 1918. Wind Cave superintendent Roy Brazell attributed the decline to rainy weather, bad roads, rumors that nearby accommodations were either unavailable or high-priced due to the Coolidge visit, the lack of improvements and tourist accommodations in the park, and the failure of the park to advertise adequately.[1] Brazell voiced his envy and resentment of Custer State Park's popularity by pointing out that the state park was "crowded with cars," while Wind Cave National Park and the southern Black Hills saw "irate motorists" cursing the mud.[2] He predicted that Coolidge's visit and Borglum's carving of Mount Rushmore would lead to unprecedented travel, but if Wind Cave continued to decline, it would not receive its "share" of Black Hills visitors.[3]

Tourists' complaints about the roads humiliated the superintendent, who was chagrined that local residents' tended to blame him for their condition. In February 1928, he wrote to Norbeck describing the situation and pleading for help. He asked the senator to give him some positive message "that I may pass on to the local people, or—to exaggerate slightly—mobbing will be the least I can expect, the meer [sic] losing of my job being considered of no importance at all."[4] Later that spring, he wrote the National Park Service director that, though one could drive from Chicago and into the Black Hills without getting off pavement or gravel, the road through Wind Cave was the "weak link" in this route. At one point, Brazell found thirty-nine cars stuck on the road north of the headquarters. The ensuing traffic jam required horses and a tractor to rectify, and Brazell sarcastically noted, "Considerable tact and diplomacy was necessary to send satisfied visitors on their way rejoicing and boosting for Wind Cave." Word of the bad roads circulated among tourist camps, decreasing visitation to the national park.[5]

The National Park Service finally did focus new attention on Wind Cave National Park, but not with results that Roy Brazell enjoyed. Officials initiated an investigation of conditions at the park in May 1928, and the investigator, H. M. Gillman, reported, among other things, that he found the facilities at Wind Cave poorly maintained. He noted that the superintendent's office needed painting, the registration counter was dirty, and the women's restroom was "bare and cheerless."[6] As a result of the investigation, Brazell resigned, and Anton J. Snyder, who had worked as a ranger in the park since 1925, was appointed superintendent.[7]

Visitation at the park increased during 1928, and Snyder deemed it the most successful year in the park's history. Still, he termed Wind Cave National Park conditions a "pitiful state of affairs" and saw the park "facing a crisis of development and improvement."[8] He also concurred with the former superintendent concerning the unfavorable impression Wind Cave created in comparison with Custer State Park. "Our shabby appearance stands out in bold relief against its comparatively immaculate background," he wrote, "and makes us a target for much unfair criticism."[9] Unlike other areas in which national parks set the standards for the local tourism industry, Wind Cave National Park took a back seat to its state-controlled neighbor in the southern Black Hills.

During 1928, National Park Service Director Stephen Mather and members of the Subcommittee of the Senate Committee on Public Lands visited Wind Cave as part of a national tour, and Thomas C. Vint, chief landscape architect with the National Park Service, also reviewed conditions that year. Subsequently, appropriations for Wind Cave did increase, resulting in some long-needed improvements, but there were particular motivations and pressures behind these new activities. For years, the National Park Service and Congress had harbored reservations about the value of Wind Cave as a national park, and Horace Albright, who succeeded Stephen Mather as director in 1929, discussed with congressmen the option of eliminating the park from the system.[10] Early in 1930, Congressman Lewis Cramton of Michigan, a member of the House Committee on Appropriations and a leading congressional supporter of the service, sent Norbeck and William Williamson a copy of legislation he proposed to introduce. The bill called for abolishing Wind Cave as a national park and making it a part of Custer State Park, in order, he said, "to take from our National Park system one unit which is not up to National Park standards."[11] Both Williamson and Norbeck supported this plan, but they wanted to delay the change. Wind Cave had been included on the route of the Park to Park Highway, which linked a number of national parks, and local residents were enthusiastic about the publicity Wind Cave might generate. Much more importantly, the senator and the congressman wanted the National Park Service to complete the long-needed improvements with congressional appropriations before the property was transferred to the state.[12]

Norbeck was in a position to promote such an arrangement. He had developed close relationships with Stephen Mather and with Horace Albright. The senator had participated in the organization of the State Park Association in the early 1920s and had assisted with passage of legisla-

tion helpful to the National Park Service.[13] Norbeck was confident the plan would succeed. Early in 1931, he commented to Charles Robertson, "We can get the whole National Park as a gift any time we want it, but the Service should make more improvements first." If his proposed appropriations were approved, he added, "Wind Cave will need nothing much more in the way of improvements the next twenty years."[14] Norbeck saw the upgrading of Wind Cave National Park as necessary preparation for its addition to a well-developed state park at little cost to the state.

The National Park Service made a variety of improvements at the park in the late 1920s and early 1930s. It installed an electric light system in the cave, constructed a ranger dormitory, upgraded the water system, and surfaced the north-south road with oil. Norbeck suggested other changes. Among the refinements he promoted was the construction of an artificial lake near the park's headquarters. Although National Park Service officials considered the lake incompatible with national park standards, Norbeck considered bodies of water to be important features in attracting tourists. He urged its construction, and the United States Biological Survey built the lake. Norbeck also encouraged his long-time Custer State Park ally, Cecil Gideon, to establish a concession business at Wind Cave for the sale of food and souvenirs.[15] Given his role as United States senator and his participation in park and conservation issues on a national level, Norbeck's interest in the park was natural. However, he had done little to address Roy Brazell's complaints over the years. Now the changes Brazell had begged for would be made, in part because the prospect of adding Wind Cave to the state park system gave Norbeck added incentive to push for improvements that complemented his methods of appealing to automobile tourists.

As the National Park Service began to improve the run-down Wind Cave, the United States Forest Service considered the situation at Jewel Cave. To a large extent, increasing local pressure to open the cave to tourists as the numbers of visitors in the area grew forced this new attention. In 1927, even before the Coolidge visit was announced, Black Hills Forest Service officials discussed with local residents ways to solve the problem of the Michaud family's claims on the cave. They also considered ideas for making the site accessible to the public. A year later, the memberships of the Custer Commercial Club, located in Custer, South Dakota, sixteen miles east of the cave, and of the Lions' Club in Newcastle, Wyoming, twenty-two miles west of the site, reached an agreement with the Forest Service that enabled the organizations to open the cave to tourists. Members of the two civic groups organized the Jewel Cave Corporation under South Dakota law. The Forest Service issued the corporation a special use permit, and in return, the group agreed to address the Michaud family claim. The corporation sold shares at twenty-five dollars per share, paid Mrs. Michaud seven hundred fifty dollars for a quit-claim deed to relinquish her rights, and began to improve the property. The enterprise was an effort to draw tourists to the area, rather than a money-making proposition in itself; the Forest Service stipulated that entrance fees should be charged only at a rate necessary to cover the cost of administration, operating expenses, and improvements.[16]

On 15 July 1928, the Jewel Cave Corporation opened the site to visitors. One of the first people to enter the cave said, "It was well worth the thirty years of waiting" since she first had heard of its existence.[17] The corporation hired guides to take visitors into the cave and offered free camping at the site, but it otherwise did little the first year to attract tourists, concentrating on improving the property instead. Despite the lack of promotion, more than eight hundred cave visitors registered during the 1928 travel season. In 1929, over two thousand people entered the cave, paying fifty cents each for the privilege.[18] This privatization of Jewel Cave solved the Forest Ser-

"JEWEL CAVE"
CUSTER, S. D.

A group of tourists, lanterns in hand, waited at the mouth of Jewel Cave.

vice's problem of administering a property with purposes outside their usual goals, satisfied local citizens who saw the cave as an asset to the local economy, and enabled Jewel Cave National Monument to become another Black Hills tourist attraction.

Peter Norbeck aided both Wind Cave National Park and Jewel Cave National Monument by obtaining federal funds to improve the highway between Newcastle, Wyoming, and Custer, South Dakota. The Park to Park Highway Act of 31 January 1931 stipulated that national park approach roads, eligible for federal funds under the act, had to begin at park boundaries. Norbeck conferred with National Park Service director Horace Albright about money for the Newcastle to Custer road, which intersected with a road leading to Wind Cave but did not reach its border. Albright suggested

Norbeck incorporate language in a proposed amendment to the bill that would allow for funding of any section of a road not less than fifteen miles long that crossed land at least ninety percent owned by the government. The road under question, which led through Forest Service land, was 8.6 miles long, so the language was changed from fifteen miles to eight miles.[19] The amendment passed, resulting in the creation of what Norbeck termed "a number one highway" from Custer west to the state line.[20]

Throughout the 1920s, similar political maneuvering and influence on public policy had helped Peter Norbeck shape the way tourism developed in the Black Hills. By the early 1930s, the successes of Norbeck and the Custer State Park Board seemed to foretell a continued application by public agencies of the entrepreneurial methods used in the state park. The potential change of jurisdiction in Wind Cave National Park and the privatization of Jewel Cave National Monument pointed in that direction. During those years, however, Norbeck had to withstand another challenge to his power in the park. The friendly William J. Bulow gubernatorial administration of 1927 to 1931, the afterglow of Coolidge's stay in the State Game Lodge, and the increasing attention to work at Mount Rushmore had helped create a peaceful interlude for Custer State Park and the senator in the last years of the 1920s, but it ended in 1930 when Republican Warren E. Green became South Dakota's governor. Although Governor Green tried to avoid aligning himself with either of the Republican factions, most members of his administration were unfriendly to Norbeck. Many in the conservative wing of the party blamed Norbeck for Governor Carl Gunderson's defeat in 1926 and the subsequent four-year Democratic control of the governor's office.[21]

Before the end of Green's first year as governor, he had replaced both John Stanley, a long-time Custer State Park Board member, and Tom Berry, a popular Democrat politician and a Bulow appointee to the board.[22] Green also installed Frank T. Fetzner of Tripp, in the southeastern part of the state, as park superintendent in place of Democrat Charles Robertson. Norbeck made a futile attempt to prevent Robertson's replacement. His frustration increased when he heard rumors that the governor had appointed the two new board members solely in order to temper the senator's influence on the park board.[23]

Controversy arose when the Green appointees fired several park employees and initiated new operating procedures. John Stanley printed editorials in his Lead newspaper supporting Norbeck and Robertson and opposing political patronage in park positions. As the public became more aware of the contentious situation in the park, the matter became politically charged. Influential citizens warned Green that his actions in park matters might destroy his support in the Black Hills and doom his reelection.[24] Norbeck observed to the new superintendent that problems always arose with a change of administration in the park and would continue to do so "until we can get the Park out of politics."[25] But the park was firmly in politics—not only as a source of patronage, but also as a battleground used to fight out political rivalries. These rivalries became particularly intense in the 1932 elections.

Norbeck was up for reelection in 1932, and as the primaries approached, the old sectional controversy regarding Custer State Park development reappeared. Norbeck opponents criticized the use of east-river taxes and fees to develop a west-river facility. They also charged that the senator's support of Mount Rushmore would cost the state a great deal of money. Norbeck's organization countered the charges, and he won the primary by an overwhelming margin.[26] As he began the race for the general election, however, Norbeck faced conditions and issues that overshadowed the controversy in the park and influenced his campaign, guaranteeing further enmity from state Republicans.

Norbeck was attuned to the feelings of South Dakota farmers who were suffering through what seemed to be interminable hard times. For South Dakotans, the Great Depression began well before the 1929 stock market crash. The fall of farm prices after World War I lowered agricultural property values and created financial hardship for farmers who had gone into debt to expand operations during the prosperous war years. State banks began failing in the early 1920s, and the Rural Credits debacle added to the bleak economic situation, burdening the state with foreclosed properties and requiring special taxes to meet bond payments. Drought conditions beginning in 1924, grasshopper infestations, and severe winter weather affected agricultural production and further weakened the state's economy. Conditions became even worse in the early 1930s.[27]

Perceiving the farmers' growing disenchantment with President Herbert Hoover's depression policies, Peter Norbeck anticipated greater than usual support for Democratic candidates in the general election, and he distanced himself from the president. Norbeck won easily, the only Republican to be elected to a major office in South Dakota, normally a Republican strong-

These CCC workers were part of Camp Narrows Company 2757, located near Blue Bell in Custer County.

hold. The state's residents gave Franklin D. Roosevelt a significant majority in the presidential race, and Democrat Tom Berry, former member of the Custer State Park Board, defeated Warren E. Green to become the state's governor. He was joined by a solidly Democratic legislature.[28]

The new state administration would have an important impact on Custer State Park, but the change in federal administration proved to be a more important impetus to tourism development in the Black Hills. The New Deal works programs initiated to alleviate the widespread unemployment and poverty in the country, including the Public Works Administration (PWA), the Works Progress Administration (WPA), and the Emergency Conservation Work (ECW) program, which encompassed the Civilian Conservation Corps (CCC), dramatically increased the tourism infrastructure in the area.[29]

The Emergency Conservation Work/Civilian Conservation Corps proved to be the most significant element in this process. Shortly after Franklin D. Roosevelt was inaugurated as president on 4 March 1933, he asked for the development of a program that would put young Americans to work on conservation projects. The Federal Unemployment Relief Act and Executive Order 6101 established the ECW, and Roosevelt appointed Robert Fechner as its director. The United States Army took responsibility for training the civilians and operating the camps, while the National Park Service and the United States Forest Service, along with the Soil Conservation Service, the Reclamation Service, and the United States Biological Survey, administered specific work programs. These included Civilian Conservation Corps projects in national parks, forests, and monuments, military parks and monuments, and state parks.[30]

South Dakota received two National Park Service administered ECW camps, one in the Badlands National Monument, sixty miles east of the Black Hills, and one at Wind Cave National Park. Superintendent Edward Freeland, who transferred from Carlsbad Caverns National Park and replaced Anton Snyder in September 1931, supervised Camp Wind Cave. The CCC men in the camp accomplished a number of improvements, many of them funded through the PWA or WPA. They constructed reservoirs, improved the park highway, upgraded the cave lighting system, assisted in installing an elevator in the cave, and improved cave trails. The workers helped build a new administration building, two employee residences, and a garage. They replaced the old structure at the cave entrance and further enhanced the approach to the cave with a new log-and-stone footbridge and new parking areas with stone curbs. They updated the water, sewer, and trash disposal systems and remodeled three residences to meet National Park Service standards. In July 1935, the Wind Cave game herds were transferred from the United States Biological Survey to the National Park Service, in effect making the entire park a game refuge. CCC workers built new fences near park boundaries to provide visitors more accessible views of the game.[31]

ECW work in the national parks proceeded according to National Park Service planning, a practice made mandatory in 1929. Coordination and subsequent development became the responsibility of the Landscape Division, created in 1927 and headed by Thomas Chalmer Vint. The Horace Albright administration of 1929 to 1933 further encouraged planning by directing that master plans be developed for many of the parks. Although planning had grown into a professional field with the Progressive Era, the New Deal funding of federal projects, notably the Tennessee Valley Authority, led social and political leaders to develop even stronger beliefs in the need for well-managed regional and national plans. The National Planning Board, established by the Public Works Administration in 1933, continued this trend by emphasizing the importance of developing guidelines for the use and conservation of resources.[32] These national efforts reinforced the priority on planning in the National Park Service, already well in place by the time of the New Deal.

In its various plans, the National Park Service included the determination of architectural styles for park buildings. At Wind Cave, designers created low buildings of native stone and stucco, perhaps because this California style, as it was often called in correspondence, was considered appropriate for the rolling hills and arid grasslands that comprised most of the park and contrasted with the timbered slopes in other sections of the Black Hills. The most imposing of the structures, the administration building, was actually a two-building unit connected by a loggia and constructed against a hillside, designed by National Park Service architect Howard Baker.[33] In 1935, Superintendent Freeland noted that the results of the work projects had made the park "one of the beauty spots of the Black Hills."[34] The New Deal works programs and the park service had reversed the long-time neglect of the park and created a new image there, although it was an image that borrowed from southwestern architectural heritage, rather than local or regional styles.

At Jewel Cave National Monument, equally dramatic changes were in store. Early in his administration, in an attempt to increase government efficiency, President Roosevelt signed Executive Order 6166, which included the transfer of jurisdiction of all national monuments administered by the Department of War and the United States Forest Service to the National Park Service as of August 1933. Upon assuming control of Jewel Cave National Monument, the park service notified the shareholders of the Jewel Cave Corporation that they would be allowed to continue operating the cave until their investment had been recouped; at that time, the park service would take over the management of the site. The Jewel Cave Corporation agreement ended in 1939; the National Park Service began operating the cave in 1940, without the benefit of the tour guides or services provided by the private group.[35]

In the meantime, a number of Civilian Conservation Corps men at Camp Wind Cave were assigned to a side camp—an extension of the main camp—

at Jewel Cave. They built a rock walkway and stairs to the cave entrance and improved stairways, rails, and trails within the cavern. In their enthusiasm to improve the area, the workers destroyed the rustic, Stick-style hotel that the Michaud family had built as an attraction for visitors in 1903. They constructed a log ranger station a short distance from the site of the hotel, thereby replacing an authentic rustic building with a designed rustic structure.[36] The ECW/CCC work in both Wind Cave National Park and Jewel Cave National Monument changed the appearance of those units. Implementing National Park Service architectural and design standards, they completed projects that would appeal to or serve tourists who visited the sites.[37]

The programs that created so much change in Wind Cave and Jewel Cave had a similar impact on Custer State Park, marking a departure from state and even individual control to significant federal influence. Since the establishment of the park in 1919, its development had been guided by a small, frequently changing group of political appointees led by Peter Norbeck, the most consistent and influential force. Norbeck used his political power to gain support and funding for the park. Except during times of political infighting, most notably the Gunderson and Green gubernatorial administrations, he was able to wield a relatively free hand in directing the development of the park according to his personal ideas and tastes and his convictions about the methods necessary to attract motoring tourists. The successes of the park, particularly the summer residency of Calvin Coolidge in 1927, had served to justify Norbeck's actions as tourism increased and national attention focused on the Black Hills. The 1932 elections ended this trajectory, creating a new balance of power on the Custer State Park Board and ushering in New Deal works programs that diminished local control over the development of the tourism infrastructure in the park.

Peter Norbeck's 1932 political victory and the election of Tom Berry to the South Dakota governor's office seemed to bode well for Norbeck's continuing aspirations for Custer State Park and for his role as the leader in the park's development. Berry, who had served on the park board during the Bulow administration and who had a congenial relationship with the senator, asked Norbeck whom he wanted as park superintendent and how they might change the make-up of the board "so that we could handle them."[38] Although Norbeck reminded Berry of his opposition to the preceding governor's partisan practices in making appointments in the park, he proposed several candidates for the board, including Harry Gandy, the Democrat and former congressman who had helped Norbeck achieve the initial park expansion. He also suggested that Charles Robertson, whom Governor Warren Green had replaced as park superintendent, be reinstated.[39]

Robertson, instead, became Tom Berry's secretary, but Berry named Harry Gandy to the park board in March and another Democrat, R. D. Cook, a few weeks later. Park Superintendent Fetzner resigned upon request, and the Custer State Park Board appointed Cecil Gideon superintendent effective 1 July 1933 despite his fears—and Norbeck's—that such a role was inappropriate for him as a park concessionaire.[40] Thus, within a few months of Berry's inauguration, all the Green appointees in the park were gone. "Governor Berry inaugurated a thorough shakeup of the State Park Board," an anonymous source noted in a newsletter circulating in the state capitol.[41] The shake-up seemed to indicate that Norbeck would have more power in Custer State Park than ever before. He was on good terms with the governor, who had experience on the park board. In addition, he had a warm relationship with the governor's secretary, who was himself a former park superintendent, with the two new board members, one of whom he had recommended, and with the new park superintendent, his long-time friend and ally, Cecil Gideon. Instead of strengthening Norbeck's position in the park, however, the election of 1932 marked the decline of his fortunes there.

One of the crucial turning points came when Cecil Gideon resigned in the fall of 1933, and Democrat Ray Milliken replaced him. Norbeck objected to the choice and voted against Milliken's appointment. The senator resented yet another untrained man being placed in the park for what he perceived as political reasons. Animosity between the two developed quickly and never dissipated. Norbeck complained that Milliken failed to keep him informed of park matters and ignored his directions; Milliken told Gandy and Cook that Norbeck interfered inappropriately with his responsibilities. At one point, Norbeck brought an auditor to the park to review the books. Milliken refused him access, saying the senator had no authority to instigate an investigation without the approval of the full board.[42] Milliken was the first park superintendent to mount a successful challenge to Norbeck's power.

Norbeck's fading political strength was another factor in his loss of influence. In the United States Senate, he was one of the few Republicans who won election in 1932. The Democrats and their charismatic leader quickly dominated the national scene. In the state, Democrats had also pushed most Republicans out of office, and many of the conservatives in his party continued to resent Norbeck for not supporting the state ticket more strongly. On the Custer State Park Board, Norbeck was the lone Republican with two Democrats as board members and a Democrat superintendent, all committed to their party. To complicate matters further, Norbeck's health was failing. For some time, he had been visiting the Mayo Clinic to be treated for chronic sores in his mouth. The condition was much more serious than he acknowledged, and it began to sap his energy and his spirit.[43]

The most significant factor in the senator's loss of influence in tourism development, however, was the creation of the New Deal works programs that brought funds and labor sources to public lands. These projects meant a rapid acceleration in the development of the tourism infrastructure in the Black Hills. In Custer State Park, this shift brought new bureaucracy and a new power structure, one that eliminated much of Norbeck's ability to control development there. As the new board members and the new superintendent worked with federal officials and employees on federally funded projects, they allied closely with National Park Service officials and embraced National Park Service standards. With the Republicans out of power on a national level and the resignation of Horace Albright as National Park Service director in 1933, Norbeck wielded less influence with park service officials than he had in the previous years.[44] The National Park Service, on the other hand, began to exercise authority in Custer State Park.

The National Park Service had supported the development of state parks since early in Director Stephen Mather's administration, but no official program to aid such development had existed until the creation of the ECW. By the fall of 1934, the National Park Service was operating more than two hundred fifty programs in state parks across the country through ECW camps. State park officials developed and carried out these programs within their parks with National Park Service approval and under its guidelines. Directors in each of the four National Park Service designated districts supervised the federally sponsored state-park programs. The districts employed federally salaried professionals, including engineers and landscape architects, to evaluate work projects and ensure that the projects did not adversely affect the natural environment of the parks. Eventually, the state parks program of the ECW became larger than the national parks and monuments component. By February 1936, the National Park Service's Branch of Planning and

State Cooperation supervised all ECW projects within the park service, no matter where they were located.[45]

Many state parks submitted plans for improvements that the Branch of Planning and State Cooperation considered inappropriate and potentially damaging to the natural environment. Eventually, however, officials began to differentiate between what was acceptable in national parks and what was acceptable in state parks. In 1935, for example, Secretary of Interior Harold Ickes stated that artificial lakes were suitable in state parks, particularly because such areas were more recreational in nature than the national parks, which should be preserving the natural environment.[46]

These conditions all combined with national trends that would further diminish Peter Norbeck's power on the park board and his vision for the park itself. In addition to an emphasis on planning, the new federal administration and the National Park Service, as well as the United States Forest Service, paid increased attention to recreational development. WPA workers built recreational facilities in state and national parks, at Bureau of Reclamation dam sites, in national forests, and on submarginal lands. The Parks, Parkway and Recreation Act of 1936 further confirmed federal support for recreation and gave the National Park Service responsibility for evaluating opportunities for recreational development on all federal lands except those administered by the Department of Agriculture. The infusion of federal funds into the National Park Service and the increase in administrative responsibilities allowed the agency to implement planning standards and recreational development, not only in national parks and monuments, but also in state parks with ECW camps.[47]

Peter Norbeck was interested in recreation only as another way to attract travelers. As his attention to scenic design and his encouragement of details such as burros in the park illustrated, he valued scenery and picturesqueness more highly than activity. He was, however, a fervent advocate of the value of efficient, long-term planning, particularly if he was doing the planning himself. Until the New Deal era, he had controlled most of the development in Custer State Park, using his political power in the state to marshal resources and deflect opposition. Now, with new federal policies, a compromised political position, an antagonistic park superintendent, and his failing health, he began to lose that control. The political maneuvering he had employed to achieve his goals now served the purposes of others who relished that control. The entrance of the National Park Service into

Peter Norbeck, who considered burros
a picturesque attraction, held the reins for
a rider at the State Game Lodge around
1927.

the park development process provided new sources of power to those who embraced park service goals and methods.

Two examples illuminate this change: the construction of the Iron Mountain Road in 1930 and 1931, before the inception of the ECW programs, and the controversy surrounding the commission for a new Sylvan Lake Hotel in 1935 and 1936, after the works programs were well underway. In developing Iron Mountain Road, Peter Norbeck employed fully his ideas about artistic development in the park, manipulating an already altered landscape to create a stunning visual and sensory experience for automobile drivers. With the Sylvan Lake Hotel issue in the mid-1930s, Norbeck fought a losing battle to extend his ideas of scenic design further as a means to appeal to motoring tourists. The two projects graphically illustrate the degree of change wrought by the inception of the ECW programs and the National Park Service influence in Custer State Park.

Early in May 1930 from the Custer State Park superintendent's office, Senator Norbeck wrote to his secretary in Washington, "The Park looks glorious. . . . Tomorrow we go on Iron Mountain to settle on a very scenic route where the great point of Attraction is Rushmore."[48] Two years later, the Iron Mountain Road, linking the park's eastern gate to Gutzon Borglum's studio near the sculpture, a distance of slightly over sixteen miles, contained elements even more dramatic than those of the Needles Highway. Cecil C. Gideon, State Game Lodge lessee, and Owen Mann, Custer State Park highway engineer, supervised the on-site design and construction of Iron Mountain Road.[49] Norbeck closely monitored the work from Washington and contributed several design elements that made the road unique. He patterned one of these on a section of road in Custer State Park that his wife called "the aisle of pines" because of the trees crowding the road's edges.[50] Anxious to give automobile drivers the experience of traveling in an isolated forest setting, Norbeck achieved another aisle of pines by convincing Forest Service officials, who shared jurisdiction in the Custer State Park Game Sanctuary, to allow the road to divide at a particular point, taking the motorists down one-way single lanes crowded by birch trees, thus creating the effect of a winding path through the woods.[51]

The "pigtail" bridges, however, proved to be one of the most important construction elements of the Iron Mountain Road. Norbeck envisioned park bridges that would provide a picturesque addition to the scenery and a heightened sense of adventure and anticipation. His fondness for switchbacks influenced the design of the pigtails, which turned under themselves, allowing motorists to look down and see where they were going or up to see where they had been. Norbeck originally planned a triple-spiral bridge at one location on the road, but he gave up the idea in deference to trusted advisors who thought the bridge was impractical. In place of the triple spiral, Cecil Gideon developed a nearly circular bridge on a trestle. The bridges were constructed with log supports and guardrails, providing the rustic effect Norbeck wanted to achieve.[52]

The road's most dramatic features were its views of Mount Rushmore, some of them framed by rock tunnels. As work on the road progressed, Norbeck warned that the tunnels' vistas of Rushmore—at that time with only Washington's head completed—should be kept confidential. This secretiveness was consistent with Norbeck's desire to present drivers with unexpected features in his scenic roads and illustrates his control of the design process. By late June 1932, the road was nearly finished, and drivers began to experience its surprises. Iron Mountain Road combined nearby scenes and distant views. From locations along the way, travelers could see the Needles, and on clear days, the Badlands to the east.[53]

The views were impressive, but motorists found themselves just as intrigued by the complexity of the drive, with Mount Rushmore as the orientation point—although disorientation seemed to be a stronger theme. Paul Bellamy, owner of the Black Hills Transportation Company, remarked that driving through the tunnels and switchbacks might lead a driver to think he had drunk too much alcohol or that someone was moving Mount Rushmore "because first he sees it in front of him, and then behind him, and then on the left, and then on the right; sometimes he is above it and sometimes he is below it, sometimes he is approaching it and other times he's going away."[54]

Similarly, *South Dakota Hiway Magazine* called the road "quite mad," appropriate for Alice in Wonderland:

> A majestic curve, and blue distance and there is Washington. A dip into clean pines. . . . A sudden space and Washington. The road dips into birch-woods. . . . Suddenly it is only a path, narrow as a footbridge. . . . Under a log bridge, the sweep of a curve, and you're over it. The bridge curves of a pattern with the road, and mountains tumbled beneath are blue that merges into purple. . . . A tunnel is carved in

Sudden scenic vistas awaited motorists exiting
tunnels on the Iron Mountain Road.

solid rock and when you're inside, you know that it's also a hill, with an elevator-like drop. . . . You climb sharply into immensity and another bridge . . . ends at solid granite. . . . Through the granite is a gap which is another tunnel—long—and sharply outlined against the end is light and the cameo-face of Washington.[55]

The "madness" of Iron Mountain Road catered to motoring tourists' tastes for adventure, excitement, and novel features in addition to natural beauty. Norbeck wanted the road to create an ambiance that would appeal to the travelers' senses. He manipulated the landscape and used the magnitude of Mount Rushmore both as a focal point for drivers' attention and as a foil for the scenery through which they traveled.

Peter Norbeck once told a friend he would rather be remembered as an artist than as a senator. In Custer State Park, he had found his canvas. Beginning with the construction of the Needles Highway in the early 1920s, continuing through the establishment of Mount Rushmore and the development of the Iron Mountain Road, Norbeck conceived, created, and manipulated features and landscapes to establish mood and effect.[56] In doing so, he helped Custer State Park become a model automobile tourists' landscape, filled with natural and man-made attractions that commanded the attention of a motorist on the move and were accessible through the windshield of a car or easily visited during a short stopover.

The election of 1932, however, diverted this path. The challenges to Norbeck's power and influence, the national trends toward wide-scale planning and development of recreational rather than purely scenic attractions for the public, and the National Park Service's management of ECW programs brought new influences to Custer State Park. The park service administered four ECW camps in the park. In addition to the usual clean-up, road maintenance, and fire suppression activities, the workers developed picnic areas, campgrounds, and hiking trails, built game fences, constructed attractive bridges, location signs, markers, and a park entrance portal, and completed landscaping projects. They also participated in more ambitious undertakings, including the creation of several artificial lakes and the construction of cabins at Blue Bell Lodge, a privately constructed lodge that was leased and later sold to the park. They built improvements at Sylvan Lake, erected a park headquarters building, and in 1935 constructed a park

The Iron Mountain Road's pigtail bridges
were engineering constructions that allowed
rapid ascent or descent in a confined space.

ON THE NEEDLES ROAD IN THE BLACK HILLS, S.D. 0754.

museum. Sioux Falls architect Howard Spitznagel designed the museum located near the State Game Lodge.[57]

This surge of activity brought unprecedented development of the park's infrastructure. Norbeck heartily supported many of the projects, but he did not always appreciate the nature of the ECW developments. He had long urged the construction of a park museum, but he criticized the finished structure, which Ray Milliken had been deeply involved in planning, as being poorly located.[58] He derided the skills of the landscape architects associated with the camps, saying they were trained adequately for small design projects but had "no more understanding of a large scenic landscape problem than they have of the Wall Street market or the Mormon creed."[59] He saw his role as park planner and visionary being usurped by federal professionals and their allies within the park. His frustration with his increasing inability to control the processes underway in Custer State Park culminated in a battle to determine the design and location of a new hotel at Sylvan Lake. In that conflict, politics, policy, and art collided.

On the last day of June 1935, the Sylvan Lake Hotel, on the shores of the man-made lake in the Custer State Park Game Sanctuary, burned to the

Beginning in 1921, the Needles Highway offered access to some of the most scenic parts of Custer State Park.

The Custer State Park Museum is a notable example of Park Rustic architecture.

ground. The Custer State Park Board quickly agreed that a new hotel must be constructed; the essential questions became where the hotel would be built and who would design it. The issue took a controversial turn when Robert D. Lusk, a Huron, South Dakota, newspaper editor and vice-president of the State Planning Board, wrote an editorial stating that the old hotel had been inappropriate for the site. He suggested that Frank Lloyd Wright, the famous Wisconsin architect, could design a building that would bring worldwide attention to Sylvan Lake and the Black Hills.[60]

Lusk's remarks appealed to Norbeck's belief in the power of artistically designed attractions in the park. Through Gutzon Borglum, a personal friend of Frank Lloyd Wright's, Norbeck contacted the architect and tried to convey a sense of the economic and political situation. Money was scarce, he told Wright, and the hotel most likely would be built at least in part by public funds. Government architects were available for public projects. Norbeck was the chairman of the Custer State Park Board, but he acknowledged that Harry Gandy had become the board's most powerful member, and Gandy would have to be convinced that the park's new hotel should be a Wright-designed building.[61]

Norbeck was the quintessential politician, and Wright was a most-impolitic architect. To Norbeck's cautionary remarks about finances, Wright replied, "Why is Custer unable to do justice to an architect if an architect does justice to Custer?"[62] In response to the senator's warning that federal professionals might be used for the work, Wright proclaimed "A Government architect is an employee therefore can create nothing and should not be allowed to destroy works of art in the womb of a nation."[63] Norbeck, who was trying to gain Wright's cooperation in managing the political situation, told Robert Lusk, "He does not seem to understand my language."[64] Indeed, Norbeck was speaking the language of politics, and Wright was using the language of art.

Despite the differences in their philosophical orientations, the two men soon shared a common goal. Norbeck became increasingly convinced of the value of a Wright-designed building in the park. For his part, Wright was enthusiastic about the prospect of a commission in the Black Hills. In 1935, the architect was 68 years old, and his long and illustrious career had reached a crossroads. His commissions had dwindled during the 1920s and early 1930s, due in part to the state of the economy and in part to a complicated and controversial personal life. He wrote, lectured, and developed an apprentice program but found little paid work. Nonetheless, he was on the verge of a new phase of his career in which he would design some of his most famous buildings.[65]

Norbeck quickly convinced Wright to visit South Dakota, examine the Sylvan Lake site, and meet Harry Gandy, but the senator could not accompany the architect himself. He asked Paul Bellamy, president of the Black Hills Transportation Company, to escort Wright to the Black Hills. Passing through Chicago early in September 1935, Bellamy telephoned Wright at his Spring Green, Wisconsin, home to make arrangements to accompany the architect back to South Dakota upon the businessman's return from a trip to the East Coast. Wright, however, insisted the journey could not wait and urged Bellamy to come to Spring Green at once. The Rapid City man did so, only to find that Wright was otherwise occupied and not ready to leave. After waiting for a day, Bellamy convinced the architect to depart for South Dakota. When the two men finally arrived at the railroad station, Wright informed his companion that he had no money. Bellamy had to buy his ticket and advance him cash for the trip.[66]

Upon arriving in the Black Hills, Wright visited Sylvan Lake in the company of Bellamy and Harold Spitznagel, the young professional who had designed the park museum building and who served as supervising architect for the Federal Housing Administration in the state. The beauty of the mirror-like Sylvan Lake and its dramatic granite outcroppings impressed Wright, and he quickly settled upon a site for the new hotel in the rocks behind and above the former structure's location. Unfortunately, Wright's outspoken manner and colorful phrases failed to impress some of his South Dakota hosts. He was particularly critical of what he termed "peeled log and boulder" architecture, a style common in the Black Hills.[67]

Wright's references to peeled logs and boulders almost certainly refer to a style of architecture that had developed within the National Park Service and became known as Park Rustic. Practitioners of Park Rustic incorporated local materials and attempted to blend and even meld buildings with the landscape. They tried to convey a rugged, primitive, hand-crafted quality by adapting historical traditions in style and craftsmanship and by avoiding refined techniques or finishing. In forested national and state parks, buildings of logs from which the bark had been removed to reveal their texture, set on foundations of minimally altered rocks in random patterns, typified Park Rustic.[68] Like the ranger station built by CCC workers at Jewel Cave National Monument, these National Park Service buildings were designed to reflect both the historical traditions and the natural setting of the areas in which they were constructed.

Wright's organic architecture also incorporated indigenous materials, and his designs were intimately associated with their natural settings. Rather than appearing part of the landscape, however, his buildings were intended to reflect their utilitarian functions while interpreting and enhancing their environment. In Wright's opinion, structures should express harmony, unity, and individuality; he opposed imitative elements or historical references in design. The architect's outspoken opposition to Park Rustic, however, contradicted most people's expectations for the new hotel at Sylvan Lake. Norbeck himself had assumed that the building might be built of logs or native stone, and Ray Milliken and National Park Service professionals agreed with each other that the typical park architecture was appropriate for the hotel. Wright's vision of a different kind of structure at Sylvan Lake represented departures from the norm and threatened the control of local and federal officials.[69]

As an additional barrier, Harry Gandy opposed Wright almost from the beginning. He feared the architect would be even harder to work with than the mercurial Gutzon Borglum, sculptor of Mount Rushmore, and he deemed the site Wright had chosen for the hotel impractical. Gandy favored a site on a ridge above the lake that had a wide view, enough room for suitable parking, and convenient access to an all-weather road.[70] The choice of site became a serious point of contention between Gandy and Norbeck. The senator insisted that the hotel should be built at or near the water. He said that from Gandy's choice of site, "Sylvan Lake does not look like a lake—it looks like a pond."[71] When Gandy brought Norbeck sketches for buildings at the upper site, Norbeck refused to look at them, calling the proposed location "a crazy thought."[72]

Shortly after Wright visited Sylvan Lake, the Custer State Park Board convened a meeting that Norbeck could not attend. The body decided to ask architects to submit preliminary sketches of proposed buildings; the board would choose the one they preferred and ask the architect who drew it to proceed with more detailed plans. Wright objected vehemently to this procedure, complaining to Gandy that participation in such a process would violate his professional standards. Wright did offer terms for acceptance of the commission, but these conditions required the board to pay a fee for preliminary sketches as well as travel expenses. If board members were satisfied with the plans, they would contract with Wright to undertake the project for a percentage of its total cost.[73]

Gandy and R. D. Cook refused to consider this proposal, even though the board received similar complaints about the process from other architects, including Howard Spitznagel, who had designed the park museum and had accompanied Wright on his visit to Sylvan Lake. Norbeck played politics, defending Wright's stance to Gandy and at the same time trying to persuade Wright to modify that stance in order to be awarded the position. Although Gandy repeated his request for sketches from Wright on at least two occasions, Wright, who badly wanted the commission, refused to comply as long as the board's selection procedure remained in place.[74]

The controversy delayed the selection of an architect. Despite Norbeck's diminished power on the Custer State Park Board, his support of Wright complicated the decision-making process. In an effort to settle the issue, Gandy wrote to Norbeck asking his opinion. Gandy carefully outlined his own concerns about a Wright commission: he believed the board's process was a businesslike, sensible way to proceed; he thought Wright's choice of site was impractical in terms of access and parking; and he doubted tourists would take an interest in any hotel beyond the price of its rooms.[75]

In a long and frank letter, Norbeck responded. He argued that Custer State Park was not a business and could not be treated as one. Norbeck called Frank Lloyd Wright a genius who could solve any practical problems connected with the site. In addressing Gandy's statement that tourists would not be attracted by a Wright hotel, Norbeck clarified his philosophy about aesthetic development in Custer State Park, using the Needles Highway as an example. The highway, he said, makes "a very favorable impression on the tourists and leads them to making unfavorable comparisons with other Parks." The road also encouraged state pride, making "boosters of our own people." Finally, the senator insisted, art "appeals to at least ninety per cent of our tourists, but in various degrees. It is, however, the magnet that draws."[76] For Norbeck, the goal of development in Custer State Park was to create an artistically designed environment that would attract motoring tourists and reflect well on the region and the state. A Frank Lloyd Wright building would serve that purpose.

Gandy, Cook, Milliken, and the National Park Service advisors, however, had other priorities. In March 1936, State Engineer Charles Trimmer, after conferring with Milliken and Cook, announced that Harold Spitznagel would design the new building to be constructed on the site of the old hotel. Newspaper reports noted that one board member, Peter Norbeck, had supported "noted architect" Frank Lloyd Wright.[77] Spitznagel had not submitted sketches as the board had requested. The young architect wrote Wright that he began working on sketches after Milliken told him the park board wanted the commission to go to a South Dakota architect and that Wright was out of the running. However, he was awarded the commission before those sketches were finished.[78]

An exchange of letters between Spitznagel and Milliken suggests a slightly different scenario. In mid-January, Spitznagel wrote to Milliken saying that he understood that Wright was no longer under consideration and that the board intended to choose "a South Dakota architect."[79] Milliken replied that he had no knowledge of the field being limited to a South Dakota architect, but he gave Spitznagel information necessary to submit a drawing and told him, "The structure should be in keeping with the surrounding ruggedness."[80] The suggestion that the decision-makers favored an architect from the state, however, is reinforced in a newspaper article written by A. A. Chenoweth, resident engineer and inspector, as the hotel was being built. Chenoweth said, "Quite properly a South Dakota architect, Harold Spitznagel, was employed by the state park board to plan a modern hotel."[81] The decision ended all hopes of a Wright hotel in the park.

The destruction of Norbeck's vision for the new hotel soon extended to the structure's location. On 13 May 1936, the Custer State Park Board, with Gandy, Cook, and Milliken present, and with the recommendation of Spitznagel, voted to change the site of the new hotel from the location of the old hotel to the elevation above the lake.[82] The decision followed on the heels of a report written at Milliken's request by a landscape architect and the architects connected with the National Park Service-administered ECW camps in Custer State Park. Submitted on park board stationary on 4 April, the report stated that the old site would crowd the hotel, presenting "an ideal photographic setting of scenic value, but of limited utility without future unified development possibilities." The site did not provide for adequate traffic flow or parking or room for "recreational" features such as swimming pools, tennis courts, and stables. John Bloom, Art Temple, Waldo Winters, and F. Bennett, the ECW professionals, suggested "a more spacious setting which would allow full unified development not as a picture, a bus depot, a lunch room, or hotel, but as a complete and conveniently organized unit dedicated to recreation."[83]

These comments summed up the aesthetic split between Norbeck, who envisioned a work of art at the lake, and Gandy, Milliken, and the ECW advisors, who preferred a practical structure with opportunities for recreation, not a "photographic setting of scenic value." With the change in site, the latter faction achieved its goal. Gandy and Milliken were able to control the process of architect selection, thereby eliminating Wright, whose ideas for the building conformed to Norbeck's wishes, without actually rejecting him. The choice of Spitznagel, who had already designed a public-works project in Custer State Park, gave them an architect more likely to be amenable to National Park Service standards. The new hotel, which opened in the fall of 1937, featured no peeled logs, but it did incorporate local rock and knotty pine, and it integrated historical references through the use of American Indian motifs.[84]

Peter Norbeck did not see the completion of the new Sylvan Lake Hotel. The senator died on 20 December 1936 of heart failure, probably exacerbated by his long illness.[85] Norbeck had guided the development of Custer State Park from early in the century. While governors, Custer State Park Board members, and park superintendents had come and gone, he had persevered in his vision of the park as a place where automobile tourists could view beautiful scenery and interesting attractions and experience the thrill of mountain roads. With the onset of the public-works programs, the balance of power had tipped against him. His ideas of artistic development clashed with the more pragmatic views of the National Park Service planners, and his antagonistic relationship with the park superintendent sealed the outcome. In the end, politics defeated the man who had used his political skills so successfully in developing tourism his way in Custer State Park.

Although Norbeck had repeatedly stated his desire to remove the park from the political arena and to end patronage as a means of filling park superintendent positions, he at times contributed to the politicization himself, using controversial events in the park to encourage opposition to political foes and recommending prospective board members and superintendents to governors. With the 1932 election, he lost control over park affairs, but those who assumed that control soon fell victim to the same political process that had given them power. In 1936, Republican Leslie Jensen of

Verne's Photo

Despite Peter Norbeck's objections, the Custer
State Park Board placed the new hotel
at Sylvan Lake some distance from the water.
South Dakota architect Harold Spitznagel
designed the building.

By the 1940s, Sylvan Lake was part of Custer State Park, and the hotel had been set back from the lake itself.

Hot Springs defeated Democrat governor Tom Berry in his reelection bid, and in August 1937, Claude Gray and W. C. Allen replaced Harry Gandy and R. D. Cook on the park board. The new board named Garret L. Owens park superintendent. Ray Milliken had anticipated the removal of Democrats connected with the park.[86] "That," he wrote to a correspondent, "is the way of politics."[87]

Peter Norbeck had been convinced that Wind Cave National Park would eventually become a part of the state system, but the transfer never took place. Instead, in the spring of 1939, the South Dakota Legislature voted to transfer Custer State Park to the federal government for national park purposes. The legislation stipulated, however, that no fees could be charged for admittance to the area. It also required the federal government to assume any obligations under pending land transactions and to agree to remit to the state all income from leases and rentals in the park for twenty years.[88]

In response to the proposed transfer, a team of National Park Service professionals toured Custer State Park in the fall of 1939. They concluded that while the park would be an appropriate part of a national recreational area, it could not be designated a national park. "Because of the extensive changes in land forms through the construction of artificial lakes, the carving of figures on Mt. Rushmore, the existence of many roads and the mining and timbering operations," the report said, "the National Park or Monument classification is precluded."[89] The following year, National Park Service director Arno Cammerer wrote South Dakota congressman Francis Case that the National Park Service was reluctant to consider absorbing Custer State Park in any form under the terms the South Dakota legislature had established.[90] The efforts to transform Custer State Park into a magnet for automobile tourists had succeeded, but in the process, the area had developed beyond the standards acceptable in national parks. The reluctance of state lawmakers to give up the income the unit generated further discouraged federal acceptance of the area. Custer State Park remained in state hands.

The decade of the 1930s brought dramatic changes to tourist-related public lands. The New Deal programs brought a wave of development while diluting local power structures and local control. The regional identity of the Black Hills as a vacation land for motoring tourists had been well established, however, and entrepreneurs and promoters within the region would build on that identity even as the works programs changed the public-tourism landscape.

5

Capitalism, Competition, and Promotion
Tourism after World War I

DEADWOOD DICK.

B.H. STUDIOS.

IN 1925, Charles McCaffree, secretary of the Atlantic, Yellowstone and Pacific Highway Association, in an address to the South Dakota Commercial Secretaries Association, discussed the value of named highways and the importance of the Black Hills in bringing people to the area. "With their blue spruce and gray granite invitation, we have an article of dependable merchandise which may be sold by the established methods," McCaffree stated. "We may secure the travelers. We may take their money away from them and send them home happy with pleasant memories to enjoy in the quiet of the home."[1] As more people became aware of this "dependable merchandise," both public and private entities in the Black Hills found ways to capitalize on the growing tourism industry and the new cadre of tourists.

At the end of World War I in 1918, most tourists in the Black Hills fell into two distinct groups: local sightseers whose day trips had minimal economic impact and upper-middle class people who could afford extended vacations at places like Hisega. Surveys conducted in 1928 and 1938 revealed a shift toward a wider audience. By the 1930s, most out-of-state tourists came from the Midwest, and the majority of them were middle-class earners: merchants, salesmen, tradesmen, farmers, teachers, students, and clerks. They stayed at camp-

A rustic design characterized the Pierre Lodge at Hisega.

grounds or in modest accommodations and enjoyed driving through the Black Hills, viewing scenery, fishing, and swimming rather than playing tennis or golf or visiting museums or sites of historical interest. The surveys present a picture of midwestern tourists of moderate means who appreciated family-oriented activities and automobile tourism rather than resort destinations.[2]

Quick sketches of seven or eight of these tourists typify the group. Joseph and Lola Washburn of Saint Paul, Minnesota, motored to San Francisco in the summer of 1932 via the Black Hills and Yellowstone National Park Highway. The couple proudly matched a friend's record by driving from Saint Paul to Rapid City in one day, a distance of 613 miles. Joe Washburn, a fan of popular western histories and western movies, particularly enjoyed the region's western flavor. Erma and Howard Derheim, natives of the depression-ravaged eastern Dakotas, had married in 1932. Although the young bride struggled to scrape together enough money for a wedding dress, the newlyweds managed a honeymoon in the Black Hills, driving from attraction to attraction while sleeping in their own tent at night.[3] Mr. and Mrs. Ross Smith traveled from Kansas to the Black Hills in 1932 and returned home with a large collection of rock, petrified wood, and crystal specimens. The *Rapid City Daily Journal* noted, "This serves to show how valued pieces of rock, that to residents of the Black Hills are just rocks, are to others who live on the prairie and have only plain stones."[4] Merrill Tucker of Rice Lake, Wisconsin, visited with a friend during the summer of 1935. They saw the Iron Mountain Road, the State Game Lodge, Sylvan Lake, Hill City, Lead, Deadwood, Spearfish, and Belle Fourche. Tucker wrote an acquaintance, "I think the Black Hills are the best vacation land in the United States."[5]

Wealthier tourists also visited the Hills. They participated in the same kinds of activities as other visitors, but on another level. Tourism in the Black Hills depended on mobility, and the Black Hills Transportation Company provides an example of a business that capitalized on that fact, appealing to a segment of society that was more well-off than the typical automobile tourist but still interested in touring rather than remaining in one location. These travelers often arrived in the Black Hills on the railroad and needed transportation to local sights, or they drove their own cars but wanted to be guided through the Hills. In 1926, Paul E. Bellamy, a Rapid City citizen and confidant of Peter Norbeck, established the Black Hills Transportation Company to serve these needs. The company conducted sightseeing tours in the Black Hills and also operated truck and bus lines. Railroads providing transportation to the Black Hills agreed to advertise the company's services and to sell travelers combination tickets that included the price of Black Hills Transportation tours, accommodations, and meals.[6]

Bellamy used touring buses with special bodies he had designed, featuring leather upholstery and canvas tops that could be rolled back to allow passengers an unobstructed view of the scenery. The company's signature colors of scarlet and dark green graced the buses, the Pendleton automobile robes designed for the company, and even the paper cups used during picnic stops.[7] Bellamy hired college men "of quite snappy and attractive appearance" as drivers in order to appeal to the company's customers, three-quarters of whom were girls and women.[8] These employees wore military-style caps, boots, French flannel shirts, and sweaters in colors of gray and black with scarlet accents.[9] The Black Hills Transportation Company served a clientele more accustomed to luxury than the tourists who drove their own cars and camped or stayed in inexpensive cabins. The company's services nevertheless underscored the fact that the Black Hills had been developed

At the top of Mt. Coolidge Black Hills S. Dak.

The removable roof of this Black Hills Transportation Company bus allowed visitors an unobstructed view of Mount Coolidge.

as a destination for drivers: visitors could access many of the offerings of the Hills only by automobile.

Most accommodations for tourists in the post–World War I era were modest. A brochure published during the early 1930s listed twenty-seven hotels, most of them simple and many built before the tourist boom. The flyer also listed forty-four cabin camps, several with tent space available; one tent-only camp; and five boarding or rooming houses. The imposing two-hundred-room Alex Johnson Hotel, which opened in downtown Rapid City in 1928, provided one significant exception to these unassuming quarters. Although not as grand as the Alex Johnson, other facilities provided some extra luxuries for certain categories of visitors. In the 1930s, for example, the Flying V Dude Ranch, thirty-five miles west of Lead near Newcastle, Wyoming, featured a modern hotel, a trout-stocked stream, and two swimming pools. Palmer Gulch Lodge, located north of Sylvan Lake, was another exception. Mr. and Mrs. Troy Parker came to South Dakota from Illinois in 1927 as part of a group of investors intent on building a resort in Palmer Gulch. Once the group recognized that plans for the relatively elaborate retreat were unreasonable for the area, the Parkers bought out the other partners and developed a complex that included cabins with running water and bathrooms. They built up a clientele of college people and professionals who returned to the lodge for extended stays each summer.[10] These types of accommodations, however, remained outnumbered by offerings that served the more transient tourists.

Many of these travelers stayed at automobile camps. Their interest in camping was as much a result of the need for economy as it was a component of the automobile travel trend. In an effort to capitalize on the popularity of car camping, municipalities sponsored free or low-cost campgrounds that attracted motoring tourists to their areas and encouraged them to spend money locally. Rapid City opened that community's municipal campground in July 1919. The city commissioners and the local commercial club worked together to establish the tourist camp on rented property in Rapid Canyon near the city. Volunteers built picnic tables and installed waste incinerators and water taps. With its mountain scenery and trout-fishing in nearby Rapid Creek, the camp gave tourists a particularly pleasant place to stop.[11]

The Rapid City municipal camp proved so successful that the city and civic groups continually worked to improve what they called "Tourist Park." In 1924, the Lions Club donated a public drinking fountain with an eleven-hundred-pound base of Black Hills rocks, constructed by master stonemason Monty Nystrom of Custer. The base supported a bronze lion's head. The town also worked to improve a small cabin that served as a community building for the camp. Local businesses and individuals donated a writing table, indoor and porch chairs, a mounted buffalo head, a mounted eagle, and draperies. A city man gave plants to the tourist park and arranged them in flower beds and cabin porch boxes.[12]

Deadwood, in the northern Black Hills, built its municipal Pine Crest Park in 1924. Located just above Deadwood on a graveled road, the park encompassed six hundred acres, with about one hundred acres cleared for parking spaces shaded by pines. The park provided stoves, wood for fires, and running water. A seating area offered a view of the city. The one-story log community house cost eight thousand dollars to construct and included writing desks, a radio, and a phonograph on the first floor and toilets, showers, and washing machines in the basement. The main room, when

cleared, could accommodate fifty dancing couples. The Deadwood post of the American Legion paid for the construction of its native-rock fireplace. Although the city charged fifty cents a night per car, the benefits offered to the tourists required a considerable investment on the part of the city in its attempts to attract motoring tourists.[13]

The fee charged at Deadwood's municipal camp illustrates a national trend from free to pay camps that developed as municipalities and travelers alike became concerned about the patronage at the camps. In 1923, W. E. Webb, the superintendent of parks in the eastern South Dakota town

The municipal tourist park in Hot Springs featured tables and fireplaces made with petrified wood and inlaid flagstones.

The close relationship between man and automobile is evident in this 1927 picture of a Black Hills tourist camp.

of Mitchell, began to investigate "the attitude of tourists, in regard to pay Camps, and its probable effect upon the number and class of tourists stopping at the different Camps."[14] In 1925, W. H. King, the secretary of the Mitchell Chamber of Commerce, summarized some of the findings in an article in *The Sunshine State,* a monthly magazine devoted to state development. He noted that free camps were initially established to cater to the early, wealthy drivers, but once the prices of cars dropped, the "class of tourists changed overnight." Although communities continued to welcome the "average" tourists, they quickly became disillusioned with transient families living out of their cars and depending on the services provided by the camps. This element, according to King, forced other tourists out, defeating the purposes of the facilities. When fees were charged, camps had more ability to regulate activities, and conditions improved.[15]

The Black Hills tourists of the 1920s and 1930s saw the results of a surge in private and local tourism development. Until the mid-1920s, the private tourism infrastructure in the Black Hills consisted principally of accommodations and direct services, including meals and tours of specific sites. With the advent of more travelers and the attention garnered by the Coolidge visit, businesses and communities followed the models established by public efforts and developed attractions geared toward automobile tourism. These businesses included souvenir production and sales activities that enticed travelers to take home mementos they found as they traveled through the region. For instance, J. J. Levinson, a jeweler in Rapid City and Lead, profited from the Coolidge visit by advertising souvenirs of the presidential visit. "Every article is artistically made and has a miniature engraving or painting of the State Game Lodge," his newspaper ad claimed.[16] Stonemason Monty Nystrom and his wife Lillian founded Artcrafters, a company that produced souvenirs. They crafted small items such as toothpick holders and paperweights, as well as larger projects such as fireplaces and monuments, from cement and local rocks, crystals, and fossils. By 1930, they employed as many as fifty women in their workshop in Custer.[17]

Several new caves became tourist attractions during this period. Wonderland Cave, discovered in 1929, opened in the early 1930s. Stagebarn Cavern, twelve miles north of Rapid City, discovered in 1924 by government trapper Rudolph C. Stoll, opened in 1935 after Stoll and two partners incorporated, improved the property, and erected highway signs on roads leading to the Black Hills as well as thoroughfares throughout the Hills. Nameless Cave near Rapid City began business in July 1935, and new owners improved and renamed Rushmore Cave, the former Hermosa Crystal Cave, in 1936. Bud and Lee Rupp, ranchers in Meade County north of Rapid City, developed Buffalo Cave on their land during the Great Depression. The brothers operated the cave until the early 1940s, when they sold their ranch and moved away.[18]

The tourists attracted to these caverns also presented other entrepreneurs with opportunities to make money. For example, Lily and Pete Scheckle, farmers and ranchers in the Piedmont area north of Rapid City, turned to tourism during the depression in order to profit from travelers' interest in caves. To draw customers to their property located on the road to the popular Crystal Cave, they added a forty-four-seat dining room to their home, where they served dinners of home-grown chicken and vegetables. During the winters, they made rock and crystal souvenirs to sell to summer tourists.[19]

Other innovative businesspeople found novel ways to appeal to motoring tourists. J. E. Handlin, Sigrid Handlin, and Monroe Handlin leased an area containing deposits of petrified wood near Piedmont and developed the Black Hills Petrified Forest in 1930. They offered guided foot tours and opened a gift stand, where they sold specimens of petrified logs and wood and souvenirs made of pieces of wood and plaster of Paris. In 1932, J. E. Handlin rented another section of land holding petrified wood and, with the land's owner, Ed Boylan, developed a road, foot paths, a parking lot, and a small museum. They named their attraction Timber of Ages Petrified Forest. In the mid-1930s, young Earl Brockelsby brought his pet rattlesnakes with him to his jobs at local tourist attractions near Rapid City and charged customers to look at them. Inspired by their interest, he borrowed money and in 1937 opened the Reptile Gardens, which became a popular stop for Black Hills vacationers motoring the area's roads.[20]

The economic opportunities available led to the development of some sites that earned the sobriquet "tourist traps." In 1927, a farmer plowing a hillside south of Rapid City discovered a twelve-hundred-foot wall that appeared man-made, although geologists from the South Dakota School of Mines in Rapid City determined it was actually a natural sandstone formation. Nevertheless, the location quickly became a tourist attraction called the Hidden City, with the owner speculating that the wall might represent a settlement of some lost civilization. The Hidden City attracted tourists throughout the 1930s, despite its local reputation for chicanery. In 1940, a consultant hired to evaluate area tourist attractions reported that the dinosaur bones at Hidden City were in fact the remains of a marine reptile brought in from another location, and a touted three-toed-horse skeleton was actually the skeleton of a modern dog. In the same vein, the expert wrote that a small zoo located at the Hidden City was ill-kept, with animals tethered or confined to cages too small for them.[21] As the Black Hills roadside attractions proliferated, automobile tourists had little ability to evaluate them before being lured off the road, and concerns about substandard offerings began to grow.

On the other hand, tourism also provided opportunities to people often excluded from more typical commerce. Women, for example, found opportunities to develop business careers. Providing meals and lodging and entertaining guests gave many a way to enter the tourist industry using traditionally feminine skills and roles. The long-time manager of the Sylvan Lake Hotel was one of these women. Myra Klepper Peters was born in Pennsylvania and grew up in Ohio and Indiana. After finishing high school, she studied music at several institutions before beginning a teaching career. She married a Methodist minister, W. R. Peters, in 1894. They initially settled in Rapid City, subsequently moving to other locations in and near the Black Hills and then to Nebraska and Missouri. W. R. Peters died suddenly in the early 1900s, leaving his young wife with three sons to raise. She returned to the Black Hills, where she served as supervisor of music in the Lead public school system for eighteen years before leasing the Sylvan Lake Hotel.[22]

Myra K. Peters managed that hotel for more than twenty years. Most of that time she was in partnership with her son, Laurel, although she was always the most prominent part of the team. A trained singer and musician of refined tastes, Peters worked to establish a cultured environment for her guests, often contending with a tight budget and an unsympathetic Custer State Park Board in order to accomplish her goals. Emotionally bound to the resort, she suffered personally through its ups and downs but remained dedicated to its success. After the original hotel burned down and the Custer State Park Board erected a temporary dining hall, she served customers well into the fall despite the lack of heat, wearing overshoes and a heavy coat. During the 1930s, she struggled to make her lease payments when business at the hotel declined. She exulted when conditions improved, allowing her to pay in full at the end of the summer.[23] Her long tenure at the hotel and her local popularity indicate her success as a Black Hills resort manager.

Like Myra K. Peters, Bernice Musekamp, born in Illinois in 1882, was a trained singer who became a well-known hostess to Black Hills tourists, but there the similarities between the two women end. Unable to live peaceably with her stepmother, Musekamp left home after completing her education. She took cooking and waitress jobs in western South Dakota and then managed a sawmill her father had established in the Black Hills. She married one of the mill workers and, with her husband and several family members, bought property west of Rapid City. A colorful woman given to blunt language, Musekamp became involved in Black Hills tourism while the industry was in its infancy. "If four or five tourists went by, you thought, 'Hell, there's a lot of tourists,'" she later remembered. Inspired, Musekamp hung out a sign advertising raspberries and cream with angel food cake and served people on her porch. "That's how I got the tourist bug," she said.

Musekamp borrowed money and slowly built a resort that included a store, dance hall, cabins, and a dining room. Her reputation for cooking delectable fried-chicken dinners with homemade breads and pies and for regaling visitors with her frank language and colorful stories made the business a popular spot. An enthusiastic poker player, she became something of a tourist attraction in her own right.[24]

Other women participated in the tourism industry in less traditional ways. Nell Perrigoue, who began a long tenure as the executive secretary of Deadwood's Chamber of Commerce in the 1930s, was instrumental in promoting the city's popular *Trial of Jack McCall*. This play, based on the murder of Wild Bill Hickok, incorporated tourists into the capture of the perpetrator and his subsequent time in court. Perrigoue also took an important role in helping to organize Deadwood's annual celebration and rodeo, the Days of '76, and she worked to counter rivals in other cities who competed for Deadwood's tourism business. Lillian Nystrom, who ran the souvenir business of Artcrafters Studio in Custer, designed items for sale and supervised staff, while her husband concentrated on constructing fireplaces, monuments, and other construction projects throughout the Black Hills. Florence Bellamy, Paul Bellamy's daughter, managed the Black Hills Transportation Company office and sold tickets for company tours.[25] For these women and others like them, tourism afforded opportunities to forge careers in marketing, public relations, production, and management.

Numbers of American Indians also participated in the growing Black Hills tourism industry. Less than two decades before the area's travel business commenced, the Black Hills themselves belonged to tribes who had signed the Fort Laramie Treaty of 1868. When the gold rush to the Black Hills began in 1875, the United States government made a futile attempt to keep the white miners out, then took the land through an act of Congress, establishing reservations for the Lakotas, or western Sioux, and promising to provide for them until they could become self-supporting. Early twentieth century conditions on the isolated, arid reservations offered a bleak contrast to economic growth in the Black Hills as that area yielded enormous wealth in gold and timber and became a marketplace for the ranchers and farmers settling on former Indian lands. Eventually, the Lakotas began discussing the inequities of their loss of this valuable region. In 1920, Congress passed legislation that allowed the Lakotas to bring the issue to the United States Court of Claims, and in 1923, attorneys for the tribe filed a

claim asking for more than $700 million in compensation for mineral and timber resources removed from the Black Hills.[26] The filing of that claim coincided with the beginning of the 1920s tourism boom in the area but seems to have created little animosity among the purveyors of tourism and those Lakotas who took part in the trade. American Indians became an integral part of the Black Hills tourism industry.

The history of American Indian participation in performances for the dominant white society raises controversial matters of exploitation, coercion, and co-opting of culture. That history also raises issues of individual agency and personal power. Historian Philip J. Deloria questions the "American myths of modernity" that suggest that American Indians were manipulated or even intimidated into participating in Wild West shows, movies, and other venues. "Some Native people," he says, "may well have been duped or bribed into some performances . . . but not for very long." Deloria continues, "It is far from clear that Native Americans in general failed to understand or to think critically about the uses of their images."[27] Indeed, the uses of those images by American Indians in the Black Hills indicate a keen understanding of what would appeal to the audiences so eager to see them.

In 1926, Frank Lockhart, the non-Indian owner of a resort in Dark Canyon outside Rapid City, and a group of Lakotas, many of them veterans of Wild West shows, reenacted an 1857 killing of northwestern Iowa settlers by Dakotas. Lockhart directed the pageant and played a leading part as the father of a pioneer family that Indians attacked, surrounding their cabin. After a brief fight, the settlers were killed, and the adults scalped. The victors performed a "scalp dance" accompanied by a drum and "blood-curdling screams of the dancers."[28] At one showing, the viewers so enjoyed the spectacle they asked for a repeat of the scalp dance, and the performers obliged, with the women participants drawing men from the audience into the dance.[29] The performances played upon dark themes of violence and conflict, but the jaunty nature of the encore indicates how removed both the participants and the audience members were from the reality of the events depicted.

The Duhamel Indian pageant, held from the late 1920s until 1942, illustrates a more serious attempt to portray local American Indian culture. The pageant originated with Nicholas Black Elk, who lived on the Pine Ridge Indian Reservation, and the Alex Duhamel family. Duhamel was the son of an early Black Hills settler who had established a successful general-merchandise business in Rapid City. In the course of their business, the Duhamels traded with many Lakotas, often taking craft items in lieu of cash and reselling them. In the late 1920s, Duhamel and Black Elk collaborated on the development of an Indian pageant that became an important part of the Duhamel family's merchandising and tourist enterprises.[30]

The Duhamel Sioux Indian Pageant is particularly notable because of its association with Black Elk. Born in 1863, he had traveled with Wild West shows in the United States and Europe. Widely recognized as a Lakota spiritual leader, Nicholas Black Elk became the subject of two well-known books, John G. Neihardt's *Black Elk Speaks: Being the Life Story of a Holy Man of the Oglala Sioux*, originally published in 1932, and *The Sacred Pipe:*

In the late 1920s, Nicholas Black Elk became one of the co-creators of the Duhamel Sioux Indian Pageant.

Black Elk's Account of the Seven Sacred Rites of the Oglala Sioux, with Joseph Epes Brown, originally published in 1953. He played a pivotal part in the Duhamel pageant's success for at least a decade, recruiting participants, organizing and directing the seasonal shows, and performing many of the leading roles. The Duhamel family and biographers of Nicholas Black Elk have maintained that his involvement in the pageant emanated from his desire to spread knowledge about Lakota culture and spirituality. [31]

The Duhamel pageant quickly became a popular summer event. At first, the participating Lakotas camped near Baken Park, a Rapid City tourist camp that included a dance hall. The Duhamel family rented the hall for the pageant performances, after which the participants paraded to the Duhamel store where the Lakotas accepted tips from the audience. The tourists were then encouraged to buy souvenirs, Lakota crafts, and more mundane necessities from the Duhamels' business. As the Great Depression deepened, the family diversified, developing limestone caverns on land they owned alongside the road leading from Rapid City to Custer State Park and purported to be a former campsite of Sitting Bull and his family. The Duhamels named the tourist attraction Sitting Bull Crystal Cavern, built an octagonal dance hall and tipi-shaped wooden ticket office close to the road, and moved the Sioux Indian Pageant to the new site. [32]

The Duhamels established a camp for the Lakota participants, providing water and food for the families who came and went during the course of the summer, with twenty-five to fifty or more performers being available at any given time. Nicholas Black Elk organized and directed the twice-daily performances there, and Alex Duhamel and his son Peter announced and narrated them. The Lakotas received twenty-five percent of the receipts and sold handicrafts to the tourists who visited their camp. The Duhamels also sold such items in the cavern's shops. The performances included a number of dances and demonstrations of healing, mourning, and burial ceremonies; one of Black Elk's granddaughters later noted that these *were* only demonstrations, since the actual sacred ceremonies were never shown to audiences. [33] To draw those audiences, the Duhamels advertised the pageant in the local newspaper. One 1935 announcement described a special event, a dog feed to be presented in addition to the regular program. "You see the dog singed, prepared for the feast, cooked, and eaten during the weird ceremony," the advertisement promised, adding, "We use 42 full-blood, old time Ogalalla Sioux." [34]

The florid language of that newspaper advertisement represents one of the compromises often inherent in Black Hills tourism in the first half of the twentieth century. In order to attract customers, tourism promoters emphasized the colorful, the exotic, and the exciting. Nicholas Black Elk, with both a deep grounding in Lakota culture and spirituality and experience in the wider world, utilized his background, knowledge, and influence to bring audiences a view—simplified though it may have been—of Lakota life and culture, in return for the opportunity to present his culture and the ability to earn money and other benefits.

Deadwood's Days of '76 celebration provides another example of American Indian participation in the industry. Beginning with its inception in 1924, Days of '76 organizers actively worked to recruit Lakotas from nearby reservations to camp above its park grounds during the event, appear in its parade, dance at its rodeo and on its main street, and take part in its historical reenactments. On the night before the opening of the Days of '76 in 1925, more than two hundred American Indians rode from their camp to a prominent Main Street site to welcome movie star Jack Hoxie to Deadwood with hours of traditional dancing. At the end of that Days of '76, many of them took part in a reenactment of the Battle of the Little Big Horn.[35] A 1939 newspaper article described the parade appearance of twenty-eight American Indian men who, with "shotguns booming," led more than one hundred men, women, and children in traditional dress up the Days of '76 parade route.[36]

State and national programs also promoted the visibility of American Indians in the region, emphasizing their cultural traditions. While these exhibitions were public, the tribal participants were private citizens who profited by selling crafts or by receiving money, food, or accommodations. In the late 1930s, Wind Cave National Park officials established a five-day encampment of nineteen Lakota families in the park. Rangers brought in a freshly killed buffalo, allowing tourists to observe the skinning, butchering, and cooking of the animal and to share in the resulting meal. On another evening, seventy-five carloads of tourists watched the group perform dances. An official report of the encampment stated, "All the ceremonies were dignified and in keeping with the best policies of the Service."[37]

In 1940, Harlan Bushfield, campaigning for governor of South Dakota, told the state's tribal population that he would devise opportunities for them to display their handicrafts and customs in a dignified manner. After

American Indians participated in Deadwood's Days of '76 celebration from its inception in 1924.

his election, Bushfield suggested that the state park board establish a model Indian village in Custer State Park. In the summer of 1941, several families from Pine Ridge erected a camp of five tipis on the northeast shore of Stockade Lake. They charged fees to tourists who viewed the village and took photographs, and they sold handicrafts from a cabin at the edge of the village grounds. Representatives of the Department of Interior's Indian Arts and Crafts Board and officials from Pine Ridge reservation and Custer State Park attended an informal opening ceremony for the camp.[38] The *Rapid City Daily Journal* called it a "proud day" for the American Indians "who entered the Black Hills, lost stronghold of their ancestors," and were welcomed by state and federal officials.[39]

One public museum was also important in attracting tourists interested in American Indian culture and therefore served as a part of Rapid City's tourism infrastructure. The Sioux Indian Museum in Rapid City, erected in 1938 as a Works Progress Administration project, was a collaboration between the city and the Department of Interior's Indian Bureau, although the city complained at one point because the Indian Bureau did not allow them to include non-Indian exhibits.[40] The museum and publicly sponsored encampments were more concerned with realism than private tourist attractions were, but like the private businesses, they wanted to attract tourists and encouraged activities that would meet that goal. Given the history of the region, however, the inclusion of Lakotas in the tourism industry indicates a measure of respect for that culture from public officials and tourism operators.

Rather than being ignored or excluded, Lakota people were presented as an integral part of the region's history. This cultural exchange, however, presented the American Indians in a particular light. Anthropologist Laura Peers points out that by the end of the nineteenth century, American Indians were seen as a part of the past, conquered peoples whose subjugation represented the march of civilization.[41] Tourists in the Black Hills found the traditional costumes, the dances, the ceremonies, and the reenactments of attacks on cabins and the Battle of the Little Big Horn enthralling because, in part, they had nothing to fear from these exotic "others," who were part of the past, artifacts of the Old West.

Just as private businesses and entrepreneurs of all cultures and sexes developed and worked in attractions for tourists, communities took steps to draw travelers, thereby benefitting the local economies. Inspired by the growing tourist industry and profiting from the public development of roads, Black Hills towns initiated or expanded existing summer celebrations in the post-World War I years. In 1924, Custer made plans to extend its Gold Discovery Day celebration "to a scale far beyond the normal conception for this event."[42] During the same summer, Deadwood initiated its Days of '76 celebration, commemorating the northern town's heritage as the locus of the Black Hills gold rush. Other celebrations included the fall Alfalfa Palace celebration in Rapid City, Automobile Days in Sturgis, and the Tri-State Roundup in Belle Fourche.[43] The celebrations served the dual purpose of entertaining residents and drawing visitors to the communities; in the process, they helped to create community identities.

Deadwood's development as a tourist destination helps to illustrate this formation of identity. The site of an early major gold strike and center of

A horse-drawn "barn dance" made its way along the Days of '76 parade route, possibly in 1930.

#6. Day's of '76 Barn Dancr

Deadwood, S.D.

territorial government activities and transportation, Deadwood was for decades after its founding the most important town in the Black Hills. The city enjoyed several boom times, but it also suffered several bust cycles. In 1920, the city was suffering yet another bust. Area mines closed, threatening the local economy. Saloons, a bedrock of Deadwood's reputation as a town of excitement and entertainment as well as an important aspect of the town's fortunes, suffered with the enactment of national prohibition. In the meantime, Rapid City, on the eastern edge of the Hills, enjoyed a strategic and geographic advantage as automobile tourism increased, and it shortly began to eclipse Deadwood as the most important city in the region. With Rapid City's ascendancy, Deadwood saw itself destined for an unaccustomed position in the region: second place.[44]

Accordingly, Deadwood began to consider tourism as a means to buttress its economy and its preeminence as a Black Hills town. As a lure to travelers, Deadwood adopted a slogan: "the historic city."[45] There was little need for embellishment of that history. Deadwood came to life as a by-product of one of the country's last and most-colorful gold rushes. While citizens on the East Coast were marveling at the development of the steam engine, the telephone, and other technological advances, Deadwood was accessible only by horse, filled with risk-taking prospectors, and home to people like Calamity Jane and Wild Bill Hickock, who was shot in the head while holding the "Dead Man's Hand" in a poker game in 1876. Immortalized in dime novels and Wild West shows, Deadwood was a commonplace name to hundreds of thousands of Americans, even if they did not know precisely where it was located. Deadwood citizens had no need to develop a mythic past; the real one was more than most people could imagine. Yet, in order to appeal to tourists, that past had to be presented in an appealing way.

The creation of the Days of '76 celebration in 1924 proved a basic part of this packaging. Like any number of other local events, the celebration became both a time for the city to enjoy its own heritage and a way to attract others to its streets. The celebration achieved national prominence when President Coolidge attended its festivities during his 1927 summer in the Black Hills. It was here the Lakotas adopted him and he donned an imposing feather headdress, to the satisfaction of press photographers. In promoting the Days of '76, Deadwood played upon its symbols, a process that the development of the character of "Deadwood Dick" exemplified.

DEADWOOD
DICK.

B.H. STUDIOS, INC.

To enhance Deadwood's historical flavor, city promoters selected former railroad worker Richard Clarke to play "Deadwood Dick," an archetype of the Old West.

Dime-novel writer Edward Wheeler had created the character of Deadwood Dick, a daring Robin Hood of the West who eventually became law-abiding, and several local Black Hills men had adopted the sobriquet over the years. Deadwood boosters decided to designate an official Deadwood Dick to represent the city in the Days of '76 celebration, drafting an elderly former railroad worker, Richard Clarke, to do the honors. Clarke's rustic appearance and ability to spin a believable tale soon endeared him to tourists. As Deadwood Dick, Clarke reached the pinnacle of his career when he rode prominently in the celebration's parade during Coolidge's 1927 attendance.[46]

The attention Clarke garnered made him an important part of Deadwood's image. When he considered building a house in the Black Hills in 1928, the Deadwood Business Men's Club formed a committee to "take action to insure Mr. Clark [*sic*] selecting Deadwood as his permanent residence."[47] Consequently, the Deadwood Dick Home Committee assisted in the construction of a house for Clarke in the city's Pine Crest tourist park. Completed in 1928 at a cost of $164.62, the cabin became a new "historic" attraction for tourists. When Clarke died in 1930, thousands of people reportedly attended his funeral and burial.[48] In making Richard Clarke a local hero, the city blurred the line between legend and reality for the sake of tourism.

Deadwood had other particular attributes to present in the Days of '76. In historian Watson Parker's words, Deadwood celebrated its heritage with "festival, pageant, parade, rodeo, and abandon."[49] Abandon had always been a hallmark of this former mining camp tucked into a narrow mountain gulch. Its citizens were accustomed to winking at transgressions of the strict letter of the law. Prostitution was always present in varying degrees of visibility. Gambling abated early in the twentieth century as Deadwood became a more respectable city, but in the 1930s, it resurfaced.[50] With the end of Prohibition, alcohol, like gambling, made a reappearance in Deadwood. The *Rapid City Daily Journal* reported that the nightlife during the 1935 Days of '76 included fifty-two nightclubs, many of them bringing back the "old glamour" through special shows.[51] As tourism in Deadwood developed, saloons, poker players, black-jack dealers, and rumors of prostitutes created a modern aura of benign lawlessness that combined with Deadwood's emphasis on its colorful past to provide visitors a particularly exciting experience.

An important component of that image emerged from the presentation of a play called the *Trial of Jack McCall* beginning in the mid-1930s. Nell Perrigoue, head of Deadwood's Chamber of Commerce, and Mrs. Pat Woods helped to develop the *Trial of Jack McCall*, which dramatized the legal proceedings against the drifter who shot James Butler ("Wild Bill") Hickok in Deadwood's Saloon No. 10 in 1876. By the end of the decade, the play, performed six nights a week during the summer, included a foot chase down Main Street and the capture of the villain. As an added attraction, tourists were recruited to play the part of jurors. The play was so successful that Perrigoue explored presenting the production in larger venues.[52]

Through its yearly celebration and summer theatrical performances, Deadwood capitalized on its history to appeal to tourists seeking an "Old West" experience. While Rapid City continued its prominence as the entrance point to the Black Hills, and the public parks and monuments in the Black Hills remained the premier tourist attractions, Deadwood carved out a significant niche as the region's most colorful, most historic, and most "western" community.

Deadwood presented the most obvious opportunity for theatrics, but other communities also used events and productions to augment their attractions to tourists. Belle Fourche, for instance, built on its history as a ranching community, promoting its longstanding rodeo celebration. Spearfish took another approach, utilizing a natural amenity to attract a significant production. In 1932, the rise of Hitler prompted the German theatrical company that presented the Passion Play to leave that country and come to the United States. After touring for several years, the group came to Spearfish in 1937, where it found a permanent home. The city purchased and donated twenty-five acres encompassing a natural amphitheatre nearby, and citizens raised twenty-eight thousand dollars in order to build an eight-thousand-seat facility that opened in 1939. Regular performances soon attracted thousands of tourists each summer.[53] The production had no historic link to the region, but it continued the trend of appealing to tourists through theatrics and entertainment.

In 1935, the Rapid City Chamber of Commerce conceived of a project, called Dinosaur Park, that could make use of federal funds and create a companion piece to Mount Rushmore within the city. In 1936, work began on the park, located on a ridge above the city near a road named Skyline Drive. Funded by the Works Progress Administration, the project was loosely based on the existence of dinosaurs in the nearby Badlands. Emmit A. Sullivan, a local lawyer and sculptor, designed the five dinosaurs that workers built in authentic proportions. The models were constructed of iron pipe set in concrete, with steel framework overlaid with wire mesh covered in concrete forming the bodies. Completed in 1938, the park featured a model of a brontosaurus that was visible from many areas of the city, although there was no evidence that dinosaurs of that type had ever lived in the area.[54] Like Mount Rushmore, Dinosaur Park offered a large-scale image with a tenuous tie to the region's past but a dramatic ability to attract modern tourists.

BLACK HILLS PASSION PLAY. SPEARFISH. S.D.

B.H. STUDIOS.

Spearfish provided suitable land and funding to create a permanent outdoor theater for the Black Hills Passion Play. The new facility opened in 1939.

As these features developed, organizations made up of local business-people and professionals assumed the responsibility for touting their own areas. City commercial clubs, which evolved into chambers of commerce during the 1930s, promoted their towns, encouraged development of services and attractions that would appeal to tourists, and attempted to band together to promote the region as a whole. The Associated Commercial Club Secretaries of the Black Hills District had formed in 1915 to bring attention to the area's main attraction for visitors. "The Black Hills district has an asset that no other part of the state can boast of—its scenery," promoter J. K. Hull explained, "and the only way to place that asset before the outside public is by concerted effort in the right kind of advertising."[55]

Individual groups took steps to provide this advertising. The Rapid City Commercial Club printed a booklet entitled *Rapid City, South Dakota: The City of Seven Valleys* about 1920. The booklet included maps showing roads and railway systems to and within the area as well as suggested routes for day trips. These maps indicated locations of a few attractions such as Custer State Park, Wind Cave National Park, and Crystal Cave, but for the most part it led drivers through natural scenery and to the sites of recreational activities such as fishing, berrying, and swimming.[56]

By the late 1920s, attractions for tourists had become more diverse, and efforts to draw them more pointed. The Associated Commercial Clubs served as a cooperative association that pooled resources to create brochures and maps, send representatives to fairs and expositions, coordinate community events, and devise other means to attract tourists into the Black Hills. The organization promoted public and commercial attractions as well as regional scenery. At the same time, however, the communities vied among themselves for tourist business, becoming increasingly competitive as greater numbers of people came to the area. During the 1930s, the competition led to the destruction of the Associated Commercial Clubs and the creation of an entirely new entity.[57]

The competition among the clubs became particularly heated as Rapid City's prominence grew. That community scored a victory when it hired Ray L. Bronson as the secretary of its commercial club in 1928. Bronson, a pharmacist, came to Belle Fourche from Iowa in 1906 and ran a pharmacy there until enlisting in the army during World War I. After the war, he returned and became secretary of the Belle Fourche Business Men's Club, where he was instrumental in beginning the Belle Fourche Roundup, the rodeo celebration that became one of the most important summer events

Set on a hill overlooking Rapid City, the massive metal and concrete sculptures of Dinosaur Park were completed in 1938.

in the Black Hills. Bronson developed a reputation as a tireless and colorful promoter, and when Rapid City lured him to its environs, he was ready to exercise all his skills.[58]

Because of his tactics, however, tension developed among community business and civic organizations. In 1929, for example, Deadwood protested the dates of a proposed Rapid City event that would detract from its Days of '76 celebration. Bronson offered to exchange days, but the Deadwood people insisted on keeping their original date and warned Rapid City against any scheduling of events immediately before or after theirs. When the Associated Commercial Club chairman solicited Standard Oil, Minnesota Northern Gas Company, and Chicago Northwestern Railway for money for a 1932 Black Hills publicity pamphlet, he found that Bronson had already contacted the businesses and gathered their donations. The firms had assumed that the booklet Bronson planned would serve the entire Black Hills, but club members suspected he intended it to be a Rapid City promotional instrument. After considerable discord and one demand to expel Rapid City from the organization, the Rapid City Commercial Club offered to increase its 1932 pledge to the Associated Commercial Club from nine hundred dollars to fifteen hundred dollars. The group, heavily in debt, accepted this olive branch and published no booklet of its own in 1932, instead distributing twenty thousand copies of the previous year's pamphlet. In the mid-1930s, the rerouting of United States Highway 16 from the northern Black Hills to the southern Hills elicited protests, especially from Deadwood interests. Although the reasons for the controversial change remained in question, many people credited Bronson with an important accomplishment: after the rerouting, Highways 16 and 14 converged in Rapid City, insuring that most visitors to the Black Hills would pass through the community.[59]

Competition in the area extended to promotion, a largely hit-or-miss effort. Despite the growing importance of the industry, no official state agency devoted to tourism promotion existed until the late 1930s. Up to that time, any public promotional efforts beyond that of civic groups emanated from the Department of Agriculture's immigration division.[60] Advertising was largely a function of individual politicians, commercial clubs, and private businesspeople. The political achievements of the 1920s, particularly the creation of Mount Rushmore National Monument and the luring of Calvin Coolidge to the Black Hills, taught industry promoters and

17th Annual Black Hills Round-up

JULY 3 4 5   JULY 3 4 5

The Old Cow Town Again Invites You To Their 17th Annual Black Hills Round-up.

July 3-4-5, 1934 Belle Fourche, S.D.

"OUT WHERE THE WEST REALLY IS"

Spend your
Vacation
in the
Scenic Black
Hills

For
Reservation
or
Information
Write Manager
Black Hills
Round-up

This
product
protected
by
Patapar

Belle Fourche's summer roundup has been known by several names; this handbill promised 1934 visitors a glimpse of "where the West really is" at the seventeenth annual Black Hills Round-up.

participants some important lessons, however, and they tried to employ them to advertise the region.

The benefits of Coolidge's visit showed the area's citizens the publicity value of association with a famous person. During the 1930s, they tried repeatedly to build on that experience. In 1930, unidentified Rapid City citizens invited infamous Chicago gangster Al Capone to visit the Black Hills. Peter Norbeck resented the ensuing publicity. "I can't say Black Hills to anybody now," Norbeck complained, "but what they remind me of the Capone invitation."[61] In 1931, Paul Bellamy, on behalf of the Black Hills Chamber of Commerce, invited President Herbert Hoover and his family to spend the summer in the Black Hills. The president did not accept, but the invitation received much attention in the press.[62] In 1932, Senator Norbeck asked Charles and Anne Lindbergh to come to Black Hills after the kidnapping and murder of their baby. Ray L. Bronson, secretary of Rapid City's commercial club, urged the invitation and promised that the Lindberghs would have complete privacy if they came to the Hills. He also noted, however, "One more recognition of the Black Hills from someone like Colonel Lindbergh and we will be on our way."[63] Although none of these personalities accepted the invitations, Black Hills promoters had taken the lesson that they could generate significant publicity if famous people came to the area.

The development of Mount Rushmore also proved instructional to Rapid City supporters. In the mid-1920s, area citizens had been slow to contribute to the Mount Rushmore project, but ten years later, they demonstrated their understanding of the value of national publicity emanating from an activity of wide significance. In 1933, the Army Air Corps and the National Geographic Society began searching for a launching site for an atmospheric balloon flight to follow that of Auguste Piccard of Switzerland, who had taken balloons to record heights in 1931 and 1932. The Rapid City Chamber of Commerce invited the committee to inspect the municipal airport, which did not meet their requirements. However, a county commissioner showed them a depression in the ground about eleven miles south of Rapid City that offered an excellent launching site. The committee agreed to use the location, which became known as the Stratobowl, if the chamber would lease the land and build a road to it. In short order, citizens of the community raised ten thousand dollars for the work. The first attempted flight, in July of 1934, failed when the balloon exploded. The next year, another July flight ended in an explosion, but on 11 November 1935 a third flight succeeded. The balloon, the *Explorer II,* reached a record-breaking height of 13.71 miles, and the men on board collected scientifically valuable atmospheric information before landing later that day near White Lake, in eastern South Dakota.[64]

The stratosphere flight put the Black Hills in the national spotlight once again. After the first failed flight, the *Rapid City Daily Journal,* encouraging continued support, reminded its readers that the region was new to tourism promotion and "is not able to finance publicity equal to the organized playground areas and for this reason an event of nation-wide importance, such as a stratosphere flight, is of incalculable value."[65] Indeed, the successful stratosphere flight resulted in news stories referring to Rapid City or the Black Hills that filled more than three thousand newspaper pages.[66] In contrast to their earlier reluctance to support Mount Rushmore, Rapid City citizens had rushed to provide money for this undertaking, knowing that the event would garner priceless publicity for their city.

A more immediate and more competitive form of promotion involved placing advertising signs in strategic spots. The highway associations that had proliferated during the 1920s had used signs and colorful markers to identify their routes and guide travelers. Tourist communities and businesses employed the same tactics. For example, during 1930 Deadwood's commercial club erected more than one hundred road markers on Black Hills highways advertising the city's Pine Crest Park. Members also placed twenty red-and-white four-foot Deadwood arrow markers at road turns and repainted a large three-sided signboard at the Spearfish-Whitewood corner. In 1935, the Deadwood Chamber of Commerce voted to place signs on all highways leading into the city and to erect signboards at each end of town pointing out the town's historic sites. Proprietors of private attractions also erected highway signs during the 1930s to draw customers.[67]

The frenzied competitiveness involved in the erection of signs stimulated complaints from many people in the tourism industry. Myra K. Peters of Sylvan Lake Lodge informed the Custer State Park Board in 1924 that a competitor had erected signs advertising his café. She had understood that the board considered road signs by concessionaires "taboo," but if this man could employ such advertising, she wanted the same opportunity.[68] In 1935, Nell Perrigoue, the secretary of the Deadwood Chamber of Commerce, notified the state's district highway engineer that Deadwood direc-

Explorer II *awaited launch from the Stratobowl in 1935.*

tional signs at the junction of two of the main Black Hills roads had been destroyed but that Rapid City signs on the same posts remained intact. The next year, Perrigoue protested because directional signs paid for by Deadwood, Spearfish, and Sundance, Wyoming, included mileage to Rapid City, even though that city had not contributed funds toward the signs.[69]

Signs became increasingly important in attracting the attention of motoring tourists. In 1936, Ted and Dorothy Hustead, who had been struggling since late in 1931 to establish their drugstore business in Wall, South Dakota, on United States Highway 14, thirty-eight miles east of Rapid City, found salvation in tourism. Dorothy Hustead conceived the idea of erecting clever signs on the highway offering free ice water at Wall Drug in order to attract the carloads of tourists constantly passing within blocks of the business on their way to the Black Hills. The first few signs drew in a steady stream of tourist traffic, and the Husteads erected more and more of them, ensuring their share of the tourist business and success for their drugstore.[70] Although the business was located outside the Black Hills, the famous Wall Drug signs soon made Wall the unofficial entry to the region. By the end of the 1930s, colorful highway signs had become a hallmark of Black Hills tourism.

The signs were only one manifestation of the importance of tourism to the region's economy. The intense competition among communities rushing to capitalize on tourism became so disruptive that prominent businessmen in the Black Hills engineered a virtual takeover of the Associated Commercial Clubs. During the fall of 1939, several of these influential leaders called meetings in Black Hills towns to address the issue. On 20 December, they established the Black Hills and Badlands Association, soliciting memberships that essentially made the Associated Commercial Clubs obsolete. In order to diminish the competitiveness among communities, the Black Hills and Badlands Association passed a formal resolution prohibiting the association from endorsing any particular highway in the area, and it recommended that each town receive the benefits of the association regardless of the level of their financial contributions.[71]

These measures did not immediately solve the problems. The Custer Commercial Club hesitated over participating in the new association because the members feared that men from the northern Hills would control the organization, but they were eventually reassured. In response to concerns about Rapid City's preeminence within the group, the Black Hills and Badlands Association instituted an administration that tempered that community's power within the group and moved its office to Sturgis. Despite the fears over Rapid City's potential dominance, the members chose Ray L. Bronson, head of that city's commercial club, to be the organization's secretary. This choice was both controversial and obvious. The people who had worked with Bronson knew that no matter how many enemies he had made, he could deliver the promotional success the organization sought. After assurances to the public that the secretary was now promoting the entire Black Hills area and after a private conversation strongly reinforcing that message to Bronson, members of the new association dropped opposition to his role.[72]

The formation of the Black Hills and Badlands Association highlighted specific concerns of the Black Hills business community that private and community competitiveness had exacerbated. The region, with its roadside attractions and modest amenities designed to appeal to automobile tourists, had developed a reputation for being a drive-through, rather than a destination, vacation spot. The new organization wanted to combat "the frequently heard statement that we are not a place to stay," hoping to retain tourists for longer periods of time. The association also opposed the existence of shoddy or exploitive attractions and services and called for a better standard of tourist accommodations and services.[73] Finally, the group advocated that the time had come to institute a professional advertising program. As Jarvis D. Davenport, president of the new group, observed to a correspondent, "The Black Hills have ridden on free publicity until the horse needs some hay."[74]

The leaders of the new group had received assurances that the State Highway Commission would assist them financially in implementing these improvements in Black Hills tourism and its promotion. However, soon after the Black Hills and Badlands Association was born, its members received discouraging news. George Starring of the Greater South Dakota Association, which had formed in 1936 to encourage agricultural, industrial, and tourism development in the state, and A. H. Pankow of the highway commission's Tourism Bureau, created in 1937, warned the men that Governor Harlan Bushfield was reluctant to make any commitment of state funds to the Black Hills and Badlands Association. The rivalry between eastern and western South Dakota continued to restrain state politicians from supporting any particular area, and this sectional tension endangered the association's future. All the parties eventually worked out an agreement by which Governor Bushfield approved the use of highway commission funds to be funneled through the Greater South Dakota Association for the benefit of the Black Hills area. The arrangement had to be kept secret, however, and the governor cautioned those involved that any public disclosure of the funding would bring dire political consequences.[75]

While developing long-term publicity goals, the Black Hills and Badlands Association depended upon its secretary, Ray Bronson, to handle immediate promotional needs. He met these challenges enthusiastically. His most visible effort was the Rapid City Port of Entry, also called the Port of Welcome. Bronson established the Port of Welcome in a cabin at the eastern edge of Rapid City, where westward-bound automobile tourists entered the Black Hills. He staffed the facility with workers who provided information to visitors about the area's attractions, encouraging them to stay in the Hills as long as possible.[76]

The fervor of the Port of Welcome staff soon created problems. The governor and other officials received reports that the workers were holding up traffic in order to have long discussions with each automobile driver passing by its doors. Additional complaints arose about proprietors of some of the less-desirable tourist attractions who frequented the facility and tried to steer customers to their businesses. Rumors also circulated that tourists were being directed to the northern Black Hills at the expense of the southern area.[77] At the end of 1940, the association recommended that the Port of Welcome be discontinued because it "has hurt and hindered our state relations and has cost more money than our present budget will allow."[78] By providing a venue for community rivalry, public dissatisfaction, political criticism, and promotion of substandard attractions, the Port of Welcome had counteracted the Black Hills and Badlands Association's goals rather than furthering them.

The group had more success in instituting a professional advertising strategy. The Black Hills and Badlands Association contracted with a national advertising agency and, with a representative of that agency, met with Governor Harlan Bushfield and the State Highway Commission to discuss publicity for the Black Hills. Governor Bushfield subsequently encouraged the legislature to appropriate money to advertise and promote the state as a whole, and the South Dakota Public Relations Bureau was formed as an avenue for generating this publicity. By 1941, the development of the Black Hills tourism infrastructure and the newly concentrated efforts to promote the area were bearing fruit. The State Highway Department showed an increase of about thirty percent in tourist traffic over the previous year. Tourism had become the state's third largest business.[79]

The future for Black Hills tourism looked bright, but World War II thwarted its progress. The Black Hills and Badlands Association issued its 1941 annual report on 13 January 1942, only a few weeks after the attack on Pearl Harbor. In it, Jarvis Davenport detailed the history of organized tourism promotion in the Black Hills. This effort, he explained, began with President Calvin Coolidge's summer vacation in 1927, was "needled" by the stratosphere balloon flights in 1934 and 1935, and was constantly buttressed by the "continued story" from Mount Rushmore. With the country's entry into World War II, tourism in the Black Hills faced a new challenge. Americans' awareness of the Black Hills would be "easily lost from the American public's mind by blitzkrieg headlines," Davenport warned. "We must not retrograde to the oblivion the Black Hills was in following World War No. 1."[80]

Within a few months, however, the organization recognized the need for a hiatus on the hectic activity of the previous two years. In 1942, with the advent of tire and gasoline rationing, automobile tourism declined rapidly. Some Black Hills tourist businesses saw as much as a fifty percent decrease in patronage. The secretary of the Black Hills and Badlands Association, E. H. ("Ax") Hanson, who had succeeded Bronson after the latter's sudden death in 1941, enlisted in the army and resigned from the association in the spring of 1942. With the end of that year's tourist season, the organization closed its office and hired a part-time secretary to take care of mail through the winter.[81]

The beginning of World War II ended the formative years of Black Hills tourism development. The growth of tourism during the interwar years had provided many incentives for travelers to come to the Black Hills. Accommodations had increased while remaining modest. Colorful, inexpensive attractions drew and entertained tourists. Communities and their civic organizations contributed to the expansion of tourism, promoting their particular areas and instituting events and productions to appeal to the travelers. The newly created Black Hills and Badlands Association implemented professional publicity efforts and encouraged increased cooperation and planning within the region.

The link between the Black Hills and Badlands Association and the South Dakota State Highway Department's publicity agency illustrates the continued dependence of Black Hills tourism on public policy and the continued importance of politics to that industry. Despite the formidable obstacles to tourism development, including an isolated location, a sparse population, the ravages of the Great Depression, and sectional and community rivalries, the area gave birth to a viable tourism industry. Black Hills tourism owed its existence to the construction of state and federally funded roads; the early development of public attractions like Custer State Park, Wind Cave National Park, and Mount Rushmore National Monument; the success of state politicians in attracting Calvin Coolidge; the improvements made by New Deal programs; and the continuing promotional and developmental efforts carried on by state officials and civic and regional groups. The success of tourism as a public enterprise allowed private tourism to flourish.

6

Conclusion
Tourism, Culture, and Society

EARLY IN 2001, the National Park Service announced that the road to Mather Point in Grand Canyon National Park would reopen after being closed for several months. The closure was part of the agency's plan to phase out car traffic in the park in favor of mass transportation, an attempt to address the problems caused by the constantly increasing numbers of automobile tourists. The park service reversed its decision after being "inundated with complaints" from businesses on the route and from tourists who preferred to enter the park in the traditional way—on the established road and in their own cars.[1] Seeing the view from Mather Point had become peripheral to the act of reaching it; travelers wanted the experience, rather than the environment, protected.

A similar adjustment to established policy occurred in the Black Hills in the late 1930s. In 1938, Congressman Francis H. Case protested the "decided eyesore" presented by Cold Springs Lake in Wind Cave National Park, which had been created with the encouragement of Peter Norbeck in the early 1930s despite National Park Service standards that held artificial lakes to be inappropriate in national park settings. Because the reservoir did not hold water properly, the lake had diminished to a permanently low level. Local residents had taken to calling the reduced body of water "Pete's

The cover of this 1930 tourism brochure
illustrated the many diversions available
to Black Hills vacationers.

Puddle," an appellation Case considered disrespectful to the late senator. He suggested that the Cold Springs Lake be returned to its intended size and appearance.[2]

After the park service conducted field investigations, National Park Service Director Arno B. Cammerer notified Case that, rather than restoring the lake, the agency intended to return the area to its "original condition as nearly as possible." However, this restoration would not extend to draining the small pond of water still present. That pool had become a well-used buffalo wallow, and a local park official reported that long lines of cars formed so that tourists could watch the animals. Returning the lake to its original size, Cammerer told Case, would eliminate this "unique display," because bison would have to use the far end of the area, where they could not be seen easily from the road.[3] A custom that had developed among tourists, therefore, dictated the National Park Service's policy. The lake would neither be eliminated to return the land to its original character nor be restored to the size and appearance Norbeck had envisioned. Like the road to Mather Point, Pete's Puddle was preserved because of tourist demands, despite its artificiality. Public policy bent to public use in order to allow visitors to enjoy traditional tourist experiences.

These episodes illustrate French geographer J. M. Miossec's model of tourism development. Miossec holds that tourism goes through several stages. In the early period, an isolated region has few amenities, tourists have little idea of the area's offerings, and local residents have mixed feelings about the value of the industry. As early businesses succeed, however, tourism begins to grow, transportation networks and attractions become increasingly complex, and local residents adopt more defined attitudes, including the acceptance or rejection of tourism or the establishment of planning mechanisms to manage its impact. By this time, tourists have received more information about what the region offers. As development continues, enjoying these offerings—the scenery, attractions, accommodations, and activities—becomes secondary to the act of being a tourist. Travelers come to the region not because of its inherent features but because it is a tourist destination.[4] As the failed attempt to close the road to Mather Point and the retention of Pete's Puddle illustrate, the experience of touring becomes a primary goal and those entities providing the services are pressed to accede to tourists' demands.

This transformation from an isolated area with special appeal for travelers to a popular tourist destination can exert a powerful influence on the region's society and culture, reordering priorities, demanding compromises, and instituting new aesthetic and commercial standards. In the Black Hills, public authorities assisted this transformation, and the public accepted and even expected the blurred line between appreciation of natural and historical resources and the development of tourism.

This phase of tourism development had been reached by the time World War II temporarily ended the industry's growth in the Black Hills. For more than twenty years, state and federal officials and programs had funded, planned, and encouraged this growth, and state and federal politics had governed the paths it took. The major initial impetus came from Peter Norbeck and the establishment of Custer State Park. With no public agency at a state or local level to plan or control tourism development and with little interest from state or local residents, Norbeck was able to stamp his own ideas on the park. These concepts revolved around the need to attract and serve motoring tourists. Norbeck encouraged the design of roads and the establishment of accommodations that would become tourist attractions in themselves. His promotion of features such as the park zoo and the burro herd were designed to catch motorists' interests and to entertain them. By urging the creation of a tourists' landscape, he hastened the advance of Black Hills tourism to the final stage of Miossec's model, and the successes of the park encouraged other public and private entities to employ similar tactics.

With the national increase in automobile tourism in the 1920s, the Black Hills had succeeded in attracting a share of the traffic, thanks in large part to political actions and policy decisions. Publicity for the Black Hills increased with the establishment of the Mount Rushmore National Memorial and Calvin Coolidge's presidential visit. Both began with efforts on the state level; both created important links between Black Hills tourism, federal funding, and national publicity. Mount Rushmore, conceived as a tourist attraction, quickly became a symbol of the nation's history, growth, and government. Coolidge, the region's most famous tourist, came to the Black Hills after heavy lobbying by South Dakota politicians. More people streamed into the area, drawn by the newspaper photographs and stories that presented an image of a scenic country favored by great men and great events. Local entrepreneurs and government officials saw Black Hills tourism with fresh eyes and initiated or enhanced offerings to visitors. The creation of Mount Rushmore, the privatization of Jewel Cave National Monument, the improvements at Wind Cave National Park, municipal efforts to attract tourists, private tourism businesses—all sought to create something the tourists wanted to see or do.

The Great Depression of the 1930s changed the trajectory of public tourism growth in the Black Hills. Public-works projects brought new funding and federal authority to the development of the industry. The Emergency Conservation Work and Civilian Conservation Corps programs introduced to the Black Hills a new approach to tourism development, focused on recreation and standardized planning. However, the nature of the earlier tourism development, based on automobile travel, ultimately determined the character of the tourism industry. Private tourism businesses, stimulated by the travel boom of the mid-1920s, instituted new services and products and eye-catching attractions designed to pull automobile travelers off the road. Citizens suffering the economic effects of the depression turned to tourism as a potential source of income. State and sectional politics continued to plague the tourism industry, and competition among Black Hills communities intensified as each area tried to capture tourist dollars. This competition led to the formation of the Black Hills and Badlands Association, a regional organization devoted to tourism planning and advertising that established a link with state government and began to incorporate the regional industry into state economic and promotional planning.

Individual public figures continued to impact tourism. After Peter Norbeck's death, other area politicians, notably Congressman Francis Case, worked to further tourism development, but the years of Norbeck's near-obsession with the development of Custer State Park continued to serve as a foundation for Black Hills tourism. Governor Harlan Bushfield, a strong supporter of the industry, could not provide financial support directly to the region, but he eventually funneled money through a state-wide organization in order to benefit the Black Hills. Throughout the interwar years, the political process and the formulation of public policy continued to influence the way Black Hills tourism developed.

The need to attract tourists affected the environment, architecture, and design in the area and influenced the kinds of businesses that appeared.

Black Hills, So. Dakota

South
Dakota
FACTS

L. G. Troth,
Secretary, Department of Agriculture
Pierre, South Dakota

SYLVAN LAKE

This booklet, printed around 1930,
featured a camping scene at Sylvan Lake.

Natural, historical, and promotional features became closely linked to tourism and eventually defined the identity of the Black Hills. Ultimately, the region became a true tourists' landscape, a culmination of Miossec's model, with a society and a culture characterized by tourism. Examination of the interwar years illuminates patterns and effects in this transformation.

As tourism evolved, a distinct separation emerged within the region. The southern Black Hills, that area south of the Rapid City and Piedmont area, and the northern Black Hills, including the communities of Lead, Deadwood, Spearfish, Sturgis, and Belle Fourche, centered on different methods of appealing to visitors. Tourism had begun in the southern Hills with the warm-water health resort at Hot Springs. Although the business there became more focused on pleasure than well-being, the resort was based upon natural features and perceived medical benefits. With the growth of the tourism industry, the southern Hills continued to build an identity dependent on natural qualities and pseudoscientific elements. The varied and novel scenery inspired roads that allowed visitors access to views of geological and natural features of the region. The preponderance of caves in the area provided attractions further steeped in geology and science. As the industry became increasingly commercialized, businesses and public attractions including the Petrified Forest, the Hidden City, the Reptile Gardens, and Dinosaur Park capitalized on this theme. Even Mount Rushmore combined man-made art with a sense that nature had somehow destined the location of the memorial, as Calvin Coolidge's statement that its cornerstone "had been laid by the hand of the Almighty" indicated.

Park Rustic architecture—the style Frank Lloyd Wright disdainfully termed "peeled log and boulder"—was enthusiastically utilized by state and national entities in the southern Black Hills during the 1930s. Ironically, that style had true local origins. The Michaud brothers had built a distinctive rustic hotel at Jewel Cave early in the century, a building destroyed by CCC workers who then proceeded to build a cabin designed to *look* rustic. Master stonemason Monty Nystrom began developing foundations and fireplaces of local, randomly placed, unaltered stones and boulders in the area during the immediate post-World War I period. The public use of rustic style, however, exerted a greater influence on the region than these local manifestations. When Custer State Park Board members and National Park Service officials considering the design of a new hotel at Sylvan Lake rejected the ideas put forth by Peter Norbeck and Frank Lloyd Wright in favor of concepts in keeping with agency standards, they helped to reinforce the emphasis on rusticity rather than moving to a more artful and sophisticated architectural interpretation in the Black Hills.

While tourism development in the southern Black Hills focused on natural features, tourism in the northern Black Hills grew around history, western images, and the use of performance and celebration. Belle Fourche capitalized on its background as a town catering to the cattle industry to develop the Belle Fourche Roundup. Deadwood, the "Historical City," utilized the Days of '76 celebration as a pageant-like display of its gold-rush history. The creation of the *Trial of Jack McCall* and the transformation of Richard Clarke into "Deadwood Dick" illustrate Deadwood's utilization of its past as colorful entertainment. Spearfish expanded upon the use of performance, bringing the Passion Play to its town. Although the varieties of tourist attractions in the northern and southern sections of the Black Hills certainly overlapped, the two areas developed distinct personalities.

Despite these distinctions, however, the types of attractions that developed in the Black Hills also followed a pattern, one initially established by public policies and with public funds, designed to attract drivers to the area and to entice them to linger. The Needles Highway and Iron Mountain Road, with their steep grades, hairpin turns, pigtail bridges and stunning, contrived views were described by drivers in terms one might use for an elaborate ride in an amusement park. The colossal dimensions of Mount Rushmore, whether glimpsed through a car window from a distance or viewed at more leisure from a nearby vantage point were awe-inspiring and mysterious. Scenes of bison grazing and wallowing near roads or mountain goats—not native to the region—balancing on cliffs transported visitors to a world both unfamiliar and safe, because they could see the wild animals from the security of their own automobiles. All of these sights and experiences were designed specifically for the enjoyment of motoring tourists, providing them unique, exciting, easily accessible adventures.

As tourism developed, towns and private entrepreneurs took these principles further. Dinosaur Park created outlines of prehistoric animals against the sky. The tipi-shaped ticket stand and octagonal dance hall at Sitting Bull Crystal Caverns hinted of an exotic culture. The Petrified Forest invited drivers to enter, briefly, an alien environment. Reptile Gardens put visitors close to species that would be threatening and frightening in another setting. The Hidden City mystified gullible travelers. The street life

The Beautiful
BLACK HILLS

Tourist Guide

Black Hills Celebrations		Map of the Black Hills
Things to See in the Black Hills	**1932**	Circle Tours of the Hills
Hotel and Resort Directory	EDITION	Scenic-Historic Highlights

and entertainment in Deadwood transported visitors to another era, and the Passion Play offered a moving, emotional experience. The attractions were adjacent to well-traveled thoroughfares, inexpensive, and entertaining. They satisfied the needs of tourists who had modest amounts of money and time to spend on their vacations, and who wanted to experience the new, the novel, and the western.

The proliferation of these offerings meant that pulling people out of their cars required increased effort. Following the examples of the named highway associations, entrepreneurs turned to brightly colored signs to promote their establishments, vying to catch the eyes of the traveling families. Communities entered into the visual competition, erecting directional markers and billboards. With the creation of the Wall Drug system of signs, Black Hills tourism became permanently linked in tourists' minds with colorful and even garish signs that became part of the built environment.

The constant need to attract tourists extended to Black Hills towns, leading them to transform their community celebrations into performances that would lure travelers. Commercial clubs and chambers of commerce applied the lessons learned from Mount Rushmore and the Coolidge visit, courting events and people that would draw attention to their locales. The struggles between communities eventually led to the formation of the Black Hills and Badlands Association, but the impetus for that group's establishment also had more complex motivations. In encouraging the construction of a Frank Lloyd Wright building at Sylvan Lake, Peter Norbeck had recognized, perhaps too late, that the area needed to find ways to diversify, to appeal to those tourists who had time and funds to enjoy a higher degree of luxury and refinement. Similarly, the Black Hills and Badlands Association leaders realized that the trajectory of tourism development in the Black Hills had led to an industry that appealed to people who passed through quickly, rather than lingering to spend time and money, and that the quality of attractions at times descended to crass hucksterism. The association's first tentative attempts to address these issues met a formidable barrier in the onset of World War II.

When tourism resumed in the United States after the war's end, it was an industry even more focused upon automobile travel. The end of gasoline and tire rationing, post-war prosperity, and the development of the interstate highway system put families back on the road. In the Black Hills, while changes occurred—particularly increased use of the public lands by

(opposite) This 1932 tourism brochure advertised the Black Hills with a striking, high-contrast graphic evoking the American Indian presence in the region.

outdoor recreationalists—automobile tourism remained cast in the mold of the inter-war years. Most accommodations remained modest and affordable to the mass of tourists. Road-side businesses, marked with boldly colored signs, proliferated. Families continued to drive the byways, pulling off to enjoy commercial attractions, then motoring on to the more uncluttered environs of the area's parks, where they might spend the night in a log tourist cabin or at a congenial campground.

In the post-war decades, Black Hills tourism continued to build on old patterns. Motorcycle races in Sturgis, instituted in the late 1930s, evolved into a nationally famous, week-long celebration drawing hundreds of thousands of bikers.[5] Beyond the obvious appeals of competition and conviviality, the motorcycle owners enjoy that Black Hills tourist tradition: negotiating the curves and turns of the roads and visiting the attractions. In the early 1940s, Korczak Ziolkowski began carving a massive monument to Lakota leader Crazy Horse, both a companion piece and a retort to the nearby Mount Rushmore.[6] Ziolkowski is dead, but the monument remains in progress and draws large numbers of tourists.

The most obvious illustration of tourism following historical patterns can be seen in Deadwood. In the late 1980s, Deadwood succeeded in gaining local and state approval to revive gambling, based on the traditional existence of that activity in the town. The law earmarked gambling proceeds for historic preservation in the city.[7] A pamphlet distributed to local voters on the issue sounded an old message, reminding residents that the region had "to attract people who are interested in more than just passing through on the way to Yellowstone."[8] After voters approved the measures, the rush to capitalize on gambling transformed Deadwood's business district into a string of gambling halls, many of them housed behind the beautifully restored facades of late nineteenth and early twentieth century buildings.

What has happened in Deadwood is a graphic example of the most basic compromises inherent in the acceptance of the tourism industry. In exchange for revenue that will keep the city alive and arrest the decay of its built environment, its citizens have served up their community's history as an offering to people who drive into Deadwood Gulch bearing nickels and quarters. Deadwood's transformation echoes the entrepreneurial spirit that has driven the development of Black Hills tourism since the 1920s.

The city has priceless resources in its setting and its history, and the people who live there have learned how to use them.

In another sense, however, Deadwood is not a typical example of Black Hills tourism. For most of the region, tourism has not co-opted local character but defined it. In a graphic illustration of Miossec's model, tourism has become the central theme in Black Hills identity. The existence and the history of tourism have become as important as the attractions themselves, as important as its "real" history. Printed handouts for tourists provide examples. The brochure for Sitting Bull Crystal Caverns explains the background of the Sioux Indian Pageant and notes, "Although the pageant ended in 1955, Sitting Bull Crystal Caverns still remains one of the Black Hill's [*sic*] leading visitor destinations."[9] An advertisement for the Black Hills Passion Play, which only recently closed, said that in 1939, Spearfish was "a small town with no tourism facilities, accessed by a two-lane highway across the state" and noted that the play had "retained its unique tradition through the years."[10] A handout promoting the still-operating 1880

*Near the end of construction,
a busload of tourists stopped to
behold the steady progress of
Mount Rushmore.*

Train says, "Help us celebrate 50 years," referring to its tenure as a tourist attraction.[11] Rather than simply touting its natural features, its history, or its attractions, the Black Hills touts the history of its tourism. This region, one might speculate, has become a large theme park, with tourism as the theme. Like other areas defined by specific enterprises—mining, fishing, logging, agriculture—the Black Hills exhibits its particular symbols. Rather than machinery or mills, docks or fields, these symbols are motels, signs, souvenir shops, and "rustic" log cabins, the amenities of a tourism industry built on automobile travel. The symbols are as valid as those of any other industry that provides an economic base and a source of pride and identity for its area's residents.

The Black Hills owes this identity to the politicians and the policies that drew automobile tourists to the area during the 1920s and the 1930s. The roads, the parks, the wild animal herds, the presidential visit, and the national monument captured drivers' attention. The modest nature of accommodations and attractions appealed to people of equally modest means newly blessed with automobiles, people more comfortable sleeping in a cabin by the road than in a luxurious hotel. Despite the imported t-shirts and curios and the national food chains, the local character of the Black Hills remains. It is a tourists' society. Like the road to Mather Point, the Black Hills has become a tourists' experience, an experience more important than the individual elements it encompasses, be they private or public, free or fee-based. The people who built and promoted Black Hills tourism inspired a regional industry and a regional identity.

Notes

Chapter 1: Birth of a Regional Industry

1. South Dakota State Highway Commission, "This Summer See South Dakota," Folder Solicitations, Black Hills, Badlands, and Lakes Association Archives, Rapid City, S.Dak.

2. Sven G. Froiland, *Natural History of the Black Hills and Badlands*, rev. ed. (Sioux Falls, S.Dak.: Center for Western Studies, Augustana College, 1990), pp. 1–11.

3. Standard Oil Company, "Visit the Black Hills," in *Black Hills of South Dakota* ([Rapid City, S.Dak.]: Rapid City Chamber of Commerce, 1932), p. [1]. This pamphlet can be found in the Vertical Files, State Archives Collection, South Dakota State Historical Society (SDSHS), Pierre, S.Dak.

4. For specific studies of the history of tourism development in the nineteenth-century United States, *see* Dona Brown, *Inventing New England: Regional Tourism in the Nineteenth Century* (Washington, D.C.: Smithsonian Institution Press, 1995); Billy M. Jones, *Health-Seekers in the Southwest, 1817-1900* (Norman: University of Oklahoma Press, 1967); Eric Purchase, *Out of Nowhere: Disaster and Tourism in the White Mountains* (Baltimore: Johns Hopkins University Press, 1999); and John F. Sears, *Sacred Places: American Tourist Attractions in the Nineteenth Century* (New York: Oxford University Press, 1989).

5. Suzanne Julin, "South Dakota Spa: A History of the Hot Springs Health Resort, 1882–1915," *South Dakota Historical Collections* 41 (1983): 201–8.

6. Ibid., pp. 208–14.

7. Ibid., pp. 206, 213–15.

8. Ibid., pp. 214–17, 249.

9. Ibid., pp. 220–22, 225–26, 249.

10. David Erpestad and David Wood, *Building South Dakota: A Historical Survey of the State's Architecture to 1945*, Historical Preservation Series, no. 1 (Pierre: South Dakota State Historical Society Press, 1997), pp. 205–6; Julin, "South Dakota Spa," pp. 224, 246–49.

11. Julin, "South Dakota Spa," pp. 249–56. A prohibition clause in the state constitution provided for fines and punishment for violations, but in many communities an informal system of licensing gave saloons quasi-legal status. Voters repealed the prohibition clause in 1897. Doane Robinson, "A Century of Liquor Legislation in Dakota," *South Dakota Historical Collections* 12 (1924): 286, 293.

12. Julin, "South Dakota Spa," pp. 218–19, 226–27, 257–58.

13. Ibid., pp. 263–65.

14. *Recent Social Trends in the United States: Report of the President's Research Committee on Social Trends*, 2 vols. (New York: McGraw-Hill Book Co., 1933), 1:172.

15. Ibid., 1:141.

16. Warren James Belasco, *Americans on the Road: From Autocamp to Motel, 1910-1945* (Baltimore: Johns Hopkins University Press, 1997), pp. 20–29.

17. Gail Bederman, *Manliness and Civilization: A Cultural History of Gender and Race in the United States, 1880-1917* (Chicago: University of Chicago Press, 1995), pp. 85–88, 192–96; Belasco, *Americans on the Road*, pp. 30–35.

18. Belasco, *Americans on the Road*, pp. 27, 90.

19. John Ise, *Our National Park Policy: A Critical History* (Baltimore: Johns Hopkins University Press for Resources for the Future, Inc., 1961), pp. 191–92.

20. Ibid., p. 197; John A. Jakle, *The Tourist: Travel in Twentieth-Century North America* (Lincoln: University of Nebraska Press, 1985), pp. 102–3, 236.

21. John W. Bohi, "Seventy-Five Years at Wind Cave: A History of the National Park," *South Dakota Historical Collections* 31 (1962): 365–70.

22. Ibid., pp. 370–92, 406–7; Julin, "South Dakota Spa," p. 251.

23. Bohi, "Seventy-Five Years at Wind Cave," pp. 369–70, 385–88, 393.

24. Ibid., pp. 393–400. Bohi's article discusses the McDonald-Stabler feud in detail.

25. Barbara Beving Long, Four Mile Research Co., *Wind Cave National Park: Historic Contexts and National Register Guidelines*, U.S., Department of the Interior, National Park Service, 1992, pp. 3/17–18; Bohi, "Seventy-Five Years at Wind Cave," pp. 416–19.

26. Eben W. Martin to E. A. Hitchcock, 13 Feb. 1902, Folder 5, Park Establishment, Box 1, Historical Files, Wind Cave National Park Library (WCNPL), Hot Springs, S.Dak. Kathy S. Mason, *Natural Museums: U. S. National Parks, 1872–1916* (East Lansing: Michigan State University Press, 2004), addresses the establishment of the early national parks, including Wind Cave.

27. Bohi, "Seventy-Five Years at Wind Cave," pp. 414–15; Ise, *Our National Park Policy*, pp. 136–37; U.S., *Statutes at Large*, vol. 32, "An Act to Set Apart Certain Lands in the State of South Dakota as a Public Park, to Be Known as Wind Cave National Park" (1903), p. 765.

28. Ise, *Our National Park Policy*, pp. 137–38; Long, "Wind Cave National Park," pp. E7, 4/30–31; Bohi, "Seventy-Five Years at Wind Cave," pp. 421–25.

29. R. S. Rising to Secretary of Interior, 9 June 1905, and Seth Bullock to Secretary of Interior, 20 June 1905, Folder 11, Cave Operations, Box 1, Historical Files, WCNPL.

30. Acting Secretary of the Interior to Eben W. Martin, 7 Oct. 1908, Folder 8, Livestock and Grazing, ibid., copy of letter in Wind Cave [WICA] Rules and Regulations, Box 554, Records of the National Park Service, Record Group [RG] 79, National Archives [NA], Washington, D.C. Wind Cave National Park Library has copied National Archives records pertaining to the park; these copies are stamped with citations.

31. Frederick M. Dille to Secretary of Interior, 25 May 1914, Folder 11, Cave Operations, Box 1, Historical Files, WCNPL, copy of letter in WICA, Employment General Pt. 3, Box 548, RG 79, NA.

32. Long, "Wind Cave National Park," App. A.l, p. 4/30; Rufus J. Pilcher to Earl M. Semingsen, 19 Oct. 1952, File 4, Box 1, Historical Files, WCNPL.

33. Superintendent [Thomas Brazell] to Director [Stephen Mather], 24 Aug. 1918, in *Superintendent's Annual Reports, Wind Cave National Park, 1908–1959*, n.p., WCNPL; Long, "Wind Cave National Park," p. 5/38. *Superintendent's Annual Reports* is a bound volume of copies of reports.

34. Martha E. Geores, *Common Ground: The Struggle for Ownership of the Black Hills National Forest* (Lanham, Md.: Rowman & Littlefield Publishers, 1996), pp. 18, 40–46; Richmond L. Clow, "Timber Users, Timber Savers: Homestake Mining Company and the First Regulated Timber Harvest," *South Dakota History* 22 (Fall 1992): 222–23.

35. Brad Naisat and Linea Sundstrom, "The Black Hills National Forest," in *Black Hills Cultural Resources Overview*, Vol. 1: *Synthetic Summary*, ed. Lance Rom, Tim Church, and Michele Church, U.S. Department of Agriculture, Forest Service, Black Hills National Forest, 1996, pp. 5e1–3; Clow, "Timber Users, Timber Savers," pp. 222–23; Harold K. Steen, *The U. S. Forest Service: A History* (Seattle: University of Washington Press, 1976), pp. 34–36, 58–59, 74–75. For a concise chronology of additions and other changes to the national forest lands in the Black Hills, *see* Naisat and Sundstrom, "Black Hills National Forest," pp. 5e-13–18. In 1954, Harney National Forest was incorporated into the Black Hills National Forest.

36. Steen, *U. S. Forest Service*, pp. 113–17; Terry L. West, *Centennial Mini-Histories of the Forest Service*, U.S. Department of Agriculture, Forest Service, 1992, pp. 52–53; William B. Greeley to Henry C. Wallace, "Report of the Forester," 1921, Owen Science and Engineering Library, Washington State University, Pullman, Wash.; Ronald A. Foresta, *America's National Parks and Their Keepers* (Washington, D.C.: Resources for the Future, Inc., 1984), pp. 17, 20–21; Jenks Cameron, *The Development of Governmental Forest Control in the United States, Studies in Administration Series* (1928; reprint ed., New York: Da Capo Press, 1972), p. 328.

37. Greeley to Wallace, "Report of the Forester," 4 Oct. 1923, p. 37; Greeley to W. M. Jardine, "Report of the Forester," 11 Oct. 1926, pp. 33,

36; Steen, *U. S. Forest Service*, pp. 209–13; West, *Centennial Mini-Histories*, pp. 51–55; Earl Pomeroy, *In Search of the Golden West: The Tourist in Western America* (New York: Alfred A. Knopf, 1957), pp. 154–55.

38. Geores, *Common Ground*, p. 63; U.S., *Statutes at Large*, vol. 39, Antiquities Act of 1906, p. 225; Hal K. Rothman, *Preserving Different Pasts: The American National Monuments* (Chicago: University of Ilinois Press, 1989), pp. xiv-xv, 43–49, 86–90.

39. Ira Michaud, "What I Have Seen and Heard," n.d., pp. 2–3, Jewel Cave National Monument Library (JCNML), Custer, S.Dak.; Karen Rogsa, *Jewel Cave: The Story behind the Scenery*, ed. Cheri C. Madison (Las Vegas: KC Publications, Inc., 1998), pp. 34–35; "Personalities: Frank and Albert Michaud," n.d., JCNML; E. [M.] Hamilton to Forester, 21 Feb. 1908, and Bertha Cain to Theodore Roosevelt, 29 May 1908, both JCNML; Gail and Michael Evans-Hatch, *Place of Passages: Historic Resource Study, Jewel Cave National Monument, South Dakota*, National Park Service, Midwestern Region (Omaha, Neb., 2006), pp. 136–54.

40. Michaud, "What I Have Seen and Heard," pp. 2–3; "Rustic House at Cave," copy of photograph in W. C. Danielson, "Report on Jewel Cave National Monument," n.d., JCNML; Rogsa, *Jewel Cave*, p. 35; "Personalities"; H. C. Neel and C. W. Fitzgerald, "Report on the Proposed Jewel Cave Game Preserve," Sept. 1907, pp. 1–3, and Overton W. Price to Smith Riley, 13 July 1906, both in JCNML. Stick architecture is distinctive in its uses of details, including decorative trusses, repetitive patterns in wall cladding, and diagonal or curved braces on porches. The Stick elements of the Jewel Cave structure are particularly evident in its porch, with intricate curved and angled details. For a discussion of Stick architecture, *see* Virginia and Lee McAlester, *A Field Guide to American Houses* (New York: Alfred A. Knopf, 1984), pp. 255–61.

41. Neel and Fitzgerald, "Report on the Proposed Jewel Cave Game Preserve," pp. 3, 6–8; Associate Forester to William H. Parker, 6 Jan. 1908, JCNML.

42. Rogsa, *Jewel Cave*, p. 36.

43. Arthur L. Lynn to W. F. Hill, 8 Feb. 1908, Bertha Cain to President [Theodore Roosevelt], 29 May 1908, Frank W. Michaud and Albert Michaud to James Wilson, 2 Jan. 1911, Secretary of Agriculture to Frank W. Michaud, 9 Mar. 1911, and Overton W. Price to E. M. Hamilton, 4 Feb. 1908, all in JCNML; Michaud, "What I Have Seen and Heard," pp. 6–8.

44. "Personalities"; Fred W. Morrell to Forester, 27 Feb. 1911, James Wilson to Frank W. Michaud, 9 Mar. 1911, and O. J. Stahl to Frank L. Michaud, 6 Jan. 1920, all in JCNML. Ira Michaud believed his father had applied for a patent but was told that the Government Land Office needed to investigate, and the patent did not come through. Ira Michaud, "What I Have Seen and Heard," p. 4.

45. Stahl to Michaud, 6 Jan. 1920; E. W. Tinker (by T. M. Moorman) to Frank Michaud, 26 Mar. 1925, Fred W. Morrell to Forest Supervisor, 18 Oct. 1913, O. J. Stahl to Forest Supervisor, 15 Feb. 1924, R. P. Imes to District Forester, 14 June 1915, and O. J. Stahl to Forest Supervisor, 5 Nov. 1923, all in JCNML; Michaud, "What I Have Seen and Heard," pp. 4–9.

46. Gilbert Courtland Fite, *Peter Norbeck: Prairie Statesman* (1948; reprint ed., Pierre: South Dakota State Historical Society Press, 2005), pp. 25–26, 33–34.

47. Ibid., pp. 9–27.

48. Ibid., pp. 28–53.

49. Ibid., p. 75; Geores, *Common Ground*, p. 69; Jessie Y. Sundstrom, *Pioneers and Custer State Park: A History of Custer State Park and Northcentral Custer County* (Custer, S.Dak.: By the Author, 1994), pp. 8–9.

50. South Dakota, *Session Laws*, 13th Leg. (1913), ch. 224, pp. 308–9; Fite, *Peter Norbeck*, p. 75.

51. George W. Roskie, "State Game Preserve," *Pahasapa Quarterly* 4 (Apr. 1915): 10–11. *Pahasapa Quarterly* was a publication of the South Dakota School of Mines in Rapid City.

52. Jessie Y. Sundstrom and Linea Sundstrom, "Transportation and Communication," in *Black Hills Cultural Resources Overview*, Vol. 1, ed. Rom, Church, and Church, pp. 5c/6-5c/10; Watson Parker, *Deadwood: The Golden Years*

(Lincoln: University of Nebraska Press, 1981), pp. 100–101.

53. Elizabeth Eiselen, "The Tourist Industry of a Modern Highway: U. S. 16 in South Dakota," *Economic Geography* 21 (1945): 221; James Cracco, "History of the South Dakota Highway Department, 1919–1941" (M. A. thesis, University of South Dakota, 1970), pp. 13–17.

54. South Dakota, *Session Laws*, 12th Leg. (1911), ch. 221, pp. 343–51; "First Report of State Highway Commission," Folder 2, Tourism and Highway Travel, State Archives Collection, SDSHS.

55. Cracco, "History of the South Dakota Highway Department," pp. 17–19. The Yellowstone Trail passed through part of northern South Dakota, then continued west through North Dakota. Harold A. Meeks, *On the Road to Yellowstone: The Yellowstone Trail and American Highways 1900–1930* (Missoula, Mont.: Pictorial Histories Publishing Co., 2000), p. 70.

56. "First Report of State Highway Commission."

57. Ibid.; Cracco, "History of the South Dakota Highway Department," pp. 22–29.

58. *Sioux Falls Press*, 7 Nov. 1915, reprinted in *Pahasapa Quarterly* 5 (Dec. 1915): 21.

59. Geores, *Common Ground*, p. 77; Bob Lee, ed., *Gold, Gals, Guns, Guts: A History of Deadwood, Lead, and Spearfish, 1874–1976* (Pierre: South Dakota State Historical Society Press, 2004), p. 170.

60. George V. Ayres, "Lawrence County Highways and How It Was Done," *Pahasapa Quarterly* 5 (Dec. 1915): 9–15; Frank S. Peck, "Roads: Past, Present, and Future," *Pahasapa Quarterly* 8 (Apr. 1919): 16; Sundstrom and Sundstrom, "Transportation and Communication," pp. 5c–11; "The Proposed Scenic Highway from Rapid City to Pactola," *Pahasapa Quarterly* 5 (Dec. 1915): 16–21.

61. A. I. Johnson, "Touring the Black Hills," *Pahasapa Quarterly* 9 (June 1920): 159–73; Sundstrom and Sundstrom, "Transportation and Communication," p. 5c/10.

62. Sundstrom, *Pioneers and Custer State Park*, pp. 90–95; *Rapid City Daily Journal*, 6 July, 3 Aug. 1918; Stanley Hood, "Sight-Seeing Trips," *Pahasapa Quarterly* 8 (Dec. 1918): 51–53. Hood described an outing at Sylvan Lake, which he called "one of the seven most wonderful spots in the world."

63. Doane Robinson, "The Picturesque Black Hills, a Paradise for Campers," *Dacotah Magazine* 2 (Oct. 1908): 81–88; *Rapid City Daily Journal*, 6 Aug. 1924.

64. Doane Robinson, "Picturesque Black Hills," p. 88; Angie Prall, "Hisega," *Pahasapa Quarterly* 6 (Feb. 1917): 26; *Rapid City Daily Journal*, 23 Aug. 1918, 6 Aug. 1919. During the summer season, the *Journal* periodically ran a column called "Hisega."

65. Robinson, quoted in Prall, "Hisega," p. 27.

66. Alice R. Gossage, "Picturesque Rapid Canyon," *Holiday Greetings from Rapid City, South Dakota, in the Black Hills* (Rapid City, S.Dak.: *Rapid City Daily Journal*, 1919–1920), copy in South Dakota Collection, Rapid City Public Library, Rapid City, S.Dak.

67. *Rapid City Daily Journal*, 26 June 1918.

68. J. H. Johnson and J. P. Snyder, "The Caves of the Black Hills," *Pahasapa Quarterly* 9 (June 1920): 175–87.

69. Watson Parker, "Booming the Black Hills," *South Dakota History* 11 (Winter 1980): 43–49; *Rapid City Daily Journal*, 6 Feb. 1918 and repeated frequently in the following weeks.

70. Committee to Samuel H. Elrod, 5 Dec. 1905, Box 1, Governor Samuel H. Elrod Papers, State Archives Collection, SDSHS; Charles McCaffree to Peter Norbeck, 1 Jan. 1919, Box 8, Governor Peter Norbeck Papers, State Archives Collection, SDSHS.

71. J. H. Steele, "A Vacation in the Black Hills," *Pahasapa Quarterly* 4 (Feb. 1915): 45.

72. H. W. Troth, "The Deadwood Business Club," ibid., pp. 11–14.

73. J. K. Hull, "Association of Commercial Club Secretaries of the Black Hills District," *Pahasapa Quarterly* 5 (Apr. 1916): 21, 23.

74. *Rapid City Daily Journal*, 3 Apr. 1918.

75. Quoted in ibid., 15 Aug. 1919, reprinting *Potter County News* of Gettysburg, S.Dak.

Chapter 2: Looking for Tourists

1. *Rapid City Daily Journal*, 10 Aug. 1920. For discussions of tourism in the United States in the early twentieth century, *see* Lynn Morrow

and Linda Myers-Phinney, *Shepherd of the Hills County: Tourism Transforms the Ozarks, 1880s–1930s* (Fayetteville: University of Arkansas Press, 1999); Earl Pomeroy, *In Search of the Golden West: The Tourist in Western America* (New York: Alfred A. Knopf, 1957); and Hal K. Rothman, *Devil's Bargains: Tourism in the Twentieth-Century American West* (Lawrence: University Press of Kansas, 1998).

2. U.S., Department of the Interior, National Park Service, *Report of the Director of the National Park Service to the Secretary of the Interior for the Fiscal Year Ended June 30, 1925, and the Travel Season, 1925,* (Washington, D.C.: Government Printing Office, 1925), p. 1.

3. Regarding the creation of these programs and their ultimate results, *see* Gilbert Courtland Fite, *Peter Norbeck: Prairie Statesman* (1948; reprint ed., Pierre: South Dakota State Historical Society Press, 2005), pp. 80–93.

4. "Permanent State Park," Message File, Box 8, Governor Peter Norbeck Papers, State Archives Collection, South Dakota State Historical Society (SDSHS), Pierre, S.Dak.

5. South Dakota, *Session Laws*, 16th Leg. (1919), ch. 164, pp. 150–51; Peter Norbeck to John A. Stanley, 17 Mar. 1921, Custer State Park, 1921–1931, Box 97, Peter Norbeck Papers, Richardson Archives, I. D. Weeks Library, University of South Dakota (USD), Vermillion, S.Dak.

6. John A. Stanley, "South Dakota's State Park," *Pahasapa Quarterly* 10 (Spring 1921): 179–81; H. S. Hedrick, "Game and Fish Conditions in the Custer State Park," ibid., pp. 189–93; Norbeck to Will O. Doolittle, 26 Sept. 1922, Theodore Shoemaker to Stanley, 31 May 1922, Stanley to John Warnke, 31 May 1922, Norbeck to Doolittle, 26 Sept. 1922, all in Custer State Park Board, C-C7.1 (Miscellaneous), 1919–1926, CCC Drawer, Custer State Park Archives [CSPA], Custer, S.Dak.

7. Norbeck to Stanley, 27 Dec. 1921, Box 70, Norbeck Papers, USD.

8. Norbeck to Stanley, 13 June 1919, Folder #5, Box 95, Norbeck Papers, USD. For a discussion of the environmental, economic, political, and cultural origins of the division between the eastern and western sides of the state, *see* James D. McLaird, "From Bib Overalls to Cowboy Boots: East River/West River Differences in South Dakota," *South Dakota History* 19 (Winter 1989): 454–91.

9. Custer State Park Board, Minutes, 3 July 1919, and Norbeck to Stanley, 13 June 1919, both Box 95, Norbeck Papers, USD; *Hot Springs Weekly Star*, 2 Nov. 1937; [Stanley] to Harold J. Cook, 30 Jan. 1923, Custer State Park Board, Correspondence, CSPA; Jessie Y. Sundstrom, *Pioneers and Custer State Park: A History of Custer State Park and Northcentral Custer County* (Custer, S.Dak.: By the Author, 1994), p. 86.

10. Norbeck to Chambers Kellar, 10 Mar. 1919, Folder #4, Box 95, Norbeck Papers, USD.

11. Norbeck to Harry L. Gandy, 20 Sept. 1919, ibid., Folder #1.

12. Gandy to Norbeck, 15 Oct. 1919, ibid.; U. S., *Statutes at Large*, vol. 41, An Act for the creation of Custer State Park Game Sanctuary, in the State of South Dakota, and for other purposes, 1920, p. 986–87; President Woodrow Wilson, "Custer State Game Park Sanctuary—South Dakota," Proclamation No. 1576, 9 Oct. 1920; Brad Noisant, "Tourism and Recreation," in *Black Hills Cultural Resources Overview*, Vol. 1: *Synthetic Summary*, ed. Lance Rom, Tim Church, Michele Church, U.S. Department of Agriculture, Forest Service, Black Hills National Forest, 1996, p. 5d-3; Fite, *Peter Norbeck*, p. 76; Stanley, "South Dakota's State Park," pp. 179–81.

13. Norbeck, "Notation for Message File," 23 Dec. 1919, Custer State Park, Box 97, and Norbeck to Gandy, 7 Aug. 1919, Folder #1, Box 95, both in Norbeck Papers, USD.

14. [A. F. Potter] to Gandy, 12 Dec. 1919, Folder #1, Box 95, ibid.

15. Gandy to Norbeck, 18 Dec. 1919, ibid.

16. South Dakota, *Session Laws*, 16th Leg., Special Sess. (1920), ch. 25, p. 25.

17. Norbeck to Elaine E. Fowler, 24 Nov. 1926, Forest Service, Box 117, Norbeck Papers, USD.

18. Norbeck to Stanley, 4 May 1921, Custer State Park, Box 70, Norbeck Papers, USD.

19. Peter Norbeck, "South Dakota State Park: The Black Hills Are Not Hills But High Mountains," *Outlook* 146 (1 June 1927): 153. *See* Paul S.

Sutter, *Driven Wild: How the Fight against Automobile Tourism Launched the Modern Wilderness Movement* (Seattle: University of Washington Press, 2002), for a thorough study of the effects of automobile tourism during this era.

20. For an overview of Norbeck's aesthetic philosophy, *see* Norbeck to Gandy, 17 Oct. 1935, Sylvan Lake Hotel, Box 70, Norbeck Papers, USD.

21. Fite, *Peter Norbeck*, pp. 95–98; William Williamson, *An Autobiography: William Williamson, Student, Homesteader, Teacher, Lawyer, Judge, Congressman, and Trusted Friend* (Rapid City, S.Dak.: By the Author, 1964), p. 131; Stanley, "South Dakota's State Park," p. 179.

22. Norbeck to Stanley, 7 July 1921, Custer State Park, Box 70, Norbeck Papers, USD.

23. Norbeck to Stanley, 14 Oct. 1921, ibid.

24. Norbeck to Scovel Johnson, 12 Apr. 1923, Box 68, ibid.

25. Norbeck to Stanley, 24 Nov. 1923, Custer State Park Board, C-C, S-1 (Cabin Lease), 1919–1925, CCC Drawer, CSPA.

26. Memorandum, Norbeck to Highway Commission, 14 Dec. 1920, Box 97, Norbeck Papers, USD.

27. Norbeck to Stanley, 7 Aug. 1923, 29 Dec. 1924, Custer State Park Board, C-C, 9.1 (Borglum), 1923–1925, CCC Drawer, CSPA.

28. Sundstrom, *Pioneers and Custer State Park*, p. 86. For examples of Norbeck's attitude toward professionals, *see* Norbeck to J. C. Denison, 8 May 1927, Custer State Park Board, Corres.-C, 16.1 (Highways), 1924–1927, CSPA; telegram, Norbeck to C. W. Robertson, 24 Mar. 1931, Box 129, Norbeck to C. C. Gideon, 23 Oct. 1931, Box 67, Paul E. Bellamy to Norbeck, 21 Jan. 1932, Box 49, Norbeck to Chauncey L. Bates, 21 Mar. 1932, Box 35, all in Norbeck Papers, USD.

29. Norbeck to J. Harper Hamilton, 22 Jan. 1932, Box 35, Norbeck Papers, USD.

30. Sven G. Froiland, *Natural History of the Black Hills and Badlands*, rev. ed. (Sioux Falls, S.Dak.: Center for Western Studies, Augustana College, 1990), p. 17; Norbeck to Scovel Johnson, 14 Nov.

1919, Folder #4, Norbeck to Stephen T. Mather, 6 Feb. 1920, Folder #3, both in Box 95, Norbeck Papers, USD; Paul E. Bellamy and G. D. Seymour, *A Guide to the Black Hills* (Rapid City, S.Dak.: Black Hills Transportation Co., 1927), pp. 13–15; Sundstrom, *Pioneers and Custer State Park*, p. 118; A. A. Schwartz, "Reconnoissence [*sic*] Estimate of the Cost of a Portion of the Proposed Scenic Highway from Sylvan Lake to Custer," 15 Sept. 1920, p. 4, Box 97, Norbeck Papers, USD; Fite, *Peter Norbeck*, p.76; Scovel Johnson to Norbeck, 27 Aug. 1920, Box 6, Governor Norbeck Papers, SDSHS; Norbeck to M. L. Shade, 7 Oct. 1921, Box 80, Scovel Johnson to Norbeck, 17 Sept., 26, 28 Oct. 1921, Box 68, all in Norbeck Papers, USD.

31. A. A. Schwartz , "Reconnoissence Estimate," pp. 2, 4; Scovel Johnson to State Highway Commission, 1 Apr. 1921, and Johnson to Peter Norbeck, 28 Oct. 1921, both Box 68, Norbeck Papers, USD; Bellamy and Seymour, *Guide to the Black Hills*, pp. 14–15; Norbeck to C. B. Powers, 18 Feb. 1920, Box 6, Governor Norbeck Papers, SDSHS.

32. Scovel Johnson to Norbeck, Box 6, Governor Norbeck Papers, SDSHS; Stanley to Norbeck, 9 Nov. 1921, Box 70, Norbeck Papers, USD.

33. P. D. Peterson, *Through the Black Hills and Bad Lands of South Dakota* (Pierre, S.Dak.: J. Fred Olander Co., 1929), p. 103.

34. N. D. MacArthur, "Black Hills Named Correctly," *Sunshine Magazine* 7 (Jan. 1927): 17–18.

35. Stanley to Beatrice Ward, 28 Apr. 1924, Historical Correspondence Materials, CSPA.

36. H. S. Hedrick, "Game and Fish Conditions in the Custer State Park," *Pahasapa Quarterly* 10 (Spring 1921): 189–93; Norbeck to Will O. Doolittle, 26 Sept. 1922, Custer State Park Board, C-C 7.1 (Miscellaneous), 1919–1926, CCC Drawer, CSPA.

37. Stanley to Norbeck, 21 Dec. 1921, Box 70, Norbeck Papers, USD.

38. Norbeck to Stanley, 27 Dec. 1921, ibid.

39. Sundstrom, *Pioneers and Custer State Park*, pp. 110–14; Stanley to Norbeck, 21 Dec. 1921; Norbeck to H. S. Hedrick, 23 Mar. 1923, Box 68, Norbeck Papers, USD.

40. Phelps Wyman to Norbeck, 26 Dec. 1920, Folder #3, and Wyman to Norbeck, 2 Mar. 1921, Folder #7, both Box 95, and Norbeck to Stanley, 14 Dec. 1921, Box 70, all in Norbeck Papers, USD.

41. Sundstrom, *Pioneers and Custer State Park*, pp. 115–16; Norbeck to Stanley, 2 Jan. 1923, Stanley to Norbeck, 28 May 1924, and Stanley to Beatrice M. Ward, 28 Apr. 1924, all in Historical Correspondence Materials, CSPA.

42. Norbeck to Percy Helm, 14 July 1919, Folder #4, Box 95, Norbeck Papers, USD.

43. Norbeck to Scovel H. Johnson, 14 Nov. 1919, ibid.

44. Stanley to Norbeck, 14 July 1920, Custer State Park Board, CC, S-1 (Cabin Lease), 1919–1925, CCC Drawer, CSPA; David Shetler, "National Register of Historic Places Inventory Nomination Form: Custer State Game Lodge," 11 June 1981, pt. 8, State Historic Preservation Office Collection, SDSHS; Hedrick, "Game and Fish Conditions," pp. 192–93.

45. John A. Stanley, *From Then until Now* (n.p., 1948), pp. 58–60; Sundstrom, *Pioneers and Custer State Park*, pp. 82–85.

46. John Warnke to Stanley, 16 May 1922, Custer State Park Board, CS-4/1-6/30, CSPA.

47. Shetler, "Custer State Game Lodge," pt. 8; Sundstrom, *Pioneers and Custer State Park*, pp. 87–89.

48. Sundstrom, *Pioneers and Custer State Park*, p. 89; Cecil C. Gideon to Norbeck, 12 Oct., 10 Dec. 1921, and Norbeck to Gideon, 22 Oct. 1921, all in Box 67, Norbeck Papers, USD.

49. Shetler, "Custer State Game Lodge," pt. 7; David Erpestad and David Wood, *Building South Dakota: A Historical Survey of the State's Architecture to 1945*, Historical Preservation Series, no. 1 (Pierre: South Dakota State Historical Society Press, 1997), pp. 207–8.

50. Stanley to Norbeck, 28 Nov. 1923, Custer State Park Board, C-C, 7.1 (Miscellaneous), 1919–1926, and Stanley to Norbeck, C-C, 5.1 (Cabin Leases), 1919–1925, both in CCC Drawer, CSPA; *Rapid City Daily Journal*, 30 Jan. 1925.

51. Norbeck to C. B. Powers, 13 Sept. 1920, Box 6, Governor Norbeck Papers, SDSHS.

52. Norbeck to Phelps Wyman, 26 Dec. 1920, Box 97, Norbeck Papers, USD.

53. Wyman to Norbeck, 28 Dec. 1920, Folder #3, Box 95, ibid.

54. Phelps Wyman, "Copy of Report on Sylvan Lake," 14 Jan. 1921, pp. 1–3, 5–7, Box 70, ibid.

55. Doolittle to Norbeck, 11 Nov. 1924, Custer State Park Board, C-C, 6.1 (Animals and Knights Templar), 1919–1925, CCC Drawer, CSPA.

56. Stanley, "South Dakota's State Park," p. 185; Stanley to Norbeck, 25 Feb. 1921, Folder #7, Box 95, David Radsliff to Norbeck, 7 Sept. 1920, Box 95, and Fred Harris to J. E. Truran, 4 Nov. 1922, Box 96, all in Norbeck Papers, USD; Sundstrom, *Pioneers and Custer State Park*, p. 95.

57. Myra K. Peters to Norbeck, 16 Aug. 1920, Folder #6, Box 95, Norbeck Papers, USD.

58. Stanley to Norbeck, 4 Mar. 1921, ibid.

59. Norbeck to Stanley, 2 Mar. 1921, Box 97, ibid.

60. Norbeck to Stanley, 19 May 1924, Historical Correspondence Materials, CSPA.

61. Norbeck to Stanley, 17 Oct., 7 Nov. 1923, ibid.

62. Norbeck to E. H. Hall, 4 Feb. 1921, Box 97, Norbeck Papers, USD.

63. Norbeck to Stanley, 2 Sept. 1923, Box 70, ibid.

64. John W. Bohi, "Seventy-Five Years at Wind Cave: A History of the National Park," *South Dakota Historical Collections* 31 (1962): 438.

65. Roy W. Brazell to Stephen Mather, 3 June, 1 Sept. 1919, in *Superintendent's Monthly Narrative Reports, Wind Cave National Park, 1909–1928*, Wind Cave National Park Library, (WCNPL), Hot Springs, S.Dak.; Bohi, "Seventy-Five Years at Wind Cave," pp. 438–39; Brazell to Horace M. Albright, 20 Sept. 1920, in *Superintendent's Annual Reports, Wind Cave National Park, 1908–1959*, WCNPL. Brazell's monthly narrative and annual reports, which are bound volumes held by Wind Cave National Park Library, detail his complaints about poor road conditions and lack of funds.

66. Brazell to Albright, 17, 20 Sept. 1919, and Brazell to Director [Mather], 12 Sept. 1921, in *Superintendent's Annual Reports*; Brazell to Director [Mather], 4 July, 6 Aug., 3 Sept. 1921, in *Superintendent's Monthly Narrative Reports*.

67. Brazell to Director [Mather], 22 Sept. 1922, 17 Sept. 1923, 14 Sept. 1924, and 10 Sept. 1925, in

Superintendent's Annual Reports; Report of the Director of the National Park Service (1925), pp. 1–2.

68. Bohi, "Seventy-Five Years at Wind Cave," p. 440.

69. Arno B. Cammerer to Stephen Mather, 13 June 1920, Box 1, Historical Files, WCNPL, copy in Wind Cave [WICA] Privileges Grazing Part 2, Box 550, Records of the National Park Service, Record Group [RG] 79, National Archives [NA], Washington, D.C.

70. Brazell to Cammerer, 28 Mar. 1927, Box 1, WCNPL, copy in WICA, Admin-Supt, Box 443, RG 79, NA.

71. Brazell to Director [Mather], 17 Sept. 1923, in *Superintendent's Annual Reports.*

72. Ibid., 12 Sept. 1921, 14 Sept. 1924, and 10 Sept. 1925; Bohi, "Seventy-Five Years at Wind Cave," pp. 442–43; Brazell to Director [Mather], 4 July, 6 Aug., and 3 Sept. 1921, in *Superintendent's Monthly Narrative Reports.*

73. Roosevelt enacted this transfer by Executive Order 6166, effective 9 Aug. 1933. Hal K. Rothman, *Preserving Different Pasts: The American National Monuments* (Urbana: University of Illinois Press, 1989), p. 187.

74. "Master Plan for the Protection and Administration of the Norbeck Wildlife Preserve," June 1927, p. 24, Black Hills National Forest, Supervisor's Office, Custer, S.Dak.

75. Henry S. Graves to D. F. Houston, 8 Oct. 1919, in "Report of the Forester," p. 19, Owen Science and Engineering Library, Washington State University, Pullman, Wash.

76. In 1920, O. J. Stahl, assistant district forester, wrote Frank L. Michaud confirming that the Forest Service was "not immediately in a position to improve the cave" even if questions about claims were resolved. Stahl to Michaud, 6 Jan. 1920, "Proclamation Jewel Cave," Jewel Cave National Monument Library (JCNML), Custer, S.Dak.

77. Conner to District Forester, 7 Nov. 1923, JCNML.

78. Stahl to Conner, 13 Nov. 1923, Conner to A. S. Peck, 14 Jan., 2 Feb. 1924, and Peck to Forester, 4 Feb. 1924, all in JCNML; Conner to Norbeck, 14 Jan. 1924, H. R. Hanly to Norbeck, 19 Jan. 1924,

Norbeck to William Williamson, 18 Jan. 1924, and Williamson to Norbeck, 25 Jan. 1924, all in Box 117, Norbeck Papers, USD.

79. Memorandum, J. F. Conner to District Forester, 30 Dec. 1926, L. F. Kneipp to Frank Michaud, 20 Feb. 1924, Kneipp to Peck, 8 Feb. 1924, Stahl to Conner, 15 Feb. 1924, and Kneipp to Michaud, 20 Feb. 1924, all in JCNML.

80. "Cycad National Monument," *Yale Alumni Weekly* 31 (5 June 1936): n.p.; John Ise, *Our National Park Policy: A Critical History* (Baltimore: Johns Hopkins University Press for the Future, Inc., 1961), p. 291; A. E. Demaray to Francis Case, 17 Apr. 1937, Fossil Cycad National Monument, Box 143, Francis H. Case Archives, Layne Library, Dakota Wesleyan University, Mitchell, S.Dak.; George R. Wieland, "Our National Monuments," *Science* 87 (14 Jan. 1938): 37–39.

81. James Cracco, "History of the South Dakota Highway Department, 1919–1941" (M.A. thesis, University of South Dakota, 1970), pp. 24–27, 54, 65–67.

82. *Rapid City, South Dakota: The City of Seven Valleys* ([Rapid City, S.Dak.]: Rapid City Commercial Club [1919]), pp. 5–6. Other highways included the Washington Highway, from Minnehaha County through Rapid City, and the King of Trails, entering the state near Sioux City, Iowa, and going through Sioux Falls and Brookings to Winnipeg, Canada. Norbeck to Thomas Sterling, 1 June 1920, Box 6, Governor Norbeck Papers, SDSHS.

83. Norbeck to Sterling, 1 June 1920.

84. Norbeck to W. D. Fisher, 30 Apr. 1920, Box 6, Governor Norbeck Papers, SDSHS.

Chapter 3: President in a Park

1. William Williamson, *An Autobiography: William Williamson, Student, Homesteader, Teacher, Lawyer, Judge, Congressman and Trusted Friend* (Rapid City, S.Dak.: By the Author, 1964), pp. 187–92; Peter Norbeck to John A. Stanley, 19 Apr. 1926, Box 80, Peter Norbeck Papers, Richardson Archives, I.D. Weeks Library, University of South Dakota (USD), Vermillion, S.Dak.; *Rapid City Daily*

Journal, 12 May, 1 June 1927.

2. *Rapid City Daily Journal*, 31 May, 1 June 1927.

3. Ibid., 31 May 1927.

4. Charles Robertson to Wilbur Robertson, 13 June 1927, Custer State Park Board, C-S, 1926-27, Custer State Park Archives (CSPA), Custer, S.Dak.

5. *Rapid City Daily Journal*, 31 May 1927.

6. Ibid., 27, 31 May, 7 June 1927; David Shetler, "National Register of Historic Places Inventory Nomination Form: Custer State Game Lodge," 11 June 1981, State Historic Preservation Office Collection, South Dakota State Historical Society (SDSHS), Pierre, S.Dak.

7. Quoted in *Rapid City Daily Journal*, 1 June 1927.

8. Norbeck to Charles Robertson, 28 May 1927, Box 13, Norbeck Papers, USD.

9. *Rapid City Daily Journal*, 1, 6 June 1927; telegrams, Norbeck to J. B. Greene, 25 May 1927, and J. B. Greene to Norbeck, 26 May 1927, Box 13, Norbeck Papers, USD.

10. Norbeck to John A. Stanley, 24 Dec. 1925, Box 70, Norbeck Papers, USD.

11. Norbeck to Cecil C. Gideon, 12 Dec. 1924, Box 67, ibid.

12. Ibid., 12 Dec. 1924, 10 Jan. 1925; Norbeck to M. L. Shade, 26 Jan. 1925, Box 71, ibid; Charles J. Dalthorp, ed., *South Dakota's Governors* (Sioux Falls, S.Dak.: Midwest Beach Co., 1953), p. 41; Gilbert C. Fite, "The History of South Dakota's Rural Credit System," *South Dakota Historical Collections* 24 (1949): 249-50, and *Peter Norbeck, Prairie Statesman* (1948; reprint ed., Pierre: South Dakota State Historical Society Press, 2005), p. 84; Herbert S. Schell, *History of South Dakota*, 4th ed., rev. John E. Miller (Pierre: South Dakota State Historical Society Press, 2004), pp. 277-80; interview of Gladys Pyle, by Paul O'Rourke, 23 June 1977, Tape 210, South Dakota Oral History Project/ American Indian Research Project (SDOHP), Institute of Indian Studies, University of South Dakota, Vermillion, S.Dak.

13. Stanley to Norbeck, 3 Feb. 1925, and Norbeck to Stanley, 24 Feb. 1925, Box 70, Norbeck Papers, USD.

14. Stanley to Norbeck, 3 Feb. 1925.

15. Schell, *History of South Dakota*, p. 277.

16. *Sioux Falls Daily Argus Leader* (clipping), [Jan. 1925], Box 70, Norbeck Papers, USD.

17. Stanley to Norbeck, 28 Jan. 1925, ibid.

18. Norbeck to Stanley, 2 Feb. 1925, ibid.

19. Norbeck to Carl Gunderson, 2 June 1925, Box 97, M. L. Shade, "Report to the State Park Board," [19 July 1926], Box 71, Stanley to Norbeck, 27 Apr. 1926, Box 70, Norbeck to Stanley, 4 May 1926, Box 70; Stanley to Norbeck, 6 May 1925, Box 70, Carl Gunderson to Norbeck, 27 June, 25 July 1925, Box 68, all in Norbeck Papers, USD; *Sioux Falls Daily Argus-Leader* (clipping), [Jan. 1925]. For details of Gunderson's reorganization, *see* South Dakota, *Session Laws*, 19th Leg. 1925, ch. 15, pp. 106-35.

20. Norbeck to Cecil C. Gideon, 14 May 1925, Box 67, Norbeck Papers, USD.

21. Norbeck to Cecil C. Gideon, 31 Dec. 1924, Box 67, and Norbeck to M. L. Shade, 3 July 1922, Box 71, both ibid.

22. Norbeck to Stanley, 8 Sept. 1925, and Stanley to Norbeck, 10 Sept. 1925, 27 Apr. 1926, Box 97, Norbeck to Stanley, 2 Mar., 25 Sept., 24 Dec. 1925, 2 Feb., 4 May 1926, Box 70, Stanley to Carl Gunderson, 21 Dec. 1925, Box 70, Norbeck to Gunderson, 18 Sept. 1925, 8 Sept. 1926, Box 68, M. L. Shade to Norbeck, 12 Dec. 1925, and Norbeck to Shade, 16 Dec. 1925, Box 71, Norbeck to Cecil C. Gideon, 15 Dec. 1925, Box 67, all in Norbeck Papers, USD; Shade, "Report to the State Park Board," [19 July 1926].

23. Norbeck to Gideon, 30 Dec. 1925, Box 67, Norbeck Papers, USD.

24. Shade, "Report to State Park Board," [19 July 1926].

25. Norbeck to Stanley, 13 Apr. 1926, Box 80, Norbeck Papers, USD.

26. Norbeck to George Elliot, 21 Sept. 1926, Folder 4, H60.1, Frank J. Hughes Papers, State Archives Collection, SDSHS.

27. Fite, "South Dakota's Rural Credit System," pp. 251-52; interview of Pyle, 23 June 1977; Norbeck to Stanley, 5 June 1927, Box 70, Norbeck Papers, USD.

28. *Rapid City Daily Journal*, 9 Aug. 1927; Norbeck

to Charles W. Robertson, 4, 25 Apr. 1927, Box 29, Norbeck to Gideon, 19 Apr. 1927, Box 67, Robertson to Norbeck, 28 Mar., 12 Apr. 1927, Box 29, all in Norbeck Papers, USD.

29. Norbeck to Stanley, 18 Apr. 1927, Box 70, Norbeck Papers, USD.

30. Norbeck to Robertson, 4 Apr., 2, 5 (two letters) May 1927, Box 29, ibid.

31. Norbeck to Robertson, 2 May 1927.

32. Telegrams, Norbeck to William Bulow, 26, 27 May 1927, and Norbeck to Bulow, 27 May 1927, Box 13, all ibid.

33. Telegram, Bulow to Norbeck, 27 May 1927.

34. South Dakota, *Session Laws*, 20th Leg., spec. sess. (1927), chs. 12, 14, pp. 29–32, 36–37; Norbeck to Gideon, 2 July 1927, Box 67, Norbeck Papers, USD; C. W. Robertson, "Highways in Custer State Park," *Black Hills Engineer* 18 (Mar. 1930): 133; *Rapid City Daily Journal*, 2 July 1927.

35. Norbeck to Gideon, 2 July 1927, Box 67, Norbeck Papers, USD. Despite this success, the official transfer of a portion of hunting-and-fishing-license revenues from Game and Fish, long sought by Norbeck, would remain particularly controversial. Sectional interests in the state held that license money should be spent on local development rather than "general state activities, whether it be the State Park, scenic highways or the entertainment of guests of the state." One newspaper editor called for the park to be turned over to the Game and Fish department if the license money was to be used to support the park. "Two Comments on Game Money in State Park," *Sunshine Magazine* 7 (Nov. 1927): 30.

36. Bulow, Lusk, quoted in *Rapid City Daily Journal*, 1 June 1927.

37. *Rapid City Daily Journal*, 6 June 1927.

38. Ibid., 16 June 1927.

39. Watson Parker, *Deadwood: The Golden Years* (Lincoln: University of Nebraska Press, 1981), p. 239; Williamson, *Autobiography*, p. 193; *Rapid City Daily Journal*, 4 Aug. 1927. A hint of controversy marred Coolidge's adoption into the tribe when Grand Short Bull, a Lakota elder from Pine Ridge, speaking through Samuel Stands, gave an interview to an Edgemont newspaperman saying that he and other elders had not given their consent to the adoption and that the name given Coolidge was not a valid one. *Rapid City Daily Journal*, 15 Aug. 1927.

40. Norbeck to W. C. Gregg, 15 Aug. 1927, Box 68, Norbeck Papers, USD. For first-person descriptions of Coolidge's stay in the Black Hills, *see* Nancy Tystad Koupal, ed., "Lydia Norbeck's 'Recollections of the Years,'" *South Dakota Historical Collections* 39 (1978): 81–86, and Williamson, *Autobiography*, pp. 187–99.

41. *Rapid City Daily Journal*, 17 Aug. 1927; Williamson, *Autobiography*, pp. 196–97; Charles H. Burke to Williamson, 6 June 1927, Norbeck to Burke, 12 June 1927, Burke to Norbeck, 15, 27 June, 14, 29 July 1927, all Box 13, Norbeck Papers, USD.

42. Burke to Williamson, 8 June 1927, Box 13, Norbeck Papers, USD. *See also* Burke to Norbeck, 8 June 1927, ibid.

43. "Hills Clubs in Favor Road to Rushmore MT," *Lead Daily Call* (clipping), [Mar. 1927], Box 70, ibid.; *Rapid City Daily Journal*, 6 May, 2 June 1927.

44. *New York Times Index* 14 (Apr.–June 1927): 177, 181–82, 15 (July–Sept. 1927): 147–48, 465; *Readers Guide to Periodical Literature*, 1925–1928 (New York: W. Wilson Co., 1929), p. 239.

45. "Dawes is Choice of Many Leaders in South Dakota," *New York Times*, 25 Aug. 1927.

46. Roland M. Jones, "What the Country is Thinking About," ibid., 30 July 1927.

47. "2,117,205 Words Wired on the Coolidge Vacation," ibid., 10 Sept. 1927.

48. "Coolidge Does Not Choose to Run in 1928," ibid., 3 Aug. 1927.

49. Gilbert C. Fite, *Mount Rushmore*, 2d ed. (Norman: University of Oklahoma Press, 1964), p. 71.

50. Doane Robinson to Norbeck, 13 Apr. 1926, Box 130, Norbeck Papers, USD.

51. Norbeck to Gutzon Borglum, 17 Apr. 1926, Box 163, ibid.

52. Suzanne Julin, comp., Introduction to *South Dakota Historical Collections Cumulative Index* (Pierre: South Dakota State Historical Society, 1989), pp. 1–3.

53. Fite, *Mount Rushmore*, pp. 5–6; "South Dakota

State Meeting of the Black and Yellow Trail Association: . . . Official Bulletin," 22 Jan. [1924], Folder 9, Tourism and Highway Travel Files, State Archives Collection, SDSHS; Robinson to Lorado Taft, 29 Dec. 1923, Folder 149, Robinson to the Editor, n. d., and Robinson to the Editor, *Deadwood Pioneer Times*, 6 Feb. 1924, Folder 15, all Box 9, Doane Robinson Papers, State Archives Collection, SDSHS; Robinson to Lorado Taft, 26 Jan. 1924, Box 130, Norbeck Papers, USD.

54. Robinson to the Editor, n.d., Folder 15, Box 9, Robinson Papers.

55. Robinson to J. B. Greene, 7 Mar. 1924, Folder 149, ibid.

56. Norbeck to Harry L. Gandy, 17 Oct. 1935, Box 70, Norbeck Papers, USD; Fite, *Mount Rushmore*, pp. 5–12, 25–27; Norbeck to Robinson, 13 Dec. 1924, Folder 161, Box 10, and Robinson to F. W. Meyers, 4 Dec. 1924, Folder 149, Box 9, Robinson Papers; Doane Robinson, "Inception and Development of the Rushmore Idea," *Black Hills Engineer* 18 (Nov. 1930): 334–35. John Taliaferro, *Great White Fathers: The Story of the Obsessive Quest to Create Mount Rushmore* (New York: BBS Public Affairs, 2002), offers a thorough treatment of the Mount Rushmore project.

57. Fite, *Mount Rushmore*, pp. 13–32; John A. Day, "Borglum: The Artist," in *Gutzon Borglum, the Artist and the Man: An Exhibition. . . .* (Vermillion, S.Dak.: Broadcaster Inc, 1984), n.p.; Arthur R. Huseboe, *An Illustrated History of the Arts in South Dakota* (Sioux Falls, S.Dak.: Center for Western Studies, Augustana College, 1989), pp. 252–53.

58. Gutzon Borglum, "The Political Importance and the Art Character of the National Memorial at Mount Rushmore," *Black Hills Engineer* 18 (Nov. 1930): 291.

59. Fite, *Mount Rushmore*, pp. 33–37.

60. Ibid., pp. 37–38.

61. Robinson to Norbeck, n.d., Box 130, Norbeck Papers, USD.

62. Norbeck to Robinson, 15, 27 (two letters), 29 Dec. 1924, Box 130, and Norbeck to Carl Gunderson, 10 Jan. 1925, Box 97, all ibid.

63. U.S., *Statutes at Large*, vol. 43, An Act to Authorize the Creation of a National Memorial in the Harney National Forest (1925), p. 1214.

64. Norbeck to Robinson, 6 Jan. 1925, Box 120, Norbeck Papers, USD; U.S., Congress, Senate, "The Creation of National Memorial in Harney National Forest," *S. Rept. 1435*, 68th Cong., 2d sess., 1925, pp. 1–2; *HR 11726*, 68th Cong., 2d sess., (16 Feb. 1925) *Congressional Record* 66, pt. 4: 3912.

65. *Statues at Large*, p. 1214.

66. Norbeck to Gunderson, 19 Jan. 1925, Box 68, Norbeck Papers, USD.

67. Robinson to Norbeck, 12 Jan. 1925, Box 130, and Gunderson to Norbeck, 16 Jan. 1925, Box 68, ibid.

68. Robinson to Norbeck, 20 Jan. 1925, Folder 162, Box 10, Robinson Papers.

69. Cora B. Johnson to Robinson, 6 Dec. 1924, Folder 149, Box 9, ibid. This folder contains correspondence between Robinson and opponents of the memorial. For Robinson's Colossus of Rhodes argument, *see* Robinson to A. T. Johnson, 2 Dec. 1924.

70. Robinson to A. T. Johnson, 2 Dec. 1924. For Cora Johnson's response to this argument, *see* Cora B. Johnson to Robinson, 6 Dec. 1924. Robinson told Johnson that he had "learned not to argue with a lady" but that he could not understand her position: "The greatest artist in the world has proposed to bring to you the must [*sic*] majestic monument in the world, *and ye would not*" (Robinson to Cora B. Johnson, 7 Dec. 1924, ibid.).

71. Robinson to Norbeck, 20 Jan. 1925, Folder 162, Box 10, ibid. For examples of public opposition, *see Hot Springs Star*, 27 Nov. 1924, 5, 12, 19 Mar., 21 May 1925.

72. Norbeck to Robinson, 28 Jan. 1925, Box 130, Norbeck Papers, USD.

73. Norbeck to Stanley, 24 Feb. 1925, Box 70, ibid.; Fite, "South Dakota's Rural Credit System," pp. 249–51; Fite, *Peter Norbeck*, p. 84; Schell, *South Dakota History*, pp. 278–80. The legislature passed a measure prohibiting additional loans; Ewert eventually was convicted of embezzlement; and the taxpayers assumed the burden of liquidating the state's indebtedness.

Fite, *Peter Norbeck*, pp. 82–85; Norbeck to Robinson, 21 Feb. 1925, Box 130, Norbeck Papers, USD. For an example of the rhetoric employed against Norbeck, *see Rapid City Daily Journal*, 25 Feb. 1925.

74. Robinson to Norbeck, 7 Feb. 1925, Box 130, Norbeck Papers, USD. *See also* ibid., 12 Jan. 1925.

75. Robinson to Norbeck, 8 Feb. 1925, Folder 162, Box 10, Robinson Papers.

76. Fite, *Mount Rushmore*, pp. 30–31; South Dakota, Legislature. *Proceedings of the House of Representatives*, 19th Leg., (1925), p. 373.

77. Robinson to Norbeck, 24 Feb. 1925, Folder 162, Box 10, Robinson Papers.

78. Fite, *Mount Rushmore*, pp. 38–39; Norbeck to Robinson, 2 Mar. 1925, Folder 162, Box 10, Robinson Papers.

79. Robinson to Norbeck, 12 Jan., 7 Feb., and 4 Mar. 1925, Box 130, Norbeck Papers, USD; Robinson to Norbeck, 8, 24 Feb. 1925, Folder 162, Box 10, Robinson Papers; South Dakota, *Session Laws*, 19th Leg. (1925), ch. 232, p. 167; Fite, *Mount Rushmore*, p. 31.

80. Fite, *Mount Rushmore*, pp. 52–53; Robinson to Norbeck, 2 Sept. 1925, Box 130, Norbeck Papers, USD; *Rapid City Daily Journal*, 1 Oct. 1925.

81. Robinson to Norbeck, 2 Oct. 1925, Norbeck to Robinson, 9 Oct. 1925, Robinson to Gutzon Borglum, 1 July 1925, all Box 130, Norbeck Papers, USD; Norbeck to Robinson, 12 Oct. 1925, Folder 162, Box 10, Robinson Papers; Gordon M. Sessions to Borglum, n.d., Box 163, Norbeck Papers, USD.

82. Frank J. Hughes, "The Beginning of the Rushmore Memorial, 1925," n.d., pp. 3, 5, 11, MORU 1002, Box 11, National Park Service, Mount Rushmore National Memorial (MRNM), Keystone, S.Dak.; J. L. Curran to "Sir," n. d., and Hughes to Robinson, 5 Mar. 1926, both Folder 11, H60.1, Hughes Papers; Norbeck to Borglum, 27 Sept. 1926, and Robinson to Borglum, 1 July 1925, both Box 130, Norbeck Papers, USD; *Deadwood Daily Pioneer Times*, 26 Apr. 1925.

83. Norbeck to Borglum, 27 Sept. 1926, and Robinson to Borglum, 1 July 1925, Box 130, Norbeck Papers, USD; *Deadwood Daily Pioneer Times*, 26 Apr. 1925; Hughes, "Beginning of the Rushmore Memorial," pp. 3–8, 11; Hughes to Borglum, 14 Apr. 1927, Folder 3, H60.1, Hughes Papers; interview of Isaac Chase, by Stephen R. Ward, 17 June 1970, Tape 64, SDOHP.

84. Hughes, "Beginning of Mount Rushmore," p. 8.

85. Norbeck to Borglum, 27 Sept. 1926, Box 130, Norbeck Papers, USD.

86. Hughes to Norbeck, 1 Apr. 1927, Folder 2, H60.1, Hughes Papers. The Homestake Mining Company eventually contributed to the Mount Rushmore project.

87. Hughes, "Beginning of the Rushmore Memorial," p. 10.

88. Norbeck to Robinson, 31 Aug. 1925, Box 130, Norbeck Papers, USD.

89. Borglum to Robinson, 26 Jan. 1925, Folder 149, Box 9, Robinson Papers.

90. Borglum, quoted in *Rapid City Daily Journal*, 24 Aug. 1926.

91. Norbeck to Robinson, 31 Aug. 1925, Box 130, Norbeck Papers, USD.

92. Herbert Myrick, "Front View of the Colossal Sculptures Designed for the Continental Memorial in the Black Hills," *Dakota Farmer* 46 (15 Dec. 1926): 1068.

93. Hughes, "Beginning of the Rushmore Memorial," p. 9.

94. Fite, *Mount Rushmore*, pp. 66–68.

95. Williamson, *Autobiography*, pp. 239–40.

96. "Address of Calvin Coolidge, President of the United States, Delivered at the Beginning of the Carving of the National Memorial on Rushmore Mountain, August 10, 1927 (program)," MORU 675, Box 3, MRNM.

97. Fite, *Mount Rushmore*, p. 83–88. For the text of Public Law 805, see U. S., *Statutes at Large*, vol. 45, p. 1300.

98. Coolidge to Norbeck, 5 Nov. 1929, Box 52, Norbeck Papers, USD.

99. John Ise, *Our National Park Policy: A Critical History* (Baltimore: Johns Hopkins University Press for Resources for the Future, Inc., 1961), pp. 412–13. After Borglum's death, his son Lincoln assumed responsibility for finishing work on the monument with what funds remained. Final drilling occurred on 31 October 1941. The monument as Gutzon Borglum conceived it was never completed. For a

discussion of operations and decisions at Mount Rushmore after Gutzon Borglum died, *see* Fite, *Mount Rushmore*, pp. 222–34.

100. *Rapid City Daily Journal*, 6 May, 15 Sept. 1927.

101. Courtney Ryley Cooper "The Last of the Argonauts," *Saturday Evening Post* 200 (17 Sept. 1927): 120.

102. Quoted in "Coolidges Depart from Rapid City," *New York Times*, 10 Sept. 1927.

103. Norbeck to Bulow, 20 Oct. 1927, Box 66, Norbeck Papers, USD.

Chapter 4: Federal Funds, Federal Control

1. Roy Brazell to Director [Stephen Mather], 26 July, 3, 9 Sept.1927, in *Superintendent's Monthly Narrative Reports, Wind Cave National Park, 1909–1928*, Wind Cave National Park Library (WCNPL), Hot Springs, S.Dak.

2. Brazell to Director, 26 July 1927, in *Superintendent's Monthly Narrative Reports.*

3. Brazell, "Review for the Year in the Parks," [1927], in *Superintendent's Annual Reports, Wind Cave National Park, 1908–1959*, WCNPL.

4. Brazell to Norbeck, 4 Feb. 1928, Box 121, Peter Norbeck Papers, Richardson Archives, I.D. Weeks Library, University of South Dakota (USD), Vermillion, S.Dak.

5. Brazell to Director, 5 Feb. 1928, ibid.

6. H. M. Gillman, Jr., to Stephen Mather, 31 May 1928, in "Report of Investigation," FREF 1914B1 #1-9, Box 1, Historical Files, WCNPL, copy in File 204, Wind Cave [WICA] Inspection, Box 443, Records of the National Park Service, Record Group [RG] 79, National Archives [NA], Washington, D.C.

7. Peter Norbeck to William V. Miner, 21 May 1928, Box 121, Norbeck Papers, USD; [Arno Cammerer] to Horace M. Albright, 18 June 1928, FREF 1914B1 #1-9, WCNPL, copy in WICA Admin-Supt. File 201-006, Box 443, RG 79, NA; *Custer Weekly Chronicle*, 25 June 1928.

8. Snyder to Director National Park Service, 1 Sept. 1928, in *Superintendent's Annual Reports.*

9. "Report of the Superintendent Wind Cave National Park Supplementing Report of Chief Landscape Architect Vint," n.d., File 6, Box 1, Investigations II of II, FREF 1914 B1 #1-9, WCNPL, copy in WICA Admin-Supt. File 204-010, Box 443, RG 79, NA.

10. Barbara Beving Long, Four Mile Research Co., *Wind Cave National Park Historic Contexts and National Register Guidelines*, U.S., Department of the Interior, National Park Service, 1992, p. 6/42; Thomas C. Vint to Director [Mather], 8 Sept. 1928, 1914 B1 #1-9, File 6, Box 1, Investigations II of II, WCNPL, copy in WICA, Admin-Supt. File 204-010; John W. Bohi, "Seventy-five Years at Wind Cave: A History of the National Park," *South Dakota Historical Collections* 31 (1962): 445; Kathy S. Mason, *Natural Museums: U.S. National Parks, 1872–1916* (East Lansing: Michigan State University Press, 2004), pp. 53–60.

11. Cramton to Norbeck, 6 Jan. 1930, Box 121, Norbeck Papers, USD.

12. Williamson to Cramton, 9 Jan. 1930, ibid.

13. Freeman Tilden, *The State Parks: Their Meaning in American Life* (New York: Alfred A. Knopf, 1962), pp. 1–6, 274–75; Gilbert Courtland Fite, *Peter Norbeck: Prairie Statesmen* (1948; reprint ed., Pierre: South Dakota State Historical Society Press, 2005), pp. 141–51; Norbeck to Mather, 8 Jan. 1923, 23 Jan. 1929, and Mather to Norbeck, 17 Jan. 1923, Box 121, and Horace M. Albright to Norbeck, 19 July 1933, Box 99, all in Norbeck Papers, USD; Harlean James, "Peter Norbeck as I Knew Him," n.d., Norbeck Memorial Association, Box 12, Paul E. Bellamy Papers, Richardson Archives, I. D. Weeks Library, USD.

14. Norbeck to Charles W. Robertson, 14 Feb. 1931, Box 121, Norbeck Papers, USD.

15. Bohi, "Seventy-Five Years at Wind Cave," pp. 446–48; Arthur E. Demaray to Stephen Mather, [11 Sept. 1928], Investigations II of II FREF 1914 B1 #1-9, Box 1, WCNPL, copy in WICA, Inspections by Hdqtrs Officers, Admin-Supt. File 204-020, Box 442, RG 79, NA; Anton J. Snyder to Director, NPS, 3 Sept. 1929, in "Wind Cave National Park," in *Superintendent's Annual Reports;* Long, "Wind Cave National Park Historic Contexts," p. 6/44; Snyder to Norbeck, 8 Feb. 1930, and Memorandum, Charles E. Peterson to Thomas Vint, 9 Apr. 1930, both Box 121, Norbeck Papers, USD.

16. "Jewel Cave National Monument: National

Register of Historic Places Multiple Property Submission, National Park Service," 21 Feb. 1995, p. E6, and Memorandum, J. F. Conner by W. [C.] Robert to District Supervisor 19 Feb. 1927, both in Jewel Cave National Monument Library (JCNML), Custer, S.Dak.; Roger W. Toll, "Report to the Director, National Park Service on Jewel Cave National Monument, South Dakota," 18 Nov. 1929, pp. 1–3, JECA 62, MORU JECA, and Certificate of Incorporation, Jewel Cave Corporation, 18 June 1928, JECA 54, MORU JC 005, both Box 1, Mount Rushmore National Memorial, Keystone, S.Dak. Jewel Cave Corporation records and other records generated while the monument was under Forest Service jurisdiction are held at Mount Rushmore National Memorial.

17. *Custer Weekly Chronicle*, 19 July 1928.

18. Ibid., 20 Sept. 1928; Toll, "Report to the Director," p. 2.

19. Albright to Norbeck, 4 Mar. 1932, Box 117, and Norbeck to Tom Berry, 2 Jan. 1933, Box 48, Norbeck Papers, USD; Edward D. Freeland, "Annual Report," 1933, in *Superintendent's Annual Reports*.

20. Norbeck to Berry, 2 Jan. 1933.

21. Fite, *Peter Norbeck*, p. 184.

22. Both men resigned, Stanley because he heard rumors that the governor was unhappy with him, and Berry because he considered it the prerogative of the party in power to fill positions in government. Warren Green to Stanley, 3 Aug. 1931, Stanley to Norbeck, 27 Aug. 1931, and Norbeck to Stanley, 1 Sept. 1931, all Box 70, Norbeck Papers, USD.

23. Norbeck to Stanley, 12, 21 Sept., 1 Oct. 1931, and John [Hirning] to Norbeck, 28 Sept. 1931, all ibid.

24. Owen Mann to Norbeck, 4 Dec. 1931, Box 69, and Charles Robertson to Norbeck, 8 Dec. 1931, Box 129, both ibid; *Pierre Capital Journal*, 15 Oct. 1931; *Lead Daily Call*, 15 Sept. 1931; Paul E. Bellamy to Norbeck, 8 Dec. 1931, Box 22, Bellamy Papers.

25. Norbeck to Frank T. Fetzner, 14 Jan. 1932, Box 129, Norbeck Papers, USD. When Cecil Gideon mildly protested several politically motivated hirings, Superintendent Fetzner told him, "to the

victor belong the spoils" (quoted in Gideon to Norbeck, 10 Jan. 1932, Box 129, ibid.).

26. *Rapid City Daily Journal*, 28 Apr., 2 May 1932; Fite, *Peter Norbeck*, p. 186.

27. Herbert S. Schell, *South Dakota History*, 4th ed., rev. John E. Miller (Pierre: South Dakota State Historical Society Press, 2004), pp. 277–83; Elizabeth Eiselen, "A Geographic Traverse across South Dakota: A Study of the Subhumid Border" (Ph.D. diss., University of Chicago, 1943), pp. 20–21.

28. Fite, *Peter Norbeck*, pp. 186–90; Schell, *History of South Dakota*, pp. 282–83.

29. For an overview of program operations in national and state parks, *see* Linda Flint McClelland, *Presenting Nature: The Historic Landscape Design of the National Park Service, 1916–1942*, U. S. Department of the Interior, National Park Service, National Register of Historic Preservation, 1993, pp. 195–270.

30. John C. Paige, *The Civilian Conservation Corps and the National Park Service, 1933–1942: An Administrative History*, U.S. Department of the Interior, National Park Service, 1985, pp. 7–13, 16; Lyle A. Derscheid, comp., *The Civilian Conservation Corps in South Dakota (1933–1942)* (Brookings: South Dakota State University Foundation Press, 1986), p. 2. The Emergency Conservation Work program was popularly called the Civilian Conservation Corps, and in 1937, the name was officially changed. The Bureau of Indian Affairs administered separate camps for American Indians. Derscheid, *Civilian Conservation Corps in South Dakota*, p. 278.

31. Long, "Wind Cave National Park Historic Contexts," App. A.1; Edward D. Freeland to Director, National Park Service, 1 Sept. 1931, in *Superintendent's Annual Reports; Derscheid, Civilian Conservation Corps in South Dakota*, pp. 189–91.

32. McClelland, *Presenting Nature*, pp. 115–16, 174–75; John Ise, *Our National Park Policy: A Critical History* (Baltimore: Johns Hopkins University Press for Resources for the Future, Inc., 1961) pp. 360–61, 367; Robert E. Ireland, "Conservation, Resource Management, and

Regional Planning: The Pioneering Role of Joseph Hyde Pratt," in *Planning the Twentieth-Century American City*, ed. Mary Corbin Sies and Christopher Silver (Baltimore: Johns Hopkins University Press, 1996), pp. 157–58. Governor Tom Berry appointed a South Dakota State Planning Board in 1934 to study the social, economic, and natural resources of the state. South Dakota State Planning Board, "Recreation in South Dakota: A Preliminary Report," n.p., Recreational Study—South Dakota, File 0-20, Records Pertaining to Recreation, Land Use, and State Cooperation—South Dakota, Central Classified Files [CCF] (1936–1952), Region II (Midwest Region), Omaha, Neb., RG 79, National Archives–Central Plains Region (NACPR), Kansas City, Mo.

33. David Erpestad and David Wood, *Building South Dakota: A Historical Survey of the State's Architecture to 1945*, Historical Preservation Series, no. 1 (Pierre: South Dakota State Historical Society Press, 1997), pp. 208–9; Edward D. Freeland to Director, 1 Sept. 1931, p. 7, and 19 Aug. 1932, p. 3, both in *Superintendent's Annual Reports*.

34. Freeland to Director, 7 July 1935, in *Superintendent's Annual Reports*.

35. Hal K. Rothman, *Preserving Different Pasts: The American National Monuments* (Chicago: University of Illinois Press, 1989), p. 187; U.S., Department of the Interior, National Park Service, Rocky Mountain Region, "Statement for Management, Jewel Cave National Monument," 1987, p. 6, and interview of Shirley Wolf, by Bruce Biltz, n.d., transcript, n.p., both JCNML.

36. Karen S. Rosga, *Jewel Cave: The Story behind the Scenery*, ed. Cheri C. Madison (Las Vegas: K. C. Publications, Inc., 1998), p. 37; Ira Michaud, "What I have Seen and Heard," n.d., p. 9; Nancy MacMillan, *Ranger Station Historic Structure Report, Jewel Cave National Monument, Custer, South Dakota*, U.S., Department of the Interior, National Park Service, 1995, p. 6. The ranger station is considered an excellent example of Park Rustic style and was included in Volume 1 of Albert H. Good, ed., *Park and Recreation Structures*, 3 vols. (Washington D. C.:

Government Printing Office, 1938).

37. The United States Forest Service conducted the programs in the majority of ECW camps in the Black Hills; a total of twenty such camps were established during the period between 1933 and 1941. Most projects involved timber management and protection, but CCC workers also built campgrounds, trails, and other amenities for forest visitors. One of the most significant projects involved the creation of the 380-acre Sheridan Lake, initially called Lake of the Pines, in Pennington County. Derscheid, *Civilian Conservation Corps in South Dakota*, pp. 89–181.

38. Berry to Norbeck, 21 Dec. 1932, Box 48, Norbeck Papers, USD.

39. Norbeck to Berry, 27, 28 Dec. 1932, 3 Jan. 1933 (telegram), ibid.

40. Gandy to Norbeck, 13 Apr. 1933, Gideon to Norbeck, 18 Apr. 1933, both Box 67, "Minutes of Meeting of Custer State Park Board," 26 June 1933, Box 97, and Norbeck to Robertson, 17 Apr. 1933, Box 129, all ibid.

41. Special Correspondence, "State Affairs," Tom Berry, Box 48, ibid.

42. Norbeck to Herbert Maier, 20 Oct. 1933, Box 96, Norbeck to Gandy, 8, 16 Apr. 1933, Box 67, Norbeck to Robertson, 12 Dec. 1930, Box 129, Norbeck to Milliken, 30 July 1934, Box 69, all in Norbeck Papers, USD; *Rapid City Daily Journal*, 20 Oct. 1933; South Dakota, *Session Laws* (1927), ch. 12, pp. 30-31; Norbeck to Milliken, 12 Feb., 3, 6, 14 Apr. 1934, Milliken to Gandy, 7 Dec. 1933, 11 Aug. 1934, Milliken to R. D. Cook, 7 Dec. 1933, all in Custer State Park Archives (CSPA), Custer, S.Dak.

43. Fite, *Peter Norbeck*, pp. 187–90. Norbeck apparently was suffering from mouth or throat cancer.

44. Ise, *Our National Park Policy*, p. 354.

45. Paige, *Civilian Conservation Corps and the National Park Service*, pp. 16, 19, 39, 60–63, 67. Depending upon the nature of the work involved, the Forest Service administered some state park camps in other areas of the country. Harold K. Steen, *The U. S. Forest Service: A History* (Seattle: University of Washington

Press, 1976), p. 215.

46. Paige, *Civilian Conservation Corps and the National Park Service*, pp. 103–6.

47. Jesse F. Steiner, *Research Memorandum on Recreation in the Depression*, Social Science Research Council, Studies in the Social Aspects of the Depression, Bulletin no. 32 (New York, 1937), pp. 59–60; Ronald A. Foresta, *America's National Parks and Their Keepers* (Washington, D.C.: Resources for the Future, Inc., 1984), p. 45. Recreation also took on greater importance in the United States Forest Service in the mid-1930s with the development of the Division of Recreation and Lands within that agency. Steen, *U. S. Forest Service*, p. 109.

48. Norbeck to Julian Blount, 6 May 1930, Box 96, Norbeck Papers, USD.

49. Scovel Johnson to Norbeck, 12 Sept. 1928, Box 68, ibid.; [Doane Robinson], "Norbeck and the Roads," n.d., Folder 240, Box 15, Doane Robinson Papers, State Archives Collection, South Dakota State Historical Society (SDSHS), Pierre, S.Dak.; Jessie Y. Sundstrom, *Pioneers and Custer State Park: A History of Custer State Park and Northcentral Custer County* (Custer, S.Dak.: By the Author, 1994) p. 124.

50. Norbeck to Robertson, 24 Mar. 1931, Box 129, Norbeck Papers, USD.

51. Francis Case, "Remarks for Ceremonies at Unveiling of Plaque to Peter Norbeck and Dedication of Norbeck Wildlife Preserve," 13 Sept. 1952, Box 12, Bellamy Papers.

52. Norbeck to Gideon, 23 Oct. 1931, Box 67, Paul E. Bellamy to Norbeck, 21 Jan. 1932 (two letters), Box 49, Norbeck to Bellamy, 26 Jan. 1932, Box 49, Gideon to Norbeck, 10 Jan., 20 Feb. 1932, Box 67, all in Norbeck Papers, USD; Frederic L. Quivik and Lon Johnson, Renewable Technologies, Inc., *Historic Bridges of South Dakota*, South Dakota Department of Transportation, June 1990, pp. 3–4.

53. Norbeck to Scovel Johnson, 6 May 1927, and Johnson to Norbeck, 8 May 1927, both Box 68, and Norbeck to J. A. Stanley, 7 July 1931, Box 70, all in Norbeck Papers, USD; *Rapid City Daily Journal*, 24 June 1932.

54. Bellamy to Norbeck, 30 Mar. 1932, Box 49,

Norbeck Papers, USD.

55. "The Black Hills of South Dakota," *South Dakota Hiway Magazine* 7 (June 1932): 9.

56. Case, "Remarks for Ceremonies"; John A. Stanley, *From Then until Now* (n.p., 1948), pp. 62–63.

57. Derscheid, *Civilian Conservation Corps in South Dakota*, pp. 197–222.

58. Norbeck to Gandy, 14 Nov. 1935, Box 96, Norbeck Papers, USD.

59. Ibid., 17 Oct. 1935, Box 70.

60. *Rapid City Daily Journal*, 1 July 1935; *Evening Huronite*, 2 July 1935; "Robert D. Lusk" in "Honor Roll," *South Dakota Historical Collections* 22 (1946): 272–74.

61. Norbeck to Lusk, 9 July, 7 Aug. 1935, and telegram, Norbeck to Frank Lloyd Wright, 19 July 1935, all Folder SC8, Box 3649A, Robert D. Lusk Papers, State Archives Collection, SDSHS; Norbeck to Gutzon Borglum, 12 July 1935, and Norbeck to Perkins and McWayne, 8 July 1935, Box 70, Norbeck Papers, USD; Norbeck to Wright, 20 Aug. 1935, NO14, Frank Lloyd Wright Foundation (FLWF), Scottsdale, Ariz., microfiche copy in J. Paul Getty Institute for the Arts and Humanities (GIAH), Los Angeles, Calif.

62. Telegram, Wright to Norbeck, 20 July 1935, Box 120, Norbeck Papers, USD.

63. Ibid., [23 July 1935], NO14, FLWF, GIAH.

64. Norbeck to Lusk, 7 Aug. 1935, Folder SC8, Box 3649A, Lusk Papers.

65. Telegram, Norbeck to Wright, 22 July 1935, ibid.; Norbeck to Gandy, 23 July 1934, Box 70, Norbeck Papers, USD; Robert D. Twombly, *Frank Lloyd Wright: His Life and His Architecture* (New York: John Wiley & Sons, 1979), pp. 17, 58–91, 173–93, 199, 305. For a closer examination of Wright's personal life, *see* Meryle Secrest, *Frank Lloyd Wright: A Biography* (New York: Alfred A. Knopf, 1992).

66. Norbeck to Wright, 2 Sept. 1935, Bellamy to Wright, 2 Sept. 1935, and Norbeck to Lusk, 15 Oct. 1935, all Folder SC8, Box 3649A, Lusk Papers.

67. "Peeled log and boulder" architectural references punctuate much of the architect's

correspondence about the Sylvan Lake project as well as an eight-page essay describing his trip to the Badlands and the Black Hills and his reactions to scenery there. This essay has been reprinted in *Frank Lloyd Wright on Architecture: Selected Writings (1894–1940)*, ed. Frederick Gutheim (New York: Grosset & Dunlap, 1941), pp. 191–96; in Frank Lloyd Wright, "The Badlands," *South Dakota History* 3 (Summer 1973): 271–84; and in Frank Lloyd Wright, *Collected Writings*, 5 vols. (New York: Rizzoli for the Frank Lloyd Wright Foundation, 1992–1995), 3:175–80.

68. Good, *Park and Recreation Structures*, 1:3–8; Laura Soulliere Harrison, *Architecture in the Parks: National Historic Landmark Theme Study*, U.S. Department of the Interior, National Park Service, pp. 4–9.

69. Twombley, *Frank Lloyd Wright*, pp. 145–51, 192–99, 303–20; Norbeck to Arno B. Cammerer, 16 July 1935, and Herbert Maier to Milliken, 28 July 1935, both Box 70, Norbeck Papers, USD; Milliken to Maier, 23 July 1935, CSPA; Warren Morrell, "Thru the Hills" (clipping), Box 12, Bellamy Papers. For Wright's discussion of the effects of organic architecture on a particular site, *see* Frank Lloyd Wright, *An Autobiography* (New York: Horizon Press, 1977), p. 503.

70. Norbeck to Lusk, 20 Oct. 1935, Folder SC8, Box 3649A, Lusk Papers; Gandy to Guy H. Harvey, 28 Sept. 1935, CSPA; Gandy to Norbeck, 17 Sept., 13 Nov. 1935, and Gandy to Floyd F. King, 14 Nov. 1935, all Box 70, Norbeck Papers, USD.

71. Norbeck to Gandy, 17 Oct. 1935, Folder SC8, Box 3649A, Lusk Papers.

72. Norbeck to Lusk, 22 Feb. 1936, Box 70, Norbeck Papers, USD.

73. Gandy to Norbeck, 17 Sept. 1935, ibid.; Gandy to Wright, 18 Sept. 1935, D06, FLWF, GIAH; Wright to Gandy, 29 Sept. 1935, Folder SC8, Box 3649A, Lusk Papers.

74. Gandy to Norbeck, 13 Nov. 1935, R. D. Cook to Gandy, 19 Nov. 1935, W. F. Blatherwick to Gandy, 1 Feb. 1936, Norbeck to Myra K. Peters, 17 Nov. 1935, Norbeck to Wright, 15 Oct. 1935, Norbeck to Gandy, 21 Nov.1935, and Gandy to Wright, 15 Jan. 1936, all Box 70, Norbeck Papers, USD; Howard Spitznagel to Ray Milliken, 1 Nov.

1935, Norbeck to Wright, 30 Oct. 1935, Gandy to Wright, 3 Nov. 1935, and Wright to Gandy, 8 Nov. 1935 (enclosure in Norbeck to Lusk, 12 Nov. 1935), all Folder SC8, Box 3649A, Lusk Papers; Carolyn Torma, "National Register of Historic Places Nomination Form: Custer State Park Museum/Visitor's Center," 1 Dec. 1982, Historic Preservation Office Collection, SDSHS; Wright to Gandy, 10 Jan. 1936, G028, FLWF, GIAH.

75. Gandy to Norbeck, 13 Nov. 1935, Box 70, Norbeck Papers, USD.

76. Norbeck to Gandy, 21 Nov. 1935, ibid.

77. *Rapid City Daily Journal*, 10 Mar. 1936; *Sioux Falls Argus Leader*, 10 Mar. 1935.

78. Spitznagel to Wright, 14 Mar. 1936, S046, FLWF, GIAH.

79. Spitznagel to Milliken, 17 Jan. 1936, CSPA.

80. Milliken to Spitznagel, 23 Jan. 1936, ibid.

81. *Hot Springs Weekly Star*, 22 June 1937.

82. Custer State Park Board, Minutes, 10, 12 May 1936, Minutes of the Custer State Park Board, 1933–1945, State Archives Collection, SDSHS.

83. Bloom, Temple, Winters, Bennett to Milliken, 4 Apr. 1936, CSPA.

84. Erpestad and Wood, *Building South Dakota*, pp. 208–9. Frank Lloyd Wright had badly wanted the Sylvan Lake commission, but by the spring of 1936, he was working on another project. His cantilevered design for a weekend home in rural Pennsylvania incorporated the rugged rocks surrounding it as well as the waterfall that gave the home its name. Fallingwater provides a dramatic example of Wright's organic architecture and his ability to interpret landscape and is considered one of the major architectural accomplishments of the twentieth century. Twombley, *Frank Lloyd Wright*, pp. 276–78.

85. Fite, *Peter Norbeck*, p. 205.

86. Ibid., pp. 190–205; Custer State Park Board, Minutes, 14 Aug. 1937, SDSHS; Milliken to A. W. Powell, 23 Mar. 1937, CSPA.

87. Milliken to W. A. Rothschild, 18 Aug. 1937, CSPA.

88. South Dakota, *Session Laws* (1939), ch. 237.

89. Howard W. Baker, "Report on the Black Hills Area, South Dakota, by Regional Office Party, October 2–5, 1939," with supplemental reports

by Carroll H. Weggeman and Frank W. Childs, p. 15, Proposed Black Hills National Area Report, File 35, Records Pertaining to Recreation, Land Use, and State Cooperation— South Dakota, CCF, Region II, RG 79, NACPR.

90. Cammerer to Case, 25 Apr. 1940, ibid.

Chapter 5: Capitalism, Competition, and Promotion

1. Charles McCaffree, "Organized Highways in South Dakota Development," *Sunshine State* 7 (Sept. 1925): 35.

2. D. A. McKinnon, "South Dakota Tourist Traffic Industry Survey," *South Dakota Hiway Magazine* 3 (Dec. 1928): 11; Form No. PU-4 (two forms) and Addenda to Form PU-4, 15 July–2 Oct. 1938, File 32, Records Pertaining to Recreation, Land Use and State Cooperation—South Dakota, Central Classified Files (1936–1952), Region II (Midwest Region), Omaha, Neb., Records of the National Park Service, Record Group 79, National Archives–Central Plains Region, Kansas City, Mo.

3. John A. Jakle, "Touring by Automobile in 1932: The American West as Stereotype," *Annals of Tourism Research* 8 (1981): 538–39; Erma Derheim, *The Depression of the Dirty Thirties: Howard and Erma's Life* (Fairfield, Wash.: Ye Galleon Press, 1992), pp. 6–10.

4. *Rapid City Daily Journal*, 16 June 1932.

5. Quoted ibid., 6 Aug. 1935.

6. Paul E. Bellamy, resume, n.d., Box 22, Paul E. Bellamy Papers, Richardson Archives, I.D. Weeks Library, University of South Dakota (USD), Vermillion, S.Dak.; *Rapid City Daily Journal*, 23 May 1926.

7. [Paul E. Bellamy], "Through the Black Hills by Bus" (revised draft of article from *Bus Age*), July 1927, Box 12, Bellamy to Fifth Avenue Uniform Company, 25 June 1934, Box 4, and Bellamy to Pendleton Woolen Mills, 15 Apr. 1940, Box 4, all in Bellamy Papers.

8. Bellamy to Fifth Avenue Uniform Company, 25 June 1934.

9. Ibid., 4 June 1929, 24 June 1931.

10. "Black Hills of South Dakota, Tourist Accommodations, Hotels, Camps, Parks," n.d.,

Box 96.1.2, Deadwood City Archives (DCA), Deadwood, S.Dak.; O. W. Coursey, "Hon. Alexander Carlton Johnson," *Sunshine Magazine* 10 (May 1929): 3; *Black Hills Weekly*, 23 June 1933; interview of Mr. and Mrs. Troy Parker, by Earl Hausle, 2 Aug. 1973, Tape 925, South Dakota Oral History Project/American Indian Research Project (SDOHP), Institute of Indian Studies, USD.

11. *Rapid City Daily Journal*, 25 July 1919.

12. Ibid., 28 May, 17 June 1924; Bob Lee, ed., *Gold, Gals, Guns, Guts: A History of Deadwood, Lead, and Spearfish, 1874–1976* (Pierre: South Dakota State Historical Society Press, 2004), p. 245.

13. Mark D. Scott, "From Sioux Falls to the Black Hills," *Sunshine State* 6 (June 1925): 30–31.

14. Webb to John A. Stanley, 21 Aug. 1923, Historical Correspondence Material, Custer State Park Archives (CSPA), Custer, S.Dak.

15. W. H. King, "Tourist Camps—Free or Fee," *Sunshine State* 6 (Mar. 1925): 9.

16. *Rapid City Daily Journal*, 23 July 1927.

17. "Custer in the Black Hills of South Dakota," *Sunshine Magazine* 10 (Apr. 1930): 8; *Custer Weekly Chronicle*, 12 Apr. 1928; Michael A. Bedeau, *Granite Faces and Concrete Critters: Automobile Tourism in the Badlands and Black Hills of South Dakota* (Rapid City, S.Dak.: Society for Commercial Archeology and South Dakota State Historical Society, 1994), p. 23.

18. Gary Schilberg and David Springhetti, eds., *1988 NSS Convention Guidebook: Caves and Associated Features of the Black Hills Area, South Dakota and Wyoming* (Huntsville, Ala.: National Speleological Society, 1988), pp. 95–96, 102–4; John R. Honerkamp, *At the Foot of the Mountain* (Piedmont, S.Dak.: By the Author, 1978), pp. 200–201.

19. Honerkamp, *At the Foot of the Mountain*, pp. 132–33.

20. Ibid., pp. 199–200; Ann Connery Frantz, "Partners in Progress," in *Gateway to the Hills: An Illustrated History of Rapid City*, by David B. Miller (Northridge, Calif.: Windsor Publications, 1985), p. 121.

21. Carl Leedy, *Black Hills Pioneer Stories* (Lead, S.Dak.: Bonanza Trails Publications, 1973), p.

141; "Black Hills Believables" (clipping), *Rapid City Journal*, n.d., History Vertical Files, Rapid City Public Library (RCPL), Rapid City, S.Dak.; James D. Bump to R. L. Bronson, 15 Apr. 1940, Black Hills, Badlands, and Lakes Association Archives (BHBLAA), Rapid City, S.Dak. *Rapid City Daily Journal*, 9 July 1935.

22. O. W. Coursey, *Who's Who in South Dakota*, vol. 5 (Mitchell, S.Dak.: Educator Supply Co., 1925), pp. 127–30.

23. *Rapid City Daily Journal*, 27 July 1932; Peters to Peter Norbeck, 15 Nov. 1935, Box 70, 2 Sept. 1933, Box 69, along with Norbeck, Notation for File, Sylvan Lake Hotel, 16 Sept. 1931, Box 69, all in Peter Norbeck Papers, Richardson Archives, I. D. Weeks Library, USD; Peters to Custer State Park Board, 9 Sept. 1935, Historical Correspondence Materials, CSPA. For examples of Peters's emotional attachment to the resort and her problems in operating the business, *see* Peters to John A. Stanley, 28 June 1924, Historical Correspondence Materials, CSPA; Peters to Norbeck, 27 Jan. 1936, Box 70, Norbeck Papers, USD. *Also see* Box 69.

24. Interview of Bernice Musekamp, by Gene Van Alstyne, 14 June 1976, transcript of Tape 1477, pp. 1–25, SDOHP.

25. Watson Parker, *Deadwood: The Golden Years* (Lincoln: University of Nebraska Press, 1981), pp. 232, 242; Frank D. Kriebs to Nell Perrigoue, 20 June 1934, 11 Oct. 1935, Folder 96.1.6, Perrigoue to Chester Arthur, 9 Mar. 1939, Folder 96.1.14, Perrigoue to Mr. Zopher, 13 Aug. 1935, Folder 96.1.16, Perrigoue to Jay Durfee, 23 Oct. 1936, Folder 96.1.16, and Durfee to Perrigoue, 26 Oct. 1936, Folder 96.1.16, all in DCA; "Director Shares Spotlight with Historical Murderer" (clipping), Folder DE16, Centennial Archives, Deadwood Public Library (DPL), Deadwood, S.Dak.; "Custer in the Black Hills of South Dakota," p. 8.; *Custer Weekly Chronicle*, 12 Apr. 1928; Bedeau, *Granite Faces and Concrete Critters*, p. 23; Florence Bellamy Young, "Just A Thinkin'," n.d., p. 14, private papers of Judge Marshall Young, Rapid City, S.Dak.

26. Richmond L. Clow, "A New Look at Indian Land Suits: The Sioux Nation's Black Hills Claim as a Case for Tribal Symbolism," *Plains Anthropologist* 28 (Nov. 1983): 315–19. For a full discussion of the Black Hills claim, *see* Edward Lazarus, *Black Hills, White Justice: The Sioux Nation versus the United States, 1775 to the Present* (New York: HarperCollins, 1991).

27. Philip J. Deloria, *Indians in Unexpected Places* (Lawrence: University Press of Kansas, 2004), pp. 54–55. For a history of American Indian participation in Wild West shows, *see* L. G. Moses, *Wild West Shows and the Images of American Indians, 1883–1933* (Albuquerque: University of New Mexico Press, 1996).

28. *Rapid City Daily Journal*, 19 June 1926.

29. Ibid., 21 June 1926.

30. David O. Born, "Black Elk and the Duhamel Sioux Indian Pageant," *North Dakota History* 61 (Winter 1994): 23–24.

31. Ibid., pp. 22–24.

32. Ibid., p. 25.

33. Ibid., pp. 23–27.

34. *Rapid City Daily Journal*, 20 July 1935.

35. *Deadwood Daily Pioneer-Times*, 11, 13 Aug. 1925; Suzanne Julin, "Native Americans and the Days of '76," 2008, Days of '76 Museum, Deadwood, S.Dak.

36. *Black Hills Weekly*, 4 Aug. 1939.

37. "Report of the First Annual Encampment in Wind Cave National Park of Oglala Sioux Indians from the Pine Ridge Reservation," [1937], n.p., File 9, Box 1, Wind Cave National Park Library, Hot Springs, S.Dak.

38. *Rapid City Daily Journal*, 17, 28 June 1941.

39. Ibid., 28 June 1941.

40. A. S. Holm to Francis Case, n.d., "Rapid City Museum" "General Project" (129), Francis H. Case Papers, Layne Library, Dakota Wesleyan University, Mitchell, S.Dak.; John E. Rau, amendment to "National Register of Historic Places Nomination Form: Rapid City Historical Museum," 23 Jan. 1989, p. 7/1; State Historic Preservation Office Collection, South Dakota State Historical Society (SDSHS), Pierre, S.Dak.; Hugh M. Hamill to Jarvis Davenport, 24 Mar. 1940, BHBLAA; *Rapid City Daily Journal*, 3 Sept. 1941.

41. Laura Peers, *Playing Ourselves: Interpreting*

Native Histories at Historic Reconstructions (New York: AltaMira Press, 2007), pp. 36–39. For an examination of American Indian participation in tourism in other areas during the interwar period, *see* John R. Finger, *Cherokee Americans: The Eastern Band of Cherokees in the Twentieth Century* (Lincoln: University of Nebraska Press, 1991), pp. 54–56, 78–79, 98–117; Margaret D. Jacobs, *Engendered Encounters: Feminism and Pueblo Cultures, 1879–1934* (Lincoln: University of Nebraska Press, 1999), pp. 163–69; and Patsy West, *The Enduring Seminoles: From Alligator Wrestling to Ecotourism* (Gainesville: University Press of Florida, 1998), pp. 10–110.

42. *Rapid City Daily Journal*, 5 June 1924.

43. Parker, *Deadwood*, p. 239; *Rapid City Daily Journal*, 25 Jan. 1925.

44. Parker, *Deadwood*, pp. 228–44; Miller, *Gateway to the Hills*, pp. 64–69.

45. *Deadwood: The Historic City* ([Deadwood, S.Dak.]: Deadwood Chamber of Commerce, [1939]), copy in Historic Vertical Files, RCPL.

46. Nelson Antrim Crawford, "The Making of a Hero," *Kansas Magazine* (1949): 1–4.

47. Deadwood Business Men's Club, Minutes, 6 Mar. 1928, DCA.

48. Ibid., 13 Mar., 29 May 1928; Crawford, "The Making of a Hero," pp. 4–5.

49. Parker, *Deadwood*, p. 239.

50. Ibid., pp. 189–91, 212–13, 239; interview of J. C. ("Buzzy") Gorum, by Earl Hausle, 7 Aug. 1972, transcript of Tape 464, pp. 2, 14, SDOHP; *Rapid City Journal*, 15 Dec. 1989. For an excellent description of preparations and events in 1925, *see* "Deadwood's Celebration," *Sunshine State* 6 (July 1925): 11.

51. *Rapid City Daily Journal*, 6 Aug. 1935.

52. "Director Shares Spotlight with Historical Murderer"; Perrigoue to Chester Arthur, 9 Mar. 1939, 96.1.14, DCA; Parker, *Deadwood*, p. 242.

53. Joshua Garrett-Davis, "Dakota Images: Josef Meier," *South Dakota History* 31 (Spring 2001): 90; Program, *Passion Play*, [1943], Black Hills Vertical Files, DPL; *Black Hills Weekly*, 6 Jan. 1939.

54. Carolyn Torma, "National Register of Historic Places Registration Form: Dinosaur Park," n.d.,

pp. 7/1–2, 8/1–4, State Historic Preservation Office Collection, SDSHS. Two additional dinosaur models were added at a later date.

55. J. K. Hull, "Association of Commercial Club Secretaries in the Black Hills District," *Pahasapa Quarterly* 5 (Apr. 1916): 21.

56. *Rapid City South Dakota: The City of Seven Valleys* ([Rapid City, S.Dak.]: Rapid City Commercial Club, n.d.), pp. 4–17, 22, 38, copy in History Vertical Files, RCPL.

57. Documents suggest that this organization formed in 1926, and its link to the earlier group of "Secretaries" is unclear. Jarvis D. Davenport to Nate Crabtree, 5 Jan. 1940, BHBLAA.

58. "Ray L. Bronson, 1880–1941," *South Dakota Hiway Magazine* 16 (May 1941): n.p.

59. Deadwood Chamber of Commerce, Minutes, 12 Feb. 1929, Days of '76 Committee, Minutes of Special Meeting, 18 Feb. 1929; Associated Commercial Clubs, Minutes of Executive and Finance Committee, 4 Feb. 1932, and of Directors' Meeting, 19 Feb. 1932, all Box 96.1.2, DCA; N. H. Reed to Bert F. Bell, 28 Jan. 1932, W. L. Hayes to Bell, 1 Feb. 1932, Bert F. Bell to John A. Boland, 2 Mar. 1932, Frank D. Kriebs to Perrigoue, 20 June 1934, 11 Oct. 1935, John T. Heffron to A. A. Coburn, 3 July 1934, Heffron to Tom Berry, 29 June 1934, Berry to Heffron, 2 July 1934, W. D. Fisher (memorandum), 8 June 1934, all in DCA; Bill Honerkamp, untitled article, *Pine Tree Telegraph* (BHBLA newsletter), n.d.; Jarvis D. Davenport to Nate Crabtree, 5 Jan. 1940, BHBLAA.

60. Shebby Lee, "Traveling the Sunshine State: The Growth of Tourism in South Dakota, 1914–1939," *South Dakota History* 19 (Summer 1989): 219.

61. Norbeck to Tom Berry, 14 Apr. 1930, Box 66, Norbeck Papers, USD.

62. Joe R. Cash to Paul Bellamy, 7 Mar. 1931, Bellamy to Hoover, 17 Mar. 1931, Bellamy to Dean Gillespie, 21 Mar. 1931, all Box 22, Bellamy Papers.

63. Ray L. Bronson to Peter Norbeck, 28 May 1932, Box 66, Norbeck Papers, USD.

64. Gene Bauer, "On the Edge of Space: The *Explorer* Expeditions of 1934–1935," *South Dakota History* 12 (Spring 1982): 1–14.

65. *Rapid City Daily Journal*, 26 Aug. 1935.

66. Ibid., 15 Nov. 1935.

67. Deadwood Commercial Club, summary of minutes, 10 Mar. to 1 Nov. 1930, DCA; *Rapid City Daily Journal*, 17 July 1935; Honerkamp, *At the Foot of the Mountain*, pp. 200–201.

68. Peters to John A. Stanley, 28 June 1924, Historical Correspondence, CSPA.

69. Perrigoue to Mr. Zopher, 31 Aug. 1935, Perrigoue to Jay Durfee, 23 Oct. 1936, Durfee to Perrigoue, 26 Oct. 1936, all in Folder 96.1.16, DCA.

70. John E. Miller, *Looking for History on Highway 14* (Pierre: South Dakota State Historical Society Press, 2001), pp. 196–97; Dana Close Jennings, *The Story of Wall Drug*, 4th ed., rev. (Stickney, S.Dak.: By the Author, 1990), pp. 40–42.

71. Jarvis D. Davenport, Robert E. Driscoll, Ray L. Bronson to Harlan J. Bushfield, 24 Feb. 1940, Davenport and Driscoll to C. R. Custer, 19 Feb. 1940, and "Annual Report of the President, Black Hills and Badlands Association," 12 Dec. 1940, all in BHBLAA.

72. S. L. Stedman to Davenport, 26 Dec. 1939, Davenport to Stedman, 28 Dec. 1939, Davenport to W. A. Strimple, 15 Jan. 1940, Davenport and Driscoll to Custer, 19 Feb. 1940, Rex Joyce to Davenport, 6 Feb. 1940, Margaret S. Bridge to Davenport, 9 Feb. 1940, Davenport, Memorandum (to file), Jan. 1940, all in BHBLAA; *Black Hills Weekly*, 9 May 1941.

73. "Annual Report of the President, Black Hills and Badlands Association," 12 Dec. 1940.

74. Davenport to Guy Bailey, 20 Feb. 1940, BHBLAA.

75. "1938 Program of the Greater South Dakota Association," [1938], n.p., Folder 1, Greater South Dakota Association Papers, State Archives Collection, SDSHS; A. H. Pankow, "Prospects are Good for Increased Tourist Business in South Dakota This Summer," *South Dakota Hiway Magazine* 14 (Apr. 1939): n.p.; Carolyn Torma, "National Register of Historic Places Registration Form: Dinosaur Park," p. 8-1; Harry P. Atwater to Harlan J. Bushfield, 24 Feb. 1940, Davenport and Robert E. Driscoll to George Starring, 24 Feb. 1940, Davenport and Driscoll to A. H. Pankow, 24 Feb. 1940, Davenport, Driscoll, and Bronson to Bushfield, 24 Feb. 1940, Bushfield to Davenport, 28 Feb.

1940, E. H. Lighter to Board of Directors, Rapid City Chamber of Commerce, 11 Oct. 1941, Lighter to Davenport, 5 Jan. 1940, Sterling H. Clark to Davenport, 24 Feb. 1940, Davenport to Redford H. Cibble, 26 Mar. 1940, Pankow to Davenport, 11 Apr. 1940, all in BHBLAA. An August 1935 news story illustrates how bitter the sectional rivalry had become. A man returning to the Black Hills from Mitchell was killed in an accident just east of the Hills while driving through a construction detour. Some area residents blamed the State Highway Commission, implying that the commission favored South Dakota's east-river section and purposely disrupted west-river roads to slow tourist traffic because the industry was so beneficial to the western part of the state. *Rapid City Daily Journal*, 10 Aug. 1935.

76. Bushfield to W. P. Rooney, 12 July 1940, Bushfield to Davenport, 24 July 1940, Davenport to Pankow, 8 June 1940, all in BHBLAA.

77. Bushfield to W. P. Rooney, 12 July 1940, Bushfield to Davenport, 24 July 1940, Davenport to Pankow, 8 June 1940, Pankow to Davenport, 7 June 1940, W. O. Sisley to Sylvan Lake Hotel, 26 June 1940, Guy N. [Borge] to Davenport, 2 July 1940, all ibid.

78. "Annual Report of the President, Black Hills and Badlands Association," 12 Dec. 1940.

79. Ibid.; "Governor Bushfield Recommends Greater Publicity Program," *South Dakota Hiway Magazine* 16 (Jan. 1941): n.p.; "Black Hills and Bad Lands Association Annual Report," 13 Jan. 1942, BHBLAA; "Tourist Prospects for 1941," *South Dakota Hiway Magazine* 16 (Apr. 1941): n.p.

80. "Black Hills and Bad Lands Association Annual Report," 13 Jan. 1942.

81. Pankow, Memorandom to M. C. Laird, n.d., enclosure in Pankow to Davenport, 8 Dec. 1942, Pankow to Davenport, 16 Mar. 1942, Davenport to E. A. Snow, 21 Sept. 1942, all in BHBLAA; *Black Hills Weekly*, 9 May 1941.

Chapter 6: Conclusion

1. "Road at Grand Canyon's South Pass to Reopen," *Seattle Times*, 4 Feb. 2001.

2. Case to O. G. Taylor, 16 Mar. 1938, National

Park State Administration File, Francis H. Case Papers, Layne Library, Dakota Wesleyan University, Mitchell, S.Dak.

3. Cammerer to Case, 14 Apr. 1939, ibid.

4. Miossec's model is described and explained in Douglas Pearce, *Tourist Development*, 2d ed. (New York: John Wiley & Sons, 1989), p. 16.

5. Carlton L. Bonilla, "A South Dakota Rendezvous: The Sturgis Motorcycle Rally and Races," *South Dakota History* 28 (Fall 1998): 123–43.

6. John M. Duffy, "Dakota Images: Korczak Ziolkowski," *South Dakota History* 30 (Fall 2000): 338.

7. *Rapid City Journal*, 7 May 1989.

8. *Say Yes!* ([Deadwood, S.Dak.]: n.p., n.d.), copy in Black Hills Vertical Files, Deadwood Public Library, Deadwood, S.Dak.

9. *Sitting Bull Crystal Caverns: The Black Hill's [sic] Premier Crystal Cave* (n.p., n.d.), copy in collection of the author.

10. *Black Hills Passion Play* (n.p., n.d.), copy ibid.

11. *Ride the Train: 1880 Train Black Hills Central Railroad* ([Hill City, S.Dak.]: n.p., [2007]), copy ibid.

Bibliography

Archives and Manuscript Collections

Bellamy, Paul E. Papers. Richardson Archives. I.D. Weeks Library, University of South Dakota. Vermillion, S.Dak.

Black Hills, Badlands, and Lakes Association Archives. Rapid City, S.Dak.

Black Hills Vertical Files. Deadwood Public Library. Deadwood, S.Dak.

Case, Francis H. Papers. Layne Library. Dakota Wesleyan University. Mitchell, S.Dak.

Centennial Archives. Deadwood Public Library. Deadwood, S.Dak.

Custer State Park Archives. Custer State Park. Custer, S.Dak.

Custer State Park Board. Minutes, 1933–1945. State Archives Collection. South Dakota State Historical Society. Pierre, S.Dak.

Days of '76 Museum Collection. Deadwood, S.Dak.

Deadwood City Archives. Deadwood, S.Dak.

Elrod, Governor Samuel H. Papers. State Archives Collection. South Dakota State Historical Society. Pierre, S.Dak.

Greater South Dakota Association Papers. State Archives Collection. South Dakota State Historical Society. Pierre, S.Dak.

History Vertical Files. Rapid City Public Library. Rapid City, S.Dak.

Hughes, Frank J. Papers. State Archives Collection. South Dakota State Historical Society. Pierre, S.Dak.

Lusk, Robert D. Papers. State Archives Collection. South Dakota State Historical Society. Pierre, S.Dak.

Norbeck, Governor Peter. Papers. State Archives Collection. South Dakota State Historical Society. Pierre, S.Dak.

Norbeck, Peter. Papers. Richardson Archives. I.D. Weeks Library. University of South Dakota. Vermillion, S.Dak.

Records of Black Hills National Forest. Black Hills National Forest Supervisor's Office. Custer, S.Dak.

Records of Jewel Cave Corporation. Mount Rushmore National Memorial. Keystone, S.Dak.

Records of Jewel Cave National Monument. Jewel Cave National Monument Library. Custer, S.Dak.

Records of Jewel Cave National Monument. Mount Rushmore National Memorial. Keystone, S.Dak.

Records of Mount Rushmore National Memorial. Keystone, S.Dak.

Records of the National Park Service. Record Group 79. National Archives. Washington, D.C.

Records of the National Park Service. Record Group 79. National Archives–Central Plains Region. Kansas City, Mo.

Records of Wind Cave National Park. Wind Cave National Park Library. Hot Springs, S.Dak.

Robinson, Doane. Papers. State Archives Collection. South Dakota State Historical Society. Pierre, S.Dak.

South Dakota Collection. Rapid City Public Library. Rapid City, S.Dak.

Tourism and Highway Travel Files. State Archives Collection. South Dakota State Historical Society. Pierre, S.Dak.

Tourism pamphlets. Collection of the author. Missoula, Mont.

Wright, Frank Lloyd. Papers. Frank Lloyd Wright Foundation. Scottsdale, Ariz. Microfiche. J. Paul Getty Institute for the Arts and Humanities. Los Angeles, Calif.

Young, Judge Marshall P. Private Papers. Rapid City, S.Dak.

Interviews

Chase, Isaac. 1970. Interview by Stephen R. Ward. 17 June 1970. Tape 64. South Dakota Oral History Project/American Indian Research Project. Institute of Indian Studies. University of South Dakota. Vermillion, S.Dak.

Gorum, J. C. ("Buzzy"). 1972. Interview by Earl Hausle, 7 Aug. 1972. Transcript of Tape 464. South Dakota Oral History Project/American Indian Research Project. Institute of Indian Studies. University of South Dakota. Vermillion, S.Dak.

Musekamp, Bernice. 1976. Interview by Gene Van Alstyne. 14 June 1976. Transcript of Tape 1477. South Dakota Oral History Project/American Indian Research Project. Institute of Indian Studies. University of South Dakota. Vermillion, S.Dak.

Parker, Mr. and Mrs. Troy. 1973. Interview by Earl Hausle. 1 Aug. 1973. Tape 925. South Dakota Oral History Project/American Indian Research Project. Institute of Indian Studies. University of South Dakota, Vermillion, S.Dak.

Pyle, Gladys. 1977. Interview by Paul O'Rourke. 23 June 1977. Tape 210. South Dakota Oral History Project/American Indian Research Project. Institute of Indian Studies. University of South Dakota. Vermillion, S.Dak.

Wolf, Shirley. N.d. Interview by Bruce Biltz. N.d. Transcript. Jewel Cave National Monument Library. Custer, S.Dak.

Unpublished Manuscripts and Reports

Hughes, Frank J. "The Beginning of the Rushmore Memorial, 1925." N.d. MORU 1002, Box 11. National Park Service. Mount Rushmore National Memorial, Keystone, S.Dak.

"Jewel Cave National Monument: National Register of Historic Places Multiple Property Submission, National Park Service." 21 Feb 1995. Jewel Cave National Monument Library, Custer, S.Dak.

Julin, Suzanne. "Native Americans and the Days of '76." 2008.

Days of '76 Museum. Deadwood, S.Dak.

"Master Plan for the Protection and Administration of the Norbeck Wildlife Preserve." June 1927. Black Hills National Forest Supervisor's Office. Custer, S.Dak.

Michaud, Ira. "What I have Seen and Heard." N.d. Jewel Cave National Monument Library. Custer, S.Dak.

Neel, H. C., and C. W. Fitzgerald. "Report on the Proposed Jewel Cave Game Preserve." Sept. 1907. Jewel Cave National Monument Library. Custer, S.Dak.

Rau, John E. Amendment to "National Register of Historic Places Nomination Form: Rapid City Historical Museum." 23 Jan. 1989. State Historic Preservation Office Collection. South Dakota State Historical Society. Pierre, S.Dak.

Shetler, David. "National Register of Historic Places Inventory Nomination Form: Custer State Game Lodge." 11 June 1981. State Historic Preservation Office Collection. South Dakota State Historical Society, Pierre, S.Dak.

Torma, Carolyn. "National Register of Historic Places Nomination Form: Custer State Park Museum/Visitor's Center." 1 Dec. 1982. State Historic Preservation Office Collection. South Dakota State Historical Society. Pierre, S.Dak.

_____. "National Register of Historic Places Registration Form: Dinosaur Park." N.d. State Historic Preservation

Office Collection. South Dakota State Historical Society. Pierre, S.Dak.

Young, Florence Bellamy. "Just A Thinkin'." Judge Marshall Young Private Papers. Rapid City, S.Dak.

Government Documents

FEDERAL

Evans-Hatch, Gail and Michael. *Place of Passages: Historic Resource Study, Jewel Cave National Monument, South Dakota.* National Park Service, Midwestern Region. Omaha, Neb., 2006.

Good, Albert H., ed. *Park and Recreation Structures.* 3 vols. Washington, D. C.: Government Printing Office, 1938.

Green, Linda Wedel. *Historic Resource Study: Yosemite, the Park and Its Resources, a History of the Discovery, Management, and Physical Development of Yosemite National Park, California.* Vol. 1. U.S. Department of the Interior. National Park Service. 1987.

Harrison, Laura Soulliere. *Architecture in the Parks: National Historic Landmark Theme Study.* U.S. Department of the Interior. National Park Service. 1986.

Long, Barbara Beving. Four Mile Research Co. *Wind Cave National Park Historic Contexts and National Register Guidelines.* U. S. Department of the Interior. National Park Service. 1992.

McClelland, Linda Flint. *Preserving Nature: The Historic Landscape Design* of the National Park Service, 1916–1942. U.S. Department of the Interior. National Park Service. National Register of Historic Preservation. 1993.

MacMillan, Nancy. *Ranger Station Historic Structure Report, Jewel Cave National Monument.* U. S. Department of the Interior. National Park Service. 1995.

Paige, John C. *The Civilian Conservation Corps and the National Park Service, 1933–1942: An Administrative History.* U.S. Department of the Interior. National Park Service. 1985.

Rom, Lance, Tim Church, and Michele Church, eds. *Black Hills Cultural Resources Overview.* Vol. 1: *Synthetic Summary.* U.S. Department of Agriculture. U.S. Forest Service. Black Hills National Forest. 1996.

U.S. Congress. House. *HR11726.* 68th Cong., 2d sess. (1925). *Congressional Record* 66, pt. 4 (15 Feb. 1925).

U.S. Congress. Senate. "The Creation of a National Memorial in Harney National Forest." *S. Rept. 1435.* 68th Cong., 2d sess. (1925).

U.S. *Statutes at Large.* Vols. 32, 39, 41, 43.

West, Terry L. *Centennial Mini-Histories of the Forest Service.* U. S. Department of Agriculture. Forest Service. 1992.

STATE

Quivik, Frederic L., and Lon Johnson. Renewable Technologies, Inc. *Historic Bridges of South Dakota.*

South Dakota. Department of Transportation. June 1990.

South Dakota. Legislature. *Proceedings of the House of Representatives.* 19th Sess. 1925.

South Dakota. Legislature. *Session Laws.* 1911, 1913, 1919, 1920, 1925, 1927, 1939.

Newspapers

Black Hills Weekly, 1925, 1933, 1939, 1941.

Custer Weekly Chronicle, 1928.

Deadwood Daily Pioneer-Times, 1925.

Evening Huronite, 1935.

Hot Springs Star, 1925, 1937.

Lead Daily Call, 1927, 1932.

New York Times, 1927.

Pierre Capital Journal, 1931.

Rapid City Daily Journal, 1918–1941, 1989.

Seattle Times, 2001.

Sioux Falls Press, 1915.

Sioux Falls Argus Leader, 1925, 1935.

Books and Articles

Ayres, George V. "Lawrence County Highways and How It Was Done." *Pahasapa Quarterly* 5 (Dec. 1914): 9–15.

Bauer, Gene. "On the Edge of Space: The *Explorer* Expeditions of 1934–1935." *South Dakota History* 12 (Spring 1982): 1–16.

Bedeau, Michael A. *Granite Faces and Concrete Critters: Automobile Tourism in the Badlands and Black Hills of South Dakota.* Rapid City, S.Dak.: Society for Commercial Archeology and South Dakota State Historical Society, 1994.

Bederman, Gail. *Manliness and Civilization: A Cultural History of Gender and Race in the United States, 1880–1917.* Chicago: University of Chicago Press, 1995.

Belasco, Warren James. *Americans on the Road: From Autocamp to Motel, 1910–1943.* Baltimore: Johns Hopkins University Press, 1997.

Bellamy, Paul E., and G. D. Seymour. *A Guide to the Black Hills.* Rapid City, S.Dak.: Black Hills Transportation Co., 1927.

Black Hills of South Dakota. [Rapid City, S.Dak.]: Rapid City Chamber of Commerce, 1932.

"The Black Hills of South Dakota." *South Dakota Hiway Magazine* 7 (June 1932): 9.

Bohi, John W. "Seventy-Five Years at Wind Cave: A History of the National Park." *South Dakota Historical Collections* 31 (1962): 365–468.

Bonilla, Carlton L. "A South Dakota Rendezvous: The Sturgis Motorcycle Rally and Races." *South Dakota History* 28 (Fall 1998): 123–43.

Borglum, Gutzon. "The Political Importance and the Art Character of the National Memorial at Mount Rushmore." *Black Hills Engineer* 18 (Nov. 1930): 285–99.

Born, David O. "Black Elk and the Duhamel Sioux Indian Pageant." *North Dakota History* 61 (Winter 1994): 21–29.

Brown, Dona. *Inventing New England: Regional Tourism in the Nineteenth Century.* Washington, D.C.: Smithsonian Institution Press, 1995.

Cameron, Jenks. *The Development of Governmental Forest Control in the United States.* Studies in Administration Series, 1928. Reprint ed. New York: Da Capo Press, 1972.

Clow, Richmond L. "A New Look at Indian Land Suits: The Sioux Nation's Black Hills Claim as a Case for Tribal Symbolism." *Plains Anthropologist* 28 (Nov. 1983): 315–24.

_____. "Timber Users, Timber Savers: Homestake Mining Company and the First Regulated Timber Harvest." *South Dakota History* 22 (Fall 1992): 213–37.

Cooper, Courtney Ryley. "The Last of the Argonauts." *Saturday Evening Post* 200 (17 Sept. 1927): 120.

Coursey, O. W. "Hon. Alexander Carlton Johnson." *Sunshine Magazine* 10 (May 1929): 3.

_____. *Who's Who in South Dakota.* Vol. 5. Mitchell, S.Dak.: Educator Supply Co., 1925.

Cox, Thomas R. *The Park Builders: A History of State Parks in the Pacific Northwest.* Seattle: University of Washington Press, 1988.

Crawford, Nelson Antrim. "The Making of a Hero." *Kansas Magazine* (1949): 1–4.

"Custer in the Black Hills of South Dakota." *Sunshine Magazine* 10 (Apr. 1930): 8.

"Cycad National Monument." *Yale Alumni Weekly* 31 (5 June 1936): n.p.

Dalthorp, Charles J., ed. *South Dakota's Governors.* Sioux Falls, S.Dak.: Midwest Beach Co., 1953.

Day, John A. "Borglum: The Artist." In *Gutzon Borglum, the Artist and the Man: An Exhibition Organized and Sponsored by the University of South Dakota Art Galleries, the Oscar Howe Art Center, and the Rushmore-Borlgum Story Museum.* Vermillion, S.Dak.: Broadcaster, Inc., 1984.

Deadwood: The Historic City. [Deadwood, S.Dak.]: Deadwood Chamber of Commerce, [1939].

"Deadwood's Celebration." *Sunshine State* 6 (July 1925): 11.

Deloria, Philip J. *Indians in Unexpected Places.* Lawrence: University Press of Kansas, 2004.

Derheim, Erma. *The Depression of the Dirty Thirties: Howard and Erma's Life.* Fairfield, Wash.: Ye Galleon Press, 1992.

Derscheid, Lyle A., comp. *The Civilian Conservation Corps in South Dakota (1933–1942).* Brookings: South Dakota State University Foundation Press, 1986.

Duffy, John M. "Dakota Images: Korczak Ziolkowski." *South Dakota History* 30 (Fall 2000): 338.

Eiselen, Elizabeth. "The Tourist Industry of a Modern Highway: U. S. 16 in South Dakota." *Economic Geography* 21 (1945): 221.

Erpestad, David, and David Wood. *Building South Dakota: A Historical Survey of the State's Architecture to 1945.* Historical Preservation Series, no. 1. Pierre: South Dakota State Historical Society Press, 1997.

Finger, John R. *Cherokee Americans: The Eastern Band of Cherokees in the Twentieth Century.* Lincoln: University of Nebraska Press, 1991.

Fite, Gilbert C. "The History of South Dakota's Rural Credit System." *South Dakota Historical Collections* 24 (1949): 220–75.

_____. *Mount Rushmore.* 2d ed. Norman: University of Oklahoma Press, 1964.

_____. *Peter Norbeck: Prairie Statesman.* 1948. Reprint ed. Pierre: South Dakota State Historical Society Press, 2005.

Foresta, Ronald A. *America's National Parks and Their Keepers.* Washington, D.C.: Resources for the Future, Inc., 1984.

Frantz, Ann Connery. "Partners in Progress." In *Gateway to the Hills: An Illustrated History of Rapid City.* By David B. Miller. Northridge, Calif.: Windsor Publications, 1985.

Froiland, Sven G. *Natural History of the Black Hills and Badlands.* Rev. ed. Sioux Falls, S.Dak.: Center for Western Studies, Augustana College, 1990.

Garrett-Davis, Joshua. "Dakota Images: Josef Meier." *South Dakota History* 31 (Spring 2001): 90.

Geores, Martha E. *Common Ground: The Struggle for Ownership of the Black Hills National Forest.* Lanham, Md.: Rowman & Littlefield Publishers, 1996.

Gossage, Alice R. "Picturesque Rapid Canyon." In *Holiday Greetings from Rapid City, South Dakota, in the Black*

Hills. Rapid City, S.Dak.: *Rapid City Daily Journal,* 1919–1920.

"Governor Bushfield Recommends Greater Publicity Program." *South Dakota Hiway Magazine* 16 (Jan. 1941): n.p.

Hedrick, H. S. "Game and Fish Conditions in the Custer State Park." *Pahasapa Quarterly* 10 (Spring 1921): 188–93.

Honerkamp, Bill. Untitled article. *Pine Tree Telegraph,* n.d.

Honerkamp, John R. *At the Foot of the Mountain.* Piedmont, S.Dak.: By the Author, 1978.

Hood, Stanley. "Sight-Seeing Trips." *Pahasapa Quarterly* 8 (Dec. 1918): 49–53.

Hull, J. K. "Association of Commercial Club Secretaries of the Black Hills District." *Pahasapa Quarterly* 5 (Apr. 1916): 21.

Huseboe, Arthur R. *An Illustrated History of the Arts in South Dakota.* Sioux Falls, S.Dak.: Center for Western Studies, Augustana College, 1989.

Ise, John. *Our National Park Policy: A Critical History.* Baltimore: Johns Hopkins University Press for Resources for the Future, Inc., 1961.

Jacobs, Margaret D. *Engendered Encounters: Feminism and Pueblo Cultures, 1879–1934.* Lincoln: University of Nebraska Press, 1999.

Jakle, John A. "Touring by Automobile in 1932: The American West as Stereotype." *Annals of Tourism Research* 8 (1981): 538–39.

_____. *The Tourist: Travel in Twentieth-Century North America.* Lincoln: University of Nebraska Press, 1985.

Jennings, Dana Close. *The Story of Wall Drug.* 4th ed., rev. Stickney, S.Dak.: By the Author, 1990.

Johnson, A. I. "Touring the Black Hills." *Pahasapa Quarterly* 9 (June 1920): 159–73.

Johnson, J. H., and J. P. Snyder. "The Caves of the Black Hills." *Pahasapa Quarterly* 9 (June 1920): 175–87.

Jones, Billy M. *Health-Seekers in the Southwest, 1817–1900.* Norman: University of Oklahoma Press, 1967.

Julin, Suzanne. "South Dakota Spa: A History of the Hot Springs Health Resort, 1882–1915." *South Dakota Historical Collections* 41 (1982): 193–271.

_____, comp. *South Dakota Historical Collections Cumulative Index.* Pierre: South Dakota State Historical Society, 1989.

King, W. H. "Tourist Camps: Free or Fee." *Sunshine State* 6 (Mar. 1925): 9.

Koupal, Nancy Tystad, ed. "Lydia Norbeck's Recollections of the Years." *South Dakota Historical Collections* 39 (1978): 1–146.

Lazarus, Edward. *Black Hills, White Justice: The Sioux Nation versus the United States, 1775 to the Present.* New York: HarperCollins, 1991.

Lee, Bob. *Gold, Gals, Guns, Guts: A History of Deadwood, Lead, and Spearfish, 1874–1976.* Pierre: South Dakota State Historical Society Press, 2004.

Lee, Shebby. "Traveling the Sunshine State: The Growth of Tourism in South Dakota, 1914–1939." *South Dakota*

History 19 (Summer 1989): 194–223.

Leedy, Carl. *Black Hills Pioneer Stories.* Lead, S.Dak.: Bonanza Trails Publications, 1973.

McAlester, Virginia and Lee. *A Field Guide to American Houses.* New York: Alfred A. Knopf, 1984.

MacArthur, N. D. "Black Hills Named Correctly." *Sunshine Magazine* 7 (Jan. 1927): 17–18.

McCaffree, Charles. "Organized Highways in South Dakota Development." *Sunshine State* 7 (Sept. 1925): 35.

McKinnon, D. A. "South Dakota Tourist Traffic Industry Survey." *South Dakota Hiway Magazine* 3 (Dec. 1928): 11.

McLaird, James D. "From Bib Overalls to Cowboy Boots: East River/West River Differences in South Dakota." *South Dakota History* 19 (Winter 1989): 454–91.

Mason, Kathy S. *Natural Museums: U.S. National Parks, 1872–1916.* East Lansing: Michigan State University Press, 2004.

Meeks, Harold A. *On the Road to Yellowstone: The Yellowstone Trail and American Highways 1900–1930.* Missoula, Mont.: Pictorial Histories Publishing Co., 2000.

Meyer, Roy W. *History of the Santee Sioux: United States Indian Policy on Trial.* Lincoln: University of Nebraska Press, 1967.

Miller, David B. *Gateway to the Hills: An Illustrated History of Rapid City.* Northridge, Calif.: Windsor Publications, 1985.

Miller, John E. *Looking for History on Highway 14.* Pierre:

South Dakota State Historical Society Press, 2001.

Morrow, Lynn, and Linda Myers-Phinney. *Shepherd of the Hills Country: Tourism Transforms the Ozarks, 1880s–1930s.* Fayetteville: University of Arkansas Press, 1999.

Moses, L. G. *Wild West Shows and the Images of American Indians, 1883-1933.* Albuquerque: University of New Mexico Press, 1996.

Myrick, Herbert. "Front View of the Colossal Sculptures Designed for the Continental Memorial in the Black Hills." *Dakota Farmer* 46 (15 Dec. 1926): 1068.

New York Times Index. Vol. 14 (Apr.-June 1927). Vol. 15 (July-Sept. 1927).

Norbeck, Peter. "South Dakota State Park: The Black Hills Are Not Hills But High Mountains." *Outlook* 146 (1 June 1927): 153.

Pankow, A. H. "Prospects are Good for Increased Tourist Business in South Dakota This Summer." *South Dakota Hiway Magazine* 14 (Apr. 1939): n.p.

Parker, Watson. "Booming the Black Hills." *South Dakota History* 11 (Winter 1980): 35–52.

_____. *Deadwood: The Golden Years.* Lincoln: University of Nebraska Press, 1981.

Paxson, Frederic L. "The Highway Movement, 1916–1935." *American Historical Review* 51 (Jan. 1946): 238–42.

Pearce, Douglas. *Tourist Development.* 2d ed. New York: John Wiley & Sons, 1989.

Peck, Frank S. "Roads: Past, Present, and Future." *Pahasapa Quarterly* 8 (Apr. 1919): 16.

Peers, Laura. *Playing Ourselves: Interpreting Native Histories at Historic Reconstructions.* New York: Altamira Press, 2007.

Peterson, P. D. *Through the Black Hills and Bad Lands of South Dakota.* Pierre, S.Dak.: J. Fred Olander Co., 1929.

Pomeroy, Earl. *In Search of the Golden West: The Tourist in Western America.* New York: Alfred A. Knopf, 1957.

Prall, Angie. "Hisega." *Pahasapa Quarterly* 6 (Feb. 1917): 26–28.

"The Proposed Scenic Highway from Rapid City to Pactola." *Pahasapa Quarterly* 5 (Dec. 915): 126–21.

Purchase, Eric. *Out of Nowhere: Disaster and Tourism in the White Mountains.* Baltimore: Johns Hopkins University Press, 1999.

Rapid City, South Dakota: The City of Seven Valleys. [Rapid City, S.Dak.]: Rapid City Commercial Club, [1919].

"Ray L. Bronson, 1880–1941." *South Dakota Hiway Magazine* 16 (May 1941): n.p.

Readers' Guide to Periodical Literature, 1925-1928. New York: W. Wilson Co., 1929.

Recent Social Trends in the United States: Report of the President's Research Committee on Social Trends. 2 vols. New York: McGraw-Hill Book Co., 1933.

"Robert D. Lusk" in "Honor Roll." *South Dakota Historical Collections* 22 (1946): 272–74.

Robertson, C. W. "Highways in Custer State Park." *Black Hills Engineer* 18 (Mar. 1930): 133–36.

Robinson, Doane. "A Century of Liquor Legislation in Dakota." *South Dakota Historical Collections* 12 (1924): 281–96.

_____. "Inception and Development of the Rushmore Idea." *Black Hills Engineer* 18 (Nov. 1930): 334–43.

_____. "The Picturesque Black Hills, a Paradise for Campers." *Dacotah Magazine* 2 (Oct. 1908): 81–88.

Rogsa, Karen S. *Jewel Cave: The Story behind the Scenery.* Ed. Cheri C. Madison. Las Vegas: KC Publications, 1998.

Roskie, George W. "State Game Preserve." *Pahasapa Quarterly* 4 (Apr. 1915): 9–14.

Rothman, Hal K. *Devil's Bargains: Tourism in the Twentieth-Century American West.* Lawrence: University Press of Kansas, 1998.

_____. *Preserving Different Pasts: The American National Monuments.* Chicago: University of Illinois Press, 1989.

Schell, Herbert S. *History of South Dakota.* 4th ed., rev. John E. Miller. Pierre: South Dakota State Historical Society Press, 2004.

Schilberg, Gary, and David Springhetti, eds. *1988 NSS Convention Guidebook: Caves and Associated Features of the Black Hills Area, South Dakota and Wyoming.* Huntsville, Ala.: National Speleological Society, 1988.

Scott, Mark D. "From Sioux Falls to the Black Hills." *Sunshine State* 6 (June 1925): 30–31.

Sears, John F. *Sacred Places: American Tourist Attractions in the Nineteenth Century.* New York: Oxford University Press, 1989.

Secrest, Meryle. *Frank Lloyd Wright: A Biography.* New York: Alfred A. Knopf, 1992.

Sies, Mary Corbin, and Christopher Silver. *Planning the Twentieth-Century American City.* Baltimore: Johns Hopkins University Press, 1996.

Stanley, John A. *From Then until Now.* N.p., 1948.

_____. "South Dakota's State Park." *Pahasapa Quarterly* 10 (Spring 1921): 179–86.

Steele, J. H. "A Vacation in the Black Hills." *Pahasapa Quarterly* 4 (Feb. 1915): 45.

Steen, Harold K. *The U. S. Forest Service: A History.* Seattle: University of Washington Press, 1976.

Steiner, Jesse Frederick. *Americans at Play: Recent Trends in Recreation and Leisure Time Activities.* New York: McGraw-Hill Book Co., 1933.

_____. *Research Memorandum on Recreation in the Depression.* Social Science Research Council. Studies in the Social Aspects of the Depression, Bulletin no. 32. New York, 1937.

Sundstrom, Jessie Y. *Pioneers and Custer State Park: A History of Custer State Park and Northcentral Custer County.* Custer, S.Dak.: By the Author, 1994.

Sutter, Paul S. *Driven Wild: How the Fight against Automobiles Launched the Modern Wilderness Movement.* Seattle: University of Washington Press, 2002.

Taliaferro, John. *Great White Fathers: The Story of the Obsessive Quest to Create Mount Rushmore.* New York: BBS Public Affairs, 2002.

Tilden, Freeman. *The State Parks: Their Meaning in American Life.* New York: Alfred A. Knopf, 1962.

"Tourist Prospects for 1941." *South Dakota Hiway Magazine* 16 (Apr. 1941): n.p.

Troth, H. W. "The Deadwood Business Club. *Pahasapa Quarterly* 4 (Feb. 1915): 11–14.

"Two Comments on Game Money in State Park." *Sunshine Magazine* 7 (Nov. 1927): 30.

Twombley, Robert D. *Frank Lloyd Wright: His Life and His Architecture.* New York: John Wiley & Sons, 1979.

West, Patsy. *The Enduring Seminoles: From Alligator Wrestling to Ecotourism.* Gainesville: University Press of Florida, 1998.

Wieland, George R. "Our National Monuments." *Science* 87 (4 Jan. 1938): 37–39,

Williamson, William. *An Autobiography: William Williamson, Student, Homesteader, Teacher, Lawyer, Judge, Congressman, and Trusted Friend.* Rapid City, S.Dak.: By the Author, 1964.

Wright, Frank Lloyd. *An Autobiography.* New York: Horizon Press, 1977.

_____. "The Badlands." *South Dakota History* 3 (Summer 1973): 271–84.

Wrobel, David M., and Patrick T. Long, eds. *Seeing and Being Seen: Tourism in the American West.* Lawrence: University Press of Kansas, 2001.

Theses and Dissertations

Cracco, James. "History of the South Dakota Highway Department, 1919–1941." M. A. thesis, University of South Dakota, 1970.

Eiselen, Elizabeth. "A Geographic Traverse across South Dakota: A Study of the Subhumid Border." Ph.D. diss., University of Chicago, 1943.

Index